PSYCHOANALYTIC UNDERSTANDING OF THE DREAM

PSYCHOANALYTIC UNDERSTANDING OF THE DREAM

Paul Sloane, M.D.

NEW YORK • JASON ARONSON • LONDON

Copyright© 1979 by Jason Aronson, Inc.

All rights reserved. Printed in the United States of America. No part of this book may be used or reproduced in any manner whatsoever without written permission from Jason Aronson, Inc. except in the case of brief quotations in reviews for inclusion in a newspaper, magazine, or broadcast.

ISBN: 87668-362-6

Library of Congress Catalog Number: 79-50290

Manufactured in the United States of America

to my family

CONTENTS

Acknowledgments	ix
1. Introduction	1
2. General Principles of Dream Interpretation	11
3. The Manifest Dream	33
4. Demonstration of a Supervisory Session	53
5. The Dream Wish	65
6. Early Dreams and Premature Interpretations	85

7. Transference Dreams	107
8. Resistance and Dreams	145
9. Dreams with Unpleasurable Affects	171
10. Validation of Interpretation	201
11. Terminal Dreams	237
Bibliography	261
Index	271

ACKNOWLEDGMENTS

I want to express my appreciation to Dr. Samuel A. Guttman and Dr. Henry T. Kleiner for reviewing sections of the book and for their very helpful suggestions; to Dr. Bernard Cowitz for his valuable contributions to the seminars; to Dr. Gerald I. Margolis and Miss Margot Newman for their suggestions; to my secretary, Mrs. Lynne Elberg for her devotion and patience in transcribing tapes and typing the manuscript; to Mrs. June Strickland for her generous assistance in providing me access to library materials; to Mrs. Ray Lincoln and Mr. Lesser Zussman, who guided me in dealing with the intricacies of publishing; and to the candidates who presented such interesting and instructive material at the seminars.

I would not want to let this opportunity pass without expressing my indebtedness to Herman Nunberg. Dr. Nunberg was a superb and inspiring teacher and, as evidenced in his many writings, an outstanding interpreter of dreams. Where psychoanalysis was concerned he was a person of uncompromising integrity. He never offered hypotheses without providing abundant clinical evidence, and he insisted his students do the same. He epitomized the combination of the intuitive and scientific analyst at his best.

CHAPTER 1

Introduction

The thought of preparing a book on the technique of dream analysis resulted from experiences with analytic candidates. The underlying purpose was to indicate how the average student could learn the art of dream interpretation, that is, of making the latent meaning of the dream available to both analyst and patient. The implication is an important one. If the analyst does not understand the dream he cannot properly interpret it to the patient. It was observed, in the course of supervision and conducting continuous case seminars, that candidates were largely at sea when they came to deal with dreams. After making a superficial attempt at understanding and interpreting the manifest dream, the candidate would ignore it or adopt an attitude of comparative passivity, on the assumption that the patient's associations alone would open up the meaning. When this procedure repeatedly failed to produce the desired result, the candidate considered the attempt to interpret dreams a futile expenditure of time and effort. Only if the dream contained obvious symbols would an attempt be made to offer an interpretation, and then one that was likely to be theoretical and too general to be related to the current situation.

As a result, the candidate was losing access to a most important aspect of the analysis. In addition, he was losing the opportunity to develop a technique and method of thinking that could immeasurably sharpen his analytic and therapeutic skills in other areas. Later in his career he might even come to rationalize his neglect of dreams by assuming that they are only one form in which the unconscious expresses itself, a form not necessarily superior to other manifestations of unconscious mental processes and therefore not worth the effort expended in unraveling them.

With this in mind, I offered to give a course on the technique of dream interpretation on a trial basis. The course took hold almost immediately. Many candidates considered it an eye-opener in that they learned for the first time how dreams could contribute understanding in a number of different areas: the life history of the patient, the meaning of the basic neurotic conflicts, recollection of infantile memories conveying a sense of conviction, the nature and meaning of the transference and resistance, insight into current situations otherwise appearing chaotic and confused, relative strengths of ego, superego, and id, the significance of early object relationships, and the application of clinical and metapsychological theory. Learning the art of dream interpretation also resulted in the refinement of the analyst's sensitivity in communicating with the patient in a way that proved both practical and fruitful.

These were not small gains, particularly since they carried a conviction of the soundness of Freud's fundamental concepts of analysis. One candidate at the completion of the course commented that he now felt he understood the meaning and rationale of psychoanalytic principles which until then had been purely theoretical.

This book is primarily intended as a handbook of the technique of dream analysis for psychoanalytic candidates as well as for the further instruction of experienced therapists. While therefore limited in scope, it nevertheless aims to fill an important need in the training of candidates. By no means a complete treatise on the psychology of the dream, the book is content rather to describe a method of teaching dream interpretation. The aspect I stress most is the analyst's unique method of mental functioning in assessing psychological data and in communicating with the patient. These are logical processes whose validity can be proved repeatedly by subsequent developments. There is no mystique about the method and it can be taught to others. On the other hand, it is not simply a

Introduction

matter of following cut and dried rules. Attaining the necessary skill requires some native endowment, empathic feeling for others, curiosity about how human beings function, and much painstaking effort.

I have tried to convey the approach utilized in the dream seminar, which was refined over the course of years. My object was to demonstrate how the analyst reasons in arriving at conclusions and why, in making selections from the patient's associations, he emphasizes certain aspects and not others. One of the guiding rules in teaching was to check flights of speculation and to insist that the hypotheses be supported by clinical evidence. Another principle was to indicate that the rules of dream interpretation were not capricious, pursued a definite logic, and did not require blind faith in authority. In the exchanges I was careful to confine the discussion to the immediate clinical data and to insist that formulations be neither too intellectual nor too general, be supported by the information at hand, and be within the context of the patient's life and social situation. This was designed to eliminate doubts about the validity of the process and to avoid intellectualization without a firm clinical basis. Although there was a constant correlation between practice and theory, especially clinical theory (repression, defense, resistance, transference, oedipus and castration complexes, etc.), the former held the position of primacy. One could rely on the fact that once the clinical data were ascertained a theoretical understanding would gradually evolve and be more readily assimilated. This goes along with the fact that the development of theory follows the uncovering of new clinical observations, for instance, the effects of deprivation in early infancy. One thing impressed on the students was the need to be cautious about arriving at conclusions in view of the multidetermined nature of the phenomena.

One area in which the therapist frequently has difficulty is his capacity to relate to the unconscious of another person. We do not all have the ear that enables us to tune in on the unconscious of others. Some people are more sensitive than others in picking up these vibrations. It is not easy to explain what determines this sensitivity to the unconscious. To some extent it depends on one's capacity to tolerate the discomfort of self-confrontation as reflected in the gross and unacceptable behavior and reactions of other people. One comes to know another by putting himself in the other's place and imagining how he would feel. It is therefore important for the therapist to be aware of the emotional reactions he is undergoing when working with the patient. This is totally different from understanding the patient on the basis of intellectual speculation. If he finds he cannot empathize with the patient but, on the contrary, experiences an estrangement in his reactions, he must consider the possibility that he is dealing with a psychotic or borderline individual (Kernberg, 1975). Such reactions of course are not always conscious; they frequently arise spontaneously, with no forethought or planning. They result from the therapist's introspection and empathy and, in the last analysis, stem from his life experience. A momentary identity can be felt with another, not because he is adopted as an ideal but because his present experience seems a repetition of something in the empathizer's past. This differs from true identification in the psychoanalytic sense, a process involving personality changes and the acquisition of new ideals, interests, etc. True identification is a merging with another individual, with a concomitant loss in detachment and objectivity. Identifying with the patient in the analytic situation, on the other hand, is a temporary experience which can be followed almost immediately by detachment from the patient and objective observation of the situation. Such "trial identification" (Fliess, 1942) is not necessarily a countertransference problem but something that occurs universally as a matter of course in the interaction between patient and analyst. As a matter of fact such interactions constitute an essential source of information about the patient. As Fliess aptly states, instead of trying to fulfill an infantile demand the analyst projects the striving, after he has "tasted it," back to the patient; he then finds himself in possession of inside knowledge of its nature, having thereby acquired the emotional basis for his interpretation (p. 215).

Helene Deutsch (1926) attributes the capacity for unconscious communication with the patient to the analyst's capacity for "intuitive empathy." This is the ability to experience the object by means of identification. To achieve this intuitive attitude the analyst must have gone through the same developmental processes as the patient. There is a revival of memory traces in the analyst as a result of an unconscious perception of the patient's material as contrasted with a purely intellectual deliberation (p. 137).

In the analyst's emotional reaction to the patient, whether based on realistic or on unconscious factors, one must include an identification not only with the patient but also with those to whom the patient relates. We can also assume that the emotional reaction which the therapist feels in working with the patient may be precisely what the patient is unconsciously trying to produce, in which case it is the concealed meaning of his intention. If the analyst recognizes this on the basis of his affective reaction, supported by subsequent reflection which will prevent him from acting out impulsively, he is in a position to use it for purposes of interpretation.

It will be observed that most of the reported dreams are those of patients with well-integrated and intact egos. These patients suffered for the most part from unconscious conflicts which had persisted since childhood. Each one seemed to have a fairly good functioning superego and an intact sense of reality and was able to respond to interpretations by a lifting of repressions and recall of past memories. In general the patients did not seem threatened in the analytic situation by any loss of self-esteem, nor were they averse to acknowledging their need for help or their dependency on the therapist. Their object relationships were comparatively normal. This did not result from a deliberate selection of cases for the seminar. It suggests that this type of patient is not unusual, despite the amount of attention being given patients with such ego disturbances as narcissistic and infantile personalities, severe acting out disorders, and the loose ego organization and object relationships of borderline cases and psychoses. The patients described could benefit from classical analytic procedures, characterized in the main by simple interpretation. Candidates can learn basic analytic techniques only from this type of patient. In addition, confirmation of interpretations in these cases was frequently forthcoming in the conscious recollection of genetic material, although one might also infer that the patient's acting out in the transference could have been a direct repetition of experiences of the preverbal period, which could not be remembered (Greenacre, 1968). In this connection consider Case 1 of Chapter 8. Very often a reconstruction of such early experiences may be supported by intuitive confirmation on the part of the patient ("it clicks"). At times the affect associated with very early experiences may be reproduced along with the production of mental images, neither of which can be considered true memories (Waelder, 1937).

It is essential for the candidate to become familiar with the basic technique so that he can acquire a firm grounding in classical analysis before he attempts to tackle cases that require technical modifications (parameters), such as patients with disturbed ego functions. It is the only way he can learn whether he has overstepped the bounds of psychoanalysis to the point of no return.

It will be noted that I have seldom referred to metapsychological theory and that I have placed greater emphasis on observation. I have also resorted frequently to the use of analogues of a metaphorical nature when dealing with abstractions. Such metaphors, dealing with both ideas and feelings, not only clarify ideas by making them concrete but also provide an emotional understanding of experiences. This is actually the substance of wit. As Krag-Pederson (1956) points out, the use of metapsychological theory or technical language seems impersonal by contrast and is more akin to what is required in the physical sciences. The use of higher order abstractions is undoubtedly a shortcut for the initiated and saves mental effort, but for the beginner their connotations may not be so self-evident. In the process of teaching, one must be aware that learning can take place only on the basis of previous experience and on the readiness to fall back on what is familiar. It therefore seems reasonable not to take the reader's comprehension for granted.

Two pitfalls present themselves in the teaching of dream analysis. One can err either by being too didactic, or by being so absorbed in presenting illustrative examples that the method itself is largely obscured. I have chosen to emphasize the didactic method, hopefully without becoming too pedantic, since I have found it the more effective pedagogically.

As this is intended as a handbook for those embarking on psychoanalytic careers, I have sought to express myself in a direct and uncomplicated manner, in terms of actual experience rather than jargon. In this respect I agree with Guttman (1965), who recognizes the importance of discussing hypothetical entities in terms familiar to the clinician; otherwise such entities remain esoteric and difficult to comprehend. If we are prepared to communicate with the patient by reducing our greater insight to terms that are part of the patient's experience, we must be similarly prepared in the supervision and instruction of candidates. Since the only reliable evidence of success in our didactic work is afforded us by student feedback, candidates must be allowed full opportunity to draw their own conclusions and to express these freely.

As one listens to the patient in a relaxed frame of mind, one has unspoken reactions to his dreams and free associations as they relate to his past history and life situation, as well as to his expressive style and peculiarities of speech, appearance, and gesture. Such observations frequently lead the analyst to ask himself questions about the patient that might either confirm, correct, or negate previous conjectures. Where they occur in this book, such personal reflections will be enclosed in brackets. The flavor of my inferences was frequently conveyed by the timbre and inflection of my voice as I stressed certain points. These were entirely spontaneous and seemed to reflect something in my unconscious or preconscious. The absence of these accents in the written work became plain when the transcriptions of the taped record were compared with the sound of the tapes themselves. Where the former came across rather flat, the latter had a vibrant and lively tone. It is hoped, however, that the written record might convey some of the flavor of the give-and-take of the discussions. I have designated my personal cases with a *P* and those reported by candidates with a *C*.

Since psychological experiences are not the exclusive possession of psychoanalysts, the book should be useful to others who practice psychotherapy, who deal with people's emotional problems, who are interested in the study of dream phenomena, or who can appreciate the technique of dream interpretation in a clinical setting. It should give them an idea of the sensitivity and circumspection with which one must approach the emotional reactions of other human beings.

CHAPTER 2

General Principles of Dream Interpretation

Since Freud discovered the unique contribution that an understanding of dreams can make to our knowledge of the unconscious, the interpretation of dreams has remained one of the main tools of psychoanalytic treatment—one that opens up new insights in depth. In clinical presentations it is not unusual to find that a particularly revealing dream is cited as confirmation of an interpretation, as if it were the equivalent of a laboratory test. The reason is that dreams convey authentic messages from the unconscious; they are free of artifacts and express thoughts over which the dreamer has no control. Freud referred to dream interpretation as a "sheet anchor" when he was assailed by doubts in the early years of analysis. "The successful transformation of a senseless and muddled dream into a logical and intelligible mental process in the dreamer would renew my confidence of being on the right track (1933, p. 7)." The comparative neglect which dream interpretation has suffered in recent years (Altman, 1969; Fliess, 1953; Greenson, 1970; Waldhorn, 1967) is not related to its fundamental soundness, but more likely to a reluctance to deal with unconscious psychic activity.

Dreams often yield knowledge about an individual that can be discovered in no other way. Among the contributions that the findings of dream interpretation can make are: bringing to consciousness forgotten experiences and memories which endow present-day experiences and conflicts with meaning; providing clues to the repressed traumatic situations of childhood which have given rise to derivative counterparts in typical attitudes and object relationships; correlating past emotional relationships with the analysand's shifting attitudes toward the analyst, thus clarifying the nature and state of the transference; indicating the stage of development and type of fixation to which the psyche is tethered; confirming our conjectures and interpretations; reflecting the progress of the analysis as indicated by the relative strength or weakness of the id, ego, and superego; pointing to the presence and nature of resistances; and casting light on the state of the analysis when it appears cloudy and obscure. Early dreams often depict the patient's entire problem with unusual clarity. It is not surprising that Freud regarded dream interpretation as "the foundation stone of psychoanalytic work" (1913b, p. 170).

The correct interpretation of a dream carries greater conviction to the patient than do interpretations of any other material. This results from the fact that the dream is experienced by the dreamer as part of reality. By virtue of its sensory (mainly pictorial) character and its affective quality, it recalls echoes from the past which have left an indelible impression on the dreamer's psyche. An interpretation which strikes home may therefore give rise to instantaneous recognition which requires no further proof. It is as if something has "clicked" in the dreamer's mind. The dreamer comes to regard the dream as the touchstone which holds the secret of his life.

Factors Involved in the Problem of Interpretation

It would be a mistake to assume that dream interpretation, or indeed the practice of psychoanalysis in general, is a simple matter of following technical rules, or that analysis proceeds according to a rational plan by the exercise of intellect alone. The latter may be true, as Freud has pointed out, for the opening and closing moves of analysis, as in chess, but not for the intricate intermediate moves. Since psychoanalysis is a psychology which deals primarily with the *repressed* unconscious, as distinguished from the *descriptive* unconscious—the preconscious—we must understand some of the characteristics of the former. Repressed thoughts follow an irrational logic which requires an approach completely different from the logical, "common-sense" method of dealing with conscious thoughts. They cannot be reached by direct interrogation since the individual's conscious perception has no access to them. Their meaning, however, may be inferred from observation of a number of phenomena related to the individual's voice, involuntary gestures, facial and other expressive movements, blushing, parapraxes, or discrepancies between content and affect. The significance of such unintentional phenomena can often be fathomed by gifted writers and artists, children who are as yet unhampered by social compromises, and those whose daily work depends on an understanding of human nature, such as lawyers, salesmen, detectives, and psychologists. In other words, the mind of the investigator must be sensitized to detect nuances by which the unconscious reveals itself. This talent is a sine qua non for the psychoanalyst. Without it he remains a stranger to the secrets of the mind, even though he may possess an excellent knowledge of clinical and metapsychological theory, important though these are to the practicing analyst.

Alterations of theory and technique follow and are determined by clinical practice in order to deal with new types of problems as they present themselves. Tartakoff (1974) clearly delineates the progressive development of techniques as a result of such problems. She points out that Freud experimented with a variety of methods such as hypnosis, suggestion, and abreaction, with the original intention of relieving symptoms. When he encountered resistance, however, he discovered that he could learn more about an individual if he merely listened in a relaxed way to the latter's spontaneous productions and allowed them to evoke responses in himself. By means of these free associations repressions could be overcome, thus permitting infantile sexual conflicts to become conscious and opening the way for their resolution by means of the transference and working through. When character problems were encountered, it was found that one had to deal with an understanding of how the ego managed to lose control of its inner house and allow itself to be dominated either by the instincts of the id or by a harsh and inflexible superego. This led to the introduction of the structural theory and the development of ego psychology with the aim of analyzing both unconscious ego and id derivatives in order once again to achieve dominance of the ego. When the problems of treating borderline conditions and narcissistic personalities arose, clinical theory came to be based on the early development of the child, particularly in the area of defects produced by deprivation and natural endowment. Free association, however, has continued as the basis of analytic technique. It may be added that few fundamental changes in psychoanalytic technique have occurred with the advent of ego psychology (Lipton, 1967; Kanzer and Blum, 1967).

Free association means more than the simple pouring out of words. It involves a particular condition of mind, one which approximates an intermediate state between sleep and wakefulness, in which judgmental faculties are held in abeyance and thoughts flow in the form of fantasies and pictorial images. It is this condition which lends meaning to free associations, since it indicates closeness to the type of thinking that exists in the unconscious.

One must not imagine, however, that a mere flow of words, in the manner of "stream-of-consciousness" thinking, can of itself lead to understanding. On the contrary, it can lead to a complete breakdown of disciplined thinking, so that the use of words for their own sake becomes a pleasurable exercise. Free association must therefore be combined with self-observation; it is useful only in connection with other analytic procedures, mainly interpretation.

The practice of free association involves a form of regression which is favored by the assumption of a reclining position and by the absence of distracting stimuli. It implies the ability to drop one's guard. The patient is asked to assume a relaxed mental state, let his thoughts wander in a diffuse fashion, and to report them the instant they occur to him, without dismissing them as unimportant or attempting to edit them. It is soon found that such wandering thoughts are not purposeless or haphazard, but are really connected in a causative chain of inner logic. This is not the logic of the rational mind, but rather of its irrational aspect, namely, the unconscious. Here the law of psychic determinism rules; the association of ideas is governed by an unconscious purpose and all psychical processes are found to be related one to another. This implies a high degree of regression involving the id, the early defense mechanisms of the ego, and the primitive aspects of the superego. The associations tend to go further back in a continuous series to the early experiences of childhood. The relatedness of ideas is determined by affect and not by intellect or concern for social, moral, or ethical amenities. The patient can be induced to express his thoughts, which are often unpleasant, only because of his neurotic suffering. He is supported in this endeavor by his trust in the analyst and his confidence that he will not be betrayed or made to undergo any consequences.

This was well illustrated by a patient, who from the beginning seemed to grasp the essence of free association. He could produce abundant and relevant associations which often completely clarified the latent meaning of his dreams. When asked, however, to summarize his associations, he invariably replied in effect, "I've been so busy giving the associations and getting involved in the feeling tone of the dream, that I can't think about them objectively." He was saying, "I'm doing what I'm supposed to do; it's your job to put things together and make sense of them." It was as if he realized that free association represented a different category of thinking than that involved in the logical organization of thought. This patient was a model of the good analysand; he was automatically able to assume the stance which brought him closer to the unconscious, recognizing the intent of the manifest dream, perceiving resemblances, and using concrete imagery to express his ideas. When an interpretation was made he could usually appreciate its relevance immediately, except when it touched a sensitive spot, in which case he would become resistant. He had the capacity temporarily to throw off the shackles of normal reasoning and give himself over to the world of the primary process. During this period he was unable to pass critical judgment on what he was saying, although he was able to recognize its relevance to the sense of the manifest dream. He seemed to have moved into a more primitive sphere where he could immediately adapt himself to the logic of the unconscious. To judge from the free flow of his associations and his difficulty in objectively applying them to his central problem, his mind seemed to be in a state of altered consciousness. That he was still in touch with reality, however, was indicated by the relevance of his associations as well as by the fact that he was able to swing back to a position where he could appreciate and later assimilate the analyst's summarization of his thoughts. His cooperative mood was not based on mere compliance in order to please the analyst or to appease him as a defense against his ambivalence. Rather, it was more on the order of an identification with the analyst as ego-ideal. It seemed that while he was operating wholly with his unconscious instrument, he was relegating the function of observation to the analyst as his surrogate ego and the latter was able to bring him back to a state of reflective objectivity.

The Role of the Analyst

The patient is advised to withdraw his critical faculties while giving free associations, so that ideas will flow uninterruptedly, regardless of their logical coherence. In this manner the patient's unconscious can find expression. Freud recommended that the analyst adopt a similar state of mind. This condition of relaxed attention, which he called one of "evenly suspended attention," was a counterpart of the patient's free associations and made it possible for the analyst to come into resonance with the patient's unconscious. It is characterized by a restful, passively receptive attitude and avoidance of concentration on any particular detail. This is based on the truism that concentration narrows the range of one's perception. The analyst seeks to broaden his observations beyond his conscious awareness and to become sensitized to the hidden messages coming from the patient's unconscious. The unconscious of another can be understood only through the medium of one's own unconscious. Freud compared the analyst's position to the state of mind that exists before falling asleep, when

General Principles of Dream Interpretation

"involuntary ideas" emerge seemingly of their own free will, changing into visual and acoustic images (1900, p. 102).

"The technique...is a very simple one.... It consists simply in not directing one's notice to anything in particular and in maintaining the same 'evenly suspended attention' ... in the face of all that one hears. In this way we spare ourselves a strain on our attention.... For as soon as anyone deliberately concentrates his attention to a certain degree, he begins to select from the material before him; one point will be fixed in his mind with particular clearness and some other will be correspondingly disregarded, and in making this selection he will be following his expectations or inclinations. This, however, is precisely what must not be done...

"It will be seen that the rule of giving equal notice to everything is the necessary counterpart to the demand made on the patient that he should communicate everything that occurs to him without criticism or selection. If the doctor behaves otherwise, he is throwing away most of the advantage which results from the patient's obeying the 'fundamental rule of psychoanalysis.' The rule for the doctor may be expressed: 'He should withhold all conscious influences from his capacity to attend, and give himself over completely to his unconscious memory.' Or, to put it purely in terms of technique: 'He should simply listen, and not bother about whether he is keeping anything in mind.'" [Freud, 1912b, pp. 111–112]

Others have enlarged upon this concept of the analyst's frame of mind. Kubie (952, p. 89) stated: "We have to be able to communicate better with the child who is within the man, so that we can understand him and so that his unconscious can understand us." According to Reik (1949), directed and concentrated thought, while valuable for objective and intellectual aims, does not permit the diffusion of feeling that is necessary to become sensitized to the unconscious, or attuned to what the patient is saying. The analyst should strive to catch the emotional undertones in what the patient says and must stop all cognitive speculation while he analyzes. Since the nature of an individual's unconscious motives is revealed by the effect of his action and behavior upon others (in the transference, upon the analyst), the only way of penetrating the secret of the patient's unconscious is from self-observation. One tries by introspection to perceive how he would behave under given circumstances, if he were the patient. The analyst can understand only what he himself has experienced.

What this amounts to is that without the instrument by which one's unconscious can come to understand another, psychoanalysis is extremely difficult. The analyst, however, must also be able to turn off the flow of unconscious material and view it objectively. By thus sublimating his affective responses into curiosity he succeeds in gaining mastery over them, and thereby avoids the possibility of being influenced by the countertransference. However, if he has difficulty immersing himself in the necessary depths of feeling, he may have to remain in the relatively untroubled but shallow waters of consciousness.

The happy combination of the analyst and the type of patient I have described above, is evidently what Isakower (1957; 1963) had in mind when he spoke of the "team" aspect of the analytic situation. He used the term *analyzing instrument* to denote the psychic state of the analyst and the analysand, both separately and in relation to each other. He described it as a "near dreamlike state of hovering attention" from which the analyst emerges only after the session has been broken off and he is left alone. At this point there occurs a process of reintegration within himself and he can begin to observe how things were fitted together. This coincides with the reintegration my patient had to undergo after giving his associations. According to Isakower, the analytic situation has a built-in structure for the living out of all universal fantasies and the sharing of them by both analyst and analysand. The end result is a combination of intuitive and cognitive processes in both of them. Malcove stressed the importance of empathy in the analyst, since it allows him to tune in to the patient's unconscious.

The individual who can react to ideas almost immediately so that his creative imagination is stirred by mere indications to transform these ideas into pictures, and the pictures into affects, is definitely better off in this area. The faculty of perceiving analogies is important. Freud (1900, p. 97) in a footnote quotes Aristotle to the effect that "the best interpreter of dreams was the man who can best grasp similarities; for dream-pictures, like pictures on water, are pulled out of shape by movement, and the most successful interpreter is the man who can detect the truth from the misshapen picture." As William James said, "Some people are far more sensitive to resemblances, and are far more ready to point out wherein they consist, than others are. They are the wits, the poets, the inventors, the scientific men, the practical geniuses" (1950, p. 530). A humorless person is at a distinct disadvantage in this type of situation. What is required is an empathic "living along" with the patient, and the capacity to recognize what significance a given situation has for him. The process is largely an affective one and the analyst must be prepared to expose himself to the oscillations of the patient's feelings. This constitutes a creative and imaginative venture which can be either intellectually and emotionally stimulating or very fatiguing, depending on the patient's responsiveness or resistance. Not all analysts possess the necessary qualifications in equal proportion, but those who have them to some degree can learn the art of dream interpretation.

I have taken up this subject at length because of its fundamental importance in the practice of psychoanalysis. It is something for which there are no technical rules. Rules are valuable insofar as they serve as guidelines until they become part of one's automatic thinking. However, the analyst must not allow them to interfere with his spontaneity. It is axiomatic that an analyst who has an affective rapport with his patient and knows what is going on within him will know instinctively what to do.

Preparation for Interpretation

An initial exploratory period is essential before any interpretation is offered. This consists largely of listening to the patient's productions with as little interruption as possible, so as not to interfere with the spontaneous stream of the patient's thoughts. One may, however, offer simple reassurance when necessary. The exploratory sessions should be devoted to learning as much about the patient's neurosis and his background as possible. One tries to recognize typical patterns of behavior, paying attention mainly to the patient's defense mechanisms and the state of the superego, as well as to id contents. Such a preparatory period, during which the analyst listens attentively to the patient and shows consistency, dependability, and empathic understanding, will foster the patient's positive attitude toward him. Even after the positive transference has been established, however, one tries not to intervene until resistances begin to interfere with the production of new material. Such resistances are usually related to the transference. Interventions at this point should be confined to attempts to discover the cause of the resistance and to resolve it.

The dream reflects the current experiences of the individual, particularly if he is in a state of anxiety or tension, as a patient beginning therapy is likely to be. Early dreams are apt to be naive and to reveal a great deal about the patient's character and neurosis. Too much anxiety-provoking material may appear in the dream and premature interpretation may prove traumatic and give rise to resistances before they can be dealt with adequately. The patient may reveal facts about himself that he may later regret disclosing. He then begins to feel threatened and his resulting defensiveness tends to render subsequent dreams more obscure and difficult to analyze. Early interventions should be restricted to reassuring the patient if his dreams disclose anxiety about being in a strange and threatening situation. If the patient gives associations to dreams of his own accord, however, he should be allowed to do so. This may give his analyst an idea of how he works with dreams.

When the analyst decides that the time is ripe to start analyzing dreams, he may offer some initial instructions. The patient may be asked what happened on the previous day that could have instigated the dream (day residue). The day residue may be an external event or some worry or preoccupation. Frequently it contains a reference to

General Principles of Dream Interpretation

the previous analytic session. It may be either something indifferent or something crucial. The analysand should then be advised to break the dream into fragments, to associate to each detail separately, and to proceed to the next detail when the associations to the first are exhausted; so on until the entire dream has been covered. Another method is to ask the patient what comes to his mind in connection with some outstanding detail of the dream, if he has ever experienced anything similar, or under what circumstances he has ever felt the same affect as in the dream. Some patients may be allowed to select any part of the dream they prefer.

The affect of the dream is of special importance, since it faithfully reflects the affect of the latent dream content and is rarely qualitatively distorted, although it may be diminished in intensity or altogether absent. It leads directly to the substance of the latent dream and shows where to look for its meaning. The analysand learns that associations do not as a rule reproduce actual situations from life, but merely allude to them, thereby indicating a connection. This may stimulate him to pay attention to vague similarities and not to overlook them.

The analysand may be passive and expect the analyst to keep asking for associations, or he may, on the contrary, resent the analyst's intervention as an intrusion and "clam up." In the latter instance, the analyst may wait until the patient has clearly exhausted his own resources and asks for assistance. In any case, the analyst must avoid the impression of imposing his own views on the analysand. He does best to maintain a judicious reserve.

Associations

An association may be defined as an actual part of one's previous experience, including actions, spoken words, thoughts, fantasies, and affects. It thus belongs to the individual's preconscious mental processes. This is in contrast to slips of the tongue, facial expressions, blushing and other physiological responses, acting out, involuntary movements, or sounds, all of which stem from the unconscious. Many patients seem not to know what constitutes an association and must be educated to the task. It will be found that formal rules and instructions usually have limited value and must be repeated. On the other hand, some patients adhere to the rules so closely that they work them into the ground. As a result the associations yield little useful information. This is a form of resistance which the patient may try to rationalize by declaring that he is merely doing what he was told to do, namely, to say whatever comes into his mind. The answer to this is that he must also stand back and observe what he has said. If the patient habitually overlooks the instructions, one must regard this as a form of resistance. In such cases, merely to repeat the instructions serves no gainful purpose, and plays into the patient's hands. It is therefore better to limit the opening instructions to as few rules as possible. Patients learn better from precept, especially if they can recognize the connection between the dream and the day residue or their current problems. It is often helpful to give the patient a concrete example of an association, based on a correlation between the dream and what is already known about him, preferably something related to the day residue.

Some analysands have a tendency to theorize on the basis of sophisticated social gossip or of a superficial acquaintance with analytic literature, in the mistaken belief that they are giving associations or that they understand the meaning of the dream. They must be made aware of the distinction between an association and an interpretation, and should be advised to avoid speculating until they have exhausted all associations.

In reporting the dream the analysand may interrupt the narration by giving associations and thus obscure the substance of the manifest dream. Since the manifest dream must remain uncontaminated, in "pure culture" as it were, he should be advised to withhold anything extraneous to the dream itself until he has finished communicating it. He must also be impressed with the importance of adhering to the sense of the manifest dream while giving associations, since it is the only way to judge the relevance of his associations. If the analysand tends to veer away from the dream he

General Principles of Dream Interpretation

may be asked how what he is saying fits in with the sense of the dream. If he does not pursue the associations, an occasional reminder may be given, by presenting in concrete terms what the manifest dream seems to be saying. It may be useful at times for the analyst to suggest associations based on his own knowledge of related material. These may stimulate the production of other associations. To guard against being too suggestive, however, the analyst must pay attention to the patient's responses to his interventions. No pressure should be applied. If the patient fails to recognize a connection, or to add elaborative material, it may be well to let the matter drop, and to allow him to go his own way. Even if the patient appears to be sidetracking the dream, one may treat as associations whatever the patient has said either before or after the dream was reported.

How does one succeed in stimulating the patient's interest in working with dreams? The patient can be encouraged if the connection between the dream and the central problem of the day, as reflected in the day residue, can be demonstrated. His curiosity may also be spurred if he finds that dreams reveal the continuity of motivation and behavior that has characterized his entire life. The one means of greatest instructive value for the analysand is the experience of having had a simple dream interpreted successfully.

Symbols

It is a frequent temptation to interpret symbols contained in the manifest dream directly in order to arrive at its latent meaning. This may occasionally be successful, but in general it should be discouraged, since by prejudging the material one may be prevented from evaluating the subtleties of the associations on their own merit. Off-the-cuff interpretations, even if they happen to be correct, are often only crude approximations of the actual meaning of the dream. At best such interpretations can only be considered tentative until all the evidence has been collated. The automatic use of symbols reduces dream interpretation to guesswork and carries no conviction; its habitual practice interferes with the development of the analyst's insight and empathy, so necessary to sharpen his skills. Above all, it gets away from the basic requirement of testing one's conclusions by clinical evidence. The interpretation of symbols may also be misleading, since a symbol, in addition to its typical meaning, may have a specific meaning for the patient. Only after all associations are found wanting, or if the dreamer can give associations to every detail but not to the symbol (which is characteristic of symbols in general) may we substitute its meaning, for instance the number *three* as referring to the male genitalia; the right side representing heterosexuality and the left, homosexuality; water denoting the mother; or something seen in miniature referring to childhood.

The Technique of Dream Interpretation

Dream analysis consists of transforming the manifest dream back into the latent dream content by unraveling the distortions which have helped create the former. This is accomplished by making reasonable deductions on the basis of the patient's associations, one's own empathy and intuition, and one's knowledge of the patient and of symbolism.

There seems to be confusion in some quarters about how dreams are interpreted, and whether interpretation refers to the content of the latent dream or to the manifest dream (French, 1958; French and Fromm, 1964; Spanjaard, 1969). It is true that the meaning of the dream is merely alluded to by the associations and hardly ever emerges in sharp outline. The final result, however, is not necessarily vague or inconclusive. On the contrary, when the associations are relevant it will be found that they clearly show a central trend; it is from this that the intention of the dream is deduced.

In discussing the dream of Irma's injection, for instance, Freud writes:

> While I was carrying it [the interpretation] out, I had some difficulty in keeping at bay all the ideas which were bound to be

General Principles of Dream Interpretation

provoked by a comparison between content of the dream and the concealed thoughts lying behind it. And in the meantime the "meaning" of the dream was borne in upon me. I became aware of the intention which was carried into effect by the dream and which must have been my motive for dreaming it. The dream fulfilled certain wishes which were started in me by the events of the previous evening. [1900, p. 118]

In the *New Introductory Lectures* he added:

On the one hand, the associations give us far more than we need for formulating the latent dream-thoughts—namely all the explanations, transitions, and connections which the patient's intellect is bound to produce in the course of his approach to the dream-thoughts. On the other hand, an association often comes to a stop precisely before the dream-thought; it has only come near to it and has only had contact with it through allusions. At that point we intervene on our own; we fill in the hints, draw undeniable conclusions, and give explicit utterance to what the patient has only touched on in his associations. This sounds as though we allowed our ingenuity and caprice to play with the material put at our disposal by the dreamer and as though we misused it in order to interpret it *into* his utterances what cannot be interpreted *from* them.... But you have only to carry out a dream-analysis yourselves or study a good account of one in our literature and you will be convinced of the cogent manner in which interpretative work like this proceeds. [1933, p. 12]

In the *Outline* he emphasized the same thought:

...in the great majority of cases the problem [of deducing from the manifest dream the latent content lying behind it] can be satisfactorily solved, but only with the help of the associations provided by the dreamer himself to the elements of the manifest content. Any other procedure is arbitrary and can yield no certain result. But the dreamer's associations bring to light intermediate links which we can insert in the gaps between the two [the manifest and latent contents] and by the aid of which we can reinstate the latent content of the dream and "interpret" it. When the meaning of the dream is understood it will be found that the dream "makes a demand on the ego—for the satisfaction of an instinct, if the dream originates from the id [i.e., the unconscious]; for the solution of a conflict, the removal of a doubt or the forming of an intention, if the dream originates from a residue of preconscious activity in waking life. [1940, pp. 169–170]

The resolution of a problem of waking life in the dream is thus the product of preconscious thought and has already been formed during the waking state. It constitutes only the superficial layer of the dream and it is the analyst's task to lay bare the deeper layers by tracing the chains of associations to their infantile origins. Dreams are determined by historical factors; they try to tell us more about ourselves than we are consciously aware of.

The method of offering interpretations to the patient is an art in itself and requires patience and tact. The analysand has an affective stake in interpretations, since they may give rise to an unaccustomed and at times even startling view of things. The analyst may learn a great deal from an understanding of the analysand's dreams; he cannot impart all of what he knows or surmises, however, because of the painful and disturbing nature of unconscious material. By the same token he is properly suspicious if the patient accepts interpretations too readily. In such instances the patient may be asked whether the interpretation fits in with any experience he has actually had or whether he is accepting the interpretation merely because it sounds reasonable. In the latter case the patient is probably not convinced and accepts the interpretation only intellectually.

People in general are reluctant to accept the reality of the unfamiliar. Confrontation with the unusual requires a readjustment to reality which may threaten to upset one's psychic equilibrium. We must therefore be prepared to deal with the resistance arising from the patient's inertia, which is a protective barrier against the inflow of overwhelming stimuli. The analysand is more likely to accept interpretations which do not require more of an adjustment than he is capable of making. This underscores the importance of offering interpretations on the basis of his previous insights, preferably using his own words, since they have a psychological content with which he is already familiar. The patient is more likely to be convinced if he recognizes the connection between his daily experiences and the details of the dream. He is thus quite impressed when he can see how the day residue finds expression in the manifest dream. His curiosity is further stimulated when he realizes that his waking reactions are repetitions of previous patterns.

Since interpretations must be offered in proper dosage, according to the patient's capacity to accept and integrate them, they should first deal with surface material, that is, the present-day situation. Simple logic in itself is usually ineffective; objective evidence becomes meaningful to the analysand only if he can respond to it affectively. Once he discovers what he can learn about himself from dream interpretation his interest in the analytic process grows apace and encourages him to ally himself with the analyst in the treatment process. The therapeutic or working alliance is essential to the success of the treatment; otherwise the outcome must remain in doubt.

In the analysis of every dream we must ask ourselves what the dream wish is. It is usually not obvious until the entire dream has been interpreted. This is particularly true in those dreams in which there has been considerable distortion. In determining the wish one must keep in mind the patient's entire background, including the nature of his repetition compulsion and the current state of the transference. It is of interest that in dreams with unpleasurable affects the wish is usually clear. The reason is that in view of the lack of obvious gratification there is no need for distortion or disguise.

In the type of patient who currently applies for treatment we are often likely to encounter character problems, narcissistic personalities, and borderline cases with varying degrees of immaturity. In dealing with these patients Freud's insistence on the analysis of transference and resistance becomes particularly apposite, because it is precisely in these two areas that the individual's idiosyncratic patterns of reaction are apt to become manifest. We must therefore adapt ourselves by developing changes in technique. Clinical theory has been enriched by the recognition of the effects of inborn characteristics, early arrests, and developmental defects as the result of maternal deprivation in the first two years of life (Spitz, 1965; Mahler, Pine and Bergman, 1975). Since many of these people are fixated at a stage before full structuralization of the superego, they are often characterized by the absence of internal conflict and a tendency to submit to discipline only when under the surveillance of external authority—externalized superego (A. Freud, 1974). As a result, rational interpretations are frequently ineffective. The patient is sensitive only to the analyst's acceptance or disapproval, and may regard his objectivity as cold and rejecting. Rather than expose himself by making further revelations, the patient may withhold information.

It becomes clear that an altogether different approach is required in treating these patients, particularly those whose disturbed early object relationships have left them with ego defects in the form of absence or distortion of internal object representations. Such people require much ego support before they can show any readiness to change. This calls for flexibility in the analyst's approach to the patient (Lorand, 1948). Unless he makes a deliberate effort to evaluate the patient's early life experiences, the analyst may have difficulty understanding or relating to him. The problem generally manifests itself when the analyst offers an interpretation of some aspect of the patient's attitude or behavior and meets with a sense of bewilderment and of being misunderstood. One then finds that he must learn to temper the wind to the shorn lamb, as it were. The analyst must assume the role of protective mother and become a surrogate for the missing internalized ideal parental objects. He must, however, be prepared to meet the onslaught of the patient's aggressivity. Anna Freud (1974, p. 16) holds that any improvement may be due not to real insight but to a new positive object relationship. Since the idea of the superego is not fully introjected in these patients, it becomes engrafted on them by an identification with the analyst as ego-ideal. According to her, the new relationship may also serve as a corrective emotional experience.

In these cases we see that we cannot follow the strict analytic procedure of inducing regression and the development of transference reactions. The main issue here is the personal encounter with another individual, to whom we offer a new form of relationship. Dream interpretation in the classical sense is often impossible because of the absence of internal conflict or of the patient's difficulty in accepting interpretation. The most we can be expected to do is to reconstruct the hypothetical early state of the patient as suggested by the dreams and in this manner avoid any appearance of criticizing his current attitude. Interpretations should take into consideration the patient's sensitivities and should be limited to the most prominent data ("reconstruction upwards": Bornstein, 1949; Loewenstein, 1951 and 1957). Only when the patient is assured of the analyst's continued friendliness will he be able to accept unpleasant truths about himself; in order to keep in the analyst's good graces, he will then work toward correcting them.

In view of the absence of conflict, of typical transference and resistance reactions, and the patient's difficulty in distinguishing between personal needs and external reality, it is open to serious question whether treatment in these cases constitutes psychoanalysis or whether it is psychoanalytically oriented psychotherapy. In the last analysis it would seem to depend on the degree to which the analyst must dilute his theoretical principles, the extent to which the role of nurturing parent, with its indefinite use of parameters, takes precedence over his role as representative of the reality principle.

It is obvious that if we are to be able to evaluate new treatment techniques, any extension of psychoanalytic technique must be based on a completely assimilated knowledge of Freud's basic findings. It is therefore essential that each candidate make this fundamental experience his own in the course of his personal analysis and analytic training. This implies a special method of mental functioning, namely, the use of introspection and empathy and an appreciation of primary and secondary processes in order to understand the unconscious mechanisms that determine the patient's behavior. In the analytic situation the analyst deals not only with the patient's resistances but also with difficulties residing within himself. These can create stresses, of various degrees of intensity, which interfere with his proper functioning. This is not altogether a matter that can be corrected by experience but may be the result of individual inclinations. Many analysts find that they are at home only with the classical analytic technique and cannot handle patients who vary too much from the norm.

CHAPTER 3

The Manifest Dream

The manifest dream is the dream as reported by the dreamer. Its basic significance lies in the fact that it is a translation of the unconscious content of the latent dream and serves as a bridge to its understanding. The return passage across the bridge can be made by translating back the thoughts of the manifest dream into their original form by means of the dreamer's free associations. When the process is complete the dream is seen to be a solution of an unconscious infantile conflict in the form of a wish fulfillment in the "present tense" (Freud, 1900, p. 535). Current tensions may be resolved in the manifest dream, but this is an incidental function of the dream. It can, however, provide valuable insight into the dreamer's characteristic method of resolving unconscious conflicts in the past.

The transformation of the latent dream content into the manifest dream is intended to make the primitive unconscious thoughts more acceptable to the dreamer's ego. This is accomplished by the dream work (condensation of data and displacement of affect), the use of symbols, and by secondary revision. The thought is transformed into visual images and speech and appears to be taking place in the present. The ego also has a hand in the final structure of the dream by introducing certain formal features, which consist of further modifications designed to make the dream more palatable. The dream, for instance, may be divided into several parts or scenes, each of which presents a different aspect of the same problem; it may contain commentaries on its contents in order to alter its obvious meaning. For instance, the words "It is only a dream" are meant to assure the dreamer that the dream is not to be taken seriously; it may consist of a "dream within a dream," by which it attempts to deny its real intention by picturing it as only a fantasy; or it may be represented by a blank screen, the "dream screen" (Lewin, 1948) or by the "Isakower phenomenon" (Isakower, 1938), as regressions to the infantile relationship to the mother. These changes represent the defensive aspects of the ego. Since the dream is essentially a narcissistic product, it can be assumed that the patient himself will appear in every dream, either as a participant or as an observer. The dream can therefore tell us much about the dreamer's character, his habitual patterns of behavior and defense, his relationship with others, and his cultural level. The dreamer's personality is reflected in the style of the dream, such as the replacement of action by thought, the inclusion of minute details, frequent expression of doubt and uncertainty, or vagueness.

In depicting conflicts, the manifest dream represents a compromise between psychical forces, namely, the demands of a repressed impulse seeking satisfaction and the resistance of the ego, spurred on by the superego. The result is that the id obtains partial gratification, the superego is appeased, and the ego gains its end by maintaining uninterrupted sleep. The id is manifested by sexuality or aggression, the superego by concern for moral and ethical values, ideals, and guilt, while the ego serves in a defensive and integrative capacity. As treatment proceeds the dream may show the fluctuating strength or weakness of each of the psychic agencies.

The manifest dream may not be the exact replica of the actual dream. Some of the details may be blurred, deleted, or distorted, as evidenced by the fact that they may be clarified, reinstated, or even supplemented when the analysand is asked to repeat the dream. One may then question how much reliability can be placed on the reported dream. Practically speaking, however, this is not a matter of real consequence. Since the changes have been introduced by the dreamer himself, they must be regarded as products of his own mind, that is, manifestations of the repressed or repressing forces. When thoroughly analyzed, everything reported as part of the

The Manifest Dream

dream will be found to be relevant. Indeed, as associations are given and repressions lifted, forgotten fragments of the dream may be recalled and corrections of some details made. The manifest dream utilizes aspects of the previous day's experiences (the day residue) as a framework within which the unconscious thoughts can arrange themselves. The day residue has been selected because it can serve as a connecting link with unconscious infantile drives that are seeking discharge. It may range from something trivial to a crucial problem that is occupying the patient's mind. In the latter case, the dream attempts to relieve the patient's tension by finding a suitable outlet, so that the patient can go on sleeping. Those who consider solution of contemporary problems to be the sole aim of the dream (French and Fromm, 1964) offer no satisfactory explanation for the fact that the solutions arrived at by the dreamer are not the result of "reasonable reflection" (Freud, 1925, p. 127). Such solutions are often unimpressive and could just as well have been reached during the waking state. In addition, these authors overlook the elaborate distortion undergone by the dream, which, as a consequence, appears bizarre and archaic and must be translated, thereby signifying that something in it is being concealed. This can only refer to thoughts from the repressed unconscious that are unacceptable to the conscious ego. Since these authors also minimize the importance of free associations they have forfeited the one means of access to the deeper layers of the mind.

Freud deplored the direct interpretation of the manifest dream, describing it as "a piece of unscientific virtuosity of very doubtful value" (1925, p. 128). He stated that in most cases the meaning of the dream can be found only with the help of the associations to the details of the manifest dream content, provided by the dreamer himself. "Even if, owing to one's own experience, one is in a position to understand many dreams to the interpretation of which the dreamer has contributed little, one must always remember that the certainty of such interpretations remains in doubt and one hesitates to press such conjectures upon the patient" (Freud, 1925, p. 129). In regard to the "problem-solving" aspect of the manifest dream, he said, "If we disregard the unconscious contribution to the formation of the dream and limit the dream to its latent [preconscious] thoughts, it can represent anything with which waking life has been concerned—a reflection, a warning, an intention, a preparation for the immediate future or, once again, the satisfaction of an unfulfilled wish" (1923a, p. 241). In other words, the disturbing situation is solved preconsciously and appears when the patient's associations to the day residue bring out the latent *thoughts* which are quite rational and accessible to consciousness. The latent *dream content*, on the other hand, which belongs to the repressed, or dynamic, unconscious can be reached only by continuing to follow the patient's associations to deeper levels. Freud reiterated his point of view in the *Outline of Psychoanalysis*: "In the great majority of cases the problem of [deducing the latent dream content from the manifest dream] can be satisfactorily solved, but only with the help of the associations provided by the dreamer himself to the elements of the manifest content. Any other procedure is arbitrary and can yield no certain result" (1940, p. 169). He thus never gave up his view that dreams were determined exclusively by historical factors and that they represented fulfillments of unconscious infantile wishes.

The Use of the Manifest Dream in Interpretation

The manifest dream plays a distinct role in the interpretation. One must understand, however, its scope and limitations, that is, to what extent it can serve as a guide to the uncovering of the latent dream content. Although one's initial inclination may be to regard the dream as a whole and to interpret it as such, this should be discarded in favor of relying upon the analysand's associations, as already mentioned.

Freud (1933, p. 11) has described several formal methods of approaching the interpretation of dreams. The patient may, for instance, be instructed to give associations to each detail of the dream by order of appearance; he might alternatively begin with the dream element which has made the strongest impression on him; or he may begin with the day residue. If the dreamer is already familiar

The Manifest Dream

with the technique of dream interpretation, he may be allowed to give associations in his own manner. These associations make the dream intelligible by showing the interconnection of the different parts of the dream and its latent content. The associations consist of preconscious latent thoughts, that is, past experiences which have not been repressed and are available to the patient's consciousness when attention is directed to them. From the latent thoughts one can formulate the content of the latent dream, namely, ideas in the repressed unconscious. Symbols can contribute to the meaning of the latent dream, but they must first be translated for the dreamer, since he cannot associate to them.

The Sense of the Manifest Dream

Freud (1923b, p. 110) noted that in the presence of severe resistance the formal guidelines that he proposed might not be effective. Resistances may be evidenced in any of several ways: a cessation of the flow of associations, complete blankness on the part of the patient, or a circuitous and endless chain of ideas with a tendency to get away from the substance of the manifest dream. The result is that in the presence of severe resistance a majority of dreams cannot be interpreted. Freud stated that in such instances one cannot expect collaboration from the dreamer. He suggested that the analyst desist from attempting to analyze such dreams and be content to translate some of the symbols which the patient might be prepared to understand and deal with. Such strong resistances occur frequently in analysis. In some instances, however, I have found that emphasis on the main theme, or the sense, of the manifest dream may lead to further insights.

By the sense of the manifest dream I refer to its plain or essential meaning. It may also be described as the quality or general tenor of the dream. This can usually be ascertained by considering the manifest dream in terms of its simple logic, taking into account the affect, or affects, experienced in the dream. The meaning should be evident before any associations are given. Indeed the relevance of the associations is usually determined by their accord with the main concept of the dream. When the manifest dream is fragmented, vague, or absurd it is all the more important to understand its essence.

To illustrate how one learns the drift of the manifest dream it may be well to review the Irma dream (Freud, 1900, p. 107). In the dream, the dreamer is trying to avoid responsibility for Irma's continued discomfort by blaming her for not having accepted his "solution." But his attempt at self-vindication is shaken when he finds that he may have overlooked an organic condition. He is reassured, however, by his friend Leopold, who tells him that Irma has an infection which will soon clear up. He also realizes that not he, but his colleague, Otto, was responsible for the infection because he had unwisely given her an injection of a drug and, moreover, had probably used a dirty syringe. The details of the dream converge into one central thought, namely, the dreamer is exonerated. If we turn to Freud's associations to the dream (ibid., pp. 107-118) we recognize that they are all relevant to this basic theme. The presence of a doubt in the dream, however, suggests that there is a conflict in the dreamer's mind, and we are alerted to the reasons for his self-reproach.

The usefulness of directing attention to the sense of the manifest dream became apparent in the course of supervising analytic candidates and conducting the technical dream seminar. Since there was often a scarcity of associations to the dream, and the time devoted to its interpretation was necessarily limited to the period of the supervisory session or the seminar, one naturally sought to get to the core of the patient's problem as expeditiously and accurately as possible. After the meaning of the manifest dream was uncovered it was found that, in order to understand all of its implications, it was necessary to know what the immediate stimulus of the dream (the day residue) was. This led to inquiries about the patient's emotional situation and the problems occupying his mind at the moment. These in turn were linked with the main facts of his background and personality, his relationships with others, the problem for which he sought treatment, the circumstances of its onset, and the nature and

The Manifest Dream

state of the transference. Other factors also became the subject of systematic consideration, such as peculiarities of speech and gesture, the appropriateness of the patient's behavior, his spontaneous movements, vocal intonations, etc. Special attention was paid to discrepancies between feelings and behavior since they directed attention to weak spots in the ego's defenses, where the unconscious was likely to break through to the surface. In the process one's unconscious could have free play in correlating the data with the main thought of the dream. It was then found that one had a fairly good picture of the patient and his neurosis. By learning how an understanding of the dream's meaning could lead to pertinent questions about the patient, the candidate was able to proceed in a logical manner, more or less on his own. It was stressed, however, that concentrating on the sense of the dream was an intellectual task, and should come only after the patient had given all of his associations.

As a teaching method it was valuable in emphasizing the importance of the manifest dream. I have referred to it previously as a laboratory specimen but it can also be compared to a rebus puzzle. The rebus puzzle contains nothing that does not contribute to its solution; everything that appears in it must be accounted for. The manifest dream likewise contains nothing superfluous and everything in it has meaning. It does not waste words nor does it deal with trivialities. If one can think of something consciously one does not have to dream about it, unless it is meant to tell something more than the dreamer already knows. If the dream, for instance, states specifically that the dreamer climbs the stairs to get to the upper floor instead of taking it for granted that he has to climb the stairs to get there, it is intended to attach a special meaning to the act of climbing stairs. Likewise, if a particular color is mentioned it is meant to convey a definite nuance. On that account the content of the manifest dream must be distinguished from the patient's associations. If in the process of relating the dream the patient is inclined to give associations, he should be advised to reserve them until he has finished reporting the dream.

The comparison of the dream with a rebus puzzle is apt for another reason. Just as the figures in a rebus puzzle must be translated into intelligible words, so the content of the unconscious must be guessed and translated from images and sounds into words before it can become conscious. The ability to interpret dreams is therefore facilitated by the type of mind which understands the allusive references of visual images and sounds in the formation of ideas. This is commonly found in visual thinkers, that is, those who tend to think in concrete terms and are therefore close to primary modes of reasoning.

Another resemblance of the dream to the rebus puzzle is that the solution is an approximation. The name "Stonewall Jackson," for instance, may be represented by pictures of a prison wall, a child playing jacks, and the rising sun—combining both visual and auditory images. The solution requires an imagination that flows freely and is not earthbound. In analysis of dreams we also deal with approximations: ". . . an association often comes to a stop precisely before the genuine dream-thought: it has only come near to it and has only had contact with it through allusions. At that point we intervene on our own; we fill in the hints, draw undeniable conclusions, and give explicit utterance to what the patient has only touched on in his associations" (Freud, 1933, p. 12).

Affects of the Manifest Dream

An essential element of the manifest dream is the affect expressed in it. In a sense, the logic of a dream cannot be understood without an understanding of the feeling tone of the dream. While other aspects of the latent dream content are usually distorted, the affect is not. Nunberg (1932, p. 25) states that the affect in the dream stems from a real experience. As part of the disguise of the dream it may be absent or subdued, or it may appear to be inappropriate to the content of the manifest dream. In the latter instance it may be assumed that the dream refers to a situation other than the one depicted or to an earlier period of the patient's life. For example, lack of concern over the death of a close relative in the dream may reflect a child's sense of freedom from disciplinary restraint, some

The Manifest Dream

benefit to be derived from the person's death, or that death in the dream refers to something other than death. Similarly, embarrassment upon appearing partially undressed is an ego reaction to the situation were it to happen to an adult, but it may also conceal the child's pleasure of appearing in the nude or exhibiting himself. The dreamer's affect and his associations provide more reliable clues to the real intent of the dream than does the literal content of the dream. The affect of the dream leads directly to the latent content. In this sense, it may be compared to the electronic impulses or the beam which guides the air pilot along his course. If one keeps the affect in mind he can be certain of being "on the beam," as it were, that is, on the track of the latent meaning of the dream.

If we are really to understand a person's experience, we must imagine a situation which is analagous to it. We can thus ask ourselves what circumstances could arise so that, given the nature of the individual and the situation in which he finds himself, a similar affect is likely to be evoked. T.S. Eliot refers to this as the "objective correlative," i.e., a correlation of the fact and the feeling—a metaphorical equivalent.

Dream Specimens
Illustrating the Sense of the Manifest Dream

Case 1P: *Dream:* A man dreamt that his mother asked him to look for something in her handbag. He did not recall what it was, but saw instead a box which he opened and found that it contained a watch. His mother then said, "But don't open the box; don't touch it." He wanted to replace the box without letting his mother know that he had looked into it. Later his curiosity again got the better of him and he opened various drawers in her room and found a number of watches in them.

Comment: The central thought of the dream is that the dreamer is showing curiosity about something which his mother forbids.

After reporting the dream, the patient went on to say that it was typical of his mother to ask him to do something and then blame him for doing it. In his eyes she was a deceptive person who repeatedly tricked him. I pointed out that the dream was saying just the opposite, namely, that *he* was being deceptive by doing something forbidden, in going beyond his mother's instructions. She apparently had not asked him to look for the box and he had opened it of his own accord, just as he had opened the drawers in her room. The patient's subsequent associations confirmed this understanding of the dream. It was also pointed out that he was usually the aggressor with others but invariably reacted as if he were being victimized. Thus by recognizing the simple logic of the dream it was possible not only to elicit meaningful associations but also to point out a fundamental trait of the patient's personality, that is, in the dream he used the same defenses of denial, rationalization, and projection that he habitually used in daily life. It illustrates the fact that defensive and synthetic functions of the ego influence the style of the manifest dream.

Case 2P: *Dream:* A reserved and emotionally controlled man dreamt that he had to go to the bathroom. He was unable to control his bowels, however, and to his great embarrassment, soiled the toilet seat. His wife was present with another person whom he did not recognize.

Comment: Here there can be no doubt about what the dream is saying. The only puzzle is that the dream content was entirely foreign to the general impression presented by the patient. His general appearance was that of a meticulously dressed gentleman who was always punctual, neat, and precise in his choice of words. For him to lose control of his bowels would be the last thing one might expect of him, particularly since every morning before he left the house he took care to move his bowels so as not to be taken unawares during the day. In this instance, a knowledge of the man suggested that the dream was not to be taken literally and that one had to look elsewhere for its true meaning.

In associating to the dream, the patient stated that he had to exercise complete control over every situation that confronted him. Ordinarily he restrained his anger toward anyone except his wife.

When they were alone he frequently had outbursts of violent anger, but recently he had *lost control* of himself and had humiliated her in the presence of others. Afterward he felt quite *embarrassed*. The loss of control of his temper was represented in the dream by his loss of bowel control. The dream may also have been a repetition of a childhood experience of spiting his mother during the toilet-training period.

Case 3P: *Dream:* A man dreamt that he was engaged in a tank war. Two groups were in combat. The shell fired from one tank could penetrate the armor of the patient's tank. The dreamer thought that he could outflank the enemy's tank and get to his rear by sending out a small, light tank which had the advantage of speed, even though it could be destroyed if it were hit.

Comment: The patient had been impotent with his wife the night of the dream. Afterward he was assailed by jealous thoughts of various men to whom his wife might be attracted. In the dream there was no firing but just maneuvering, resorting to a diversionary tactic by sending out a light, speedy tank. This was the simple thought of the dream. In his further associations, the patient discussed his relationships to his father, employer, and analyst, each of whom he tried to outwit. In the analysis he frequently avoided dealing with interpretations by "slipping away with his mouth" and quickly changing the subject. He thus tried to *outmaneuver* the analyst by distracting him with irrelevant material. The tank which could be penetrated by a shell, that is, a phallic-shaped object, reminded him of his fear of having his own defenses penetrated which would then betray his homosexual tendencies.

The manifest dream thus directed attention to the patient's chief form of resistance in the analysis, namely, the use of diversionary tactics in order to evade the main topic. It also implied that by outflanking the enemy and getting to his rear he could become the active, instead of the passive, homosexual partner.

Case 4P: The sense of the following dream became clear after the affects were understood in their proper context.

Dream: A patient dreamt that she was preparing succotash. A friend walked in and the patient said, "You are probably surprised at what I am making." She felt tense.

Comment: It would be difficult to understand the dream without knowing why the patient expected her friend to be surprised by the fact that she was making a common dish like succotash and why she felt tense at the end, since the dream contained nothing to warrant this type of reaction.

The patient stated that succotash is a mixture of corn and lima beans, in which the two vegetables retain their individual forms. Her husband was fond of corn, while she preferred lima beans. Knowing that she and her husband were incompatible, it seemed likely that succotash referred to her marriage. When she had informed her friends that she and her husband were planning to get married, they expressed *surprise* and thought that the marriage would not last. But why did she feel tense? She had recently been thinking of leaving her husband but had many misgivings about doing so. She related it to the guilt she felt after her grandmother's death, at which time she developed a long-standing phobia. She was afraid she would have a recurrence of the phobia if she left her husband.

Case 5C: The following dream anticipated the patient's future behavior, in addition to highlighting one of his outstanding character traits.

Dream: I am in the hallway of my school in my car. The hall is filled with rushing, foaming water, like a white water race, except that it keeps freezing. I am driving the car and am supposed to get to the end, to the threshhold, before the water freezes the car so that it can't move. I have to move fast enough to keep the water from freezing into ice. On the sidelines are many friends cheering me on. My cousin E. is also there. I'm doing very well and feel excited, as if I were winning an athletic contest, but just before I get to the threshhold, the ice freezes over and I am forced to stop.

Comment: The sense of the dream is that the dreamer, cheered on by his friends, is about to win a contest, but fails at the last moment. The patient worked for his father who held a strict hand over him.

The father objected to the patient's desire to marry out of his faith, and the son, although feeling resentful, hesitated to oppose his father. The freezing of the water was suggestive of the patient's paralysis of will. The fact that he did not reach his goal in the dream, presaged his decision to break off relations with his young lady. Symbolically, the threshhold represented a vagina, so that the dream could also suggest that his sexual wishes were forbidden, probably because they were incestuous.

Demonstration of the Use of the Manifest Dream

Case 6C: *Dream:* A woman dreamt: I came into an unfamiliar room. A student who was four or five inches taller than me lifted me by the waist to his face and kissed me. It was an affectionate kiss. I was taken aback, but I liked the idea of his lifting me up and bringing me to his face.

Background: The patient was a thirty-seven-year-old divorced social worker with three children. She had for two years been living with a man eleven years her junior and had come into analysis at his insistence that she do something about her chaotic life. She had accepted his advice only because she was afraid he would leave her if she did not get straightened out. Much of the analysis was spent in trying to help her realize that she should be in analysis for reasons of her own and not in order to please someone else. As might be expected, many aspects of her personality were quite infantile.

Day Residue: The dream occurred after a New Year's Eve party. According to her paramour she was usually more sexually aroused after parties, a fact of which she was unaware. That evening they had intercourse, but when he had a premature ejaculation, she took it to mean that he did not love her as much as she loved him. It was most important for her to be "adored" in an intense sexual way. She was also ashamed of her body because she felt she was heavy and had pendulous breasts, and for that reason preferred to get undressed in the dark and crawl under the covers before her body could be observed.

[There appears to be enough material here for us to attempt to understand what the manifest dream is saying. The patient is pleasantly surprised when she is lifted up and kissed affectionately by an adolescent boy who is taller than she. Where might a comparative situation have occurred? It seems to resemble that of a child who is being lifted up and kissed by an older man. This could refer then to a childhood experience. The fact that she has many infantile traits would confirm this impression. The striking thing is that the man in the dream is a younger person. Her paramour is younger than she is. Is it likely that she is attracted to younger men? In view of her need to be loved it could mean that she feels in command of the situation with younger men, since they are less likely to be critical of her and she can have a firmer hold on them. If this is her conscious way of overcoming her fear of being abandoned, she certainly has not been successful with her paramour, probably because of her infantile personality. This is evidenced by the fact that her paramour treats her as a child and is critical of her.]

By means of such reflections one tries to orient oneself in regard to a person whom, as yet, one hardly knows. One may thereby be in a better position to evaluate the patient's associations.

Associations: "Student": Last year there was a young boy of eighteen in one of her classes who was charming and funny, but shallow. Actually he was as tall as she, and not four or five inches taller.

Being "lifted up": At the New Year's Eve party there was a middle-aged woman artist present who went around with younger boys. She was a tiny woman and once at a night club the patient saw her being lifted up by a man. The woman seemed to be enjoying it. The patient contrasted her own body with that of the other woman and remarked that it would be difficult for anyone to lift her because of her size.

She was depressed following her experiences on New Year's Eve because she felt that her paramour did not love her. When she sought some expression of affection from him, he merely said that her reaction was unreasonable and that she should work harder in her analysis. He also criticized her for her tendency to wallow in despair.

"Young man": She said it felt good to have a young man do this to her, because it made her feel young again. She also said that a relationship with a young man was safer because it was only sexual and did not require any commitment on her part. It was important for her to feel she was needed, because it shored up her self-esteem and overcame her "bad" feelings about herself.

[These associations confirm our supposition that her preference for young men was determined by a feeling of greater security with them. But then other questions arise. Why is the student made to appear four or five inches taller? Could this refer to the therapist who is rather tall?]

Discussion: In response to my question, the presenter said that the patient was about sixty-six or sixty-seven inches tall, while he was seventy-one. This then could apply to the figures mentioned in the dream (*four or five inches taller*). He was then asked if the patient had ever expressed any interest in him. He replied that she was a very attractive woman who was really not as heavy as she claimed to be. At the start of the analysis, she used to come to sessions well-dressed and charming, but within a short time all of this changed. She began to wear sloppy, old clothes and never used makeup. Her overt attitude toward the therapist was hostile, critical, and negativistic. She often tried to ridicule him, but felt guilty because she realized that her behavior was provocative. Whenever the thought of wanting to be liked by the therapist came up, she reacted with anger. If he gingerly tried to point out evidences of her positive feelings she accused him of Freudian mumbo jumbo. She frequently sought advice from him, but when he offered a suggestion she invariably found fault with it and rejected it.

A member of the seminar inquired about her relationship with her father. The presenter replied that her father was very fond of her and when she was a child he frequently lifted her up as in the dream. Her mother's two orphaned brothers also lived in the home and were married during her latency period. As a child she was adored by them. She had been much aware of her father's sexuality. She wanted him to display affection for her but when he did she would become angry with him. This was clearly a defensive reaction. The patient slept in the parents' room until she was four or five, and several times witnessed sexual relations between them. Her father often called her by the name he used for his wife when they were having intercourse, and at such times she would become furious. This double attitude toward her father was characteristic of her.

A question was raised about her attraction to younger men. The answer was that she felt safe with them because she could control them. To them she appeared to be the "experienced woman" of whom they would become enamored, so that she could have active mastery over them. She added that they were not likely to reject her.

What was the dream wish? The dream seemed to represent two wishes: (1) to be made love to by a young boy who would not be likely to pass judgment on her and with whom she could feel secure; (2) to be treated affectionately as a cute little girl by an older man, the therapist, in the immediate situation, and her father and uncles on a deeper level. In either case she could overcome the narcissistic injury of the previous evening when she felt rejected by her paramour during lovemaking. Narcissistic mortification is often overcome by being loved.

[Understanding the dream wish is not always sufficient. In the present case it still leaves unanswered why she felt inadequate. The reasons for this must have been unconscious, since realistically speaking she was an attractive and charming woman. In studying a dream we try to find out as much as possible about the patient's personality, unconscious conflicts, and the transference in order to be in a position to better understand and deal with her.]

These questions were raised in the seminar. Someone suggested that her self-consciousness about exposing her nudity might have to do with the fact that she was a woman and lacked a penis. This, of course, was a possibility. I remarked that a likely alternative could be her inadequacy in relation to her mother because her father preferred the latter. The dream attempts to solve this problem when she is loved by a callow youth who is impressed by her "greater experience," and also in having her regress to the time when she was adored as an asexual child for her cuteness, perhaps at a time when the absence of a penis was unimportant. Could she be hoping to overcome this early trauma, namely, her feeling of inadequacy, by means of the transference?

The presenter offered a possible explanation for her resistance to accepting his interpretations. It was related to an experience at the age of twelve when her older brother was trying to help her with her mathematics. She did not understand what he was teaching her but said that she did, so that she should not appear stupid. [This might indicate that in her mind men were bright and girls stupid, a suggestion of penis envy.] When she reported this, the therapist suggested that she might be reacting similarly in the analysis. She tacitly agreed with him. Shortly thereafter she had difficulty in talking during the hour. She said she felt uncomfortable because she wanted to ask the therapist if she could borrow a magazine from the waiting room but was afraid to do so. When the therapist said, "Certainly you may," she poured out her feelings, saying that she had no right to ask for the favor because it introduced a note of informality. She had heard of what one could and could not do with one's analyst and added, "I'm not worthy enough even to have made this request."

I remarked that it obviously took courage for her to ask for the favor. It indicated that she looked upon the therapist with awe and yet felt free enough to make the request. She must have come to feel a certain degree of ease with him. The fact that he granted her the favor could increase her positive feelings for him, since he was a protective person who did not take advantage of her inadequacy or hold her up to ridicule. The presenter doubted that she could allow herself to express such feelings openly.

I remarked he could have suggested to the patient that the boy in the dream referred to him, since he was four or five inches taller than she. In addition he might have pointed out that she seemed to show greater comfort with him by venturing to ask him for the magazine. Was she possibly reassured when he told her she could borrow it? The dream thus provided information about the nature of the transference. Once a positive transference is established, the therapist has greater leverage with the patient and can offer suggestions and interpretations on a broader scale without arousing resistance.

Assuming that the patient's sense of inadequacy resulted, at least, in part from her comparison with her mother, she may have tried to overcome it by regressing to the level of a cute, little, asexual girl—in which guise she could obtain her father's love while avoiding competition with her mother. This was how she may have attempted to resolve her oedipal problem as a child. It may also explain why the patient never allowed herself to behave in a grownup manner. This was her pattern both in her daily life and in the transference. Awareness of the patient's transference reactions could have led to penetration of her problem in greater depth. A fuller interpretation of the dream could in this way open up much about the transference that had been repressed; from that one could proceed to analyze the oedipal conflict.

Summary: The contributions of the manifest dream to the understanding of the latent dream content is described. The manifest dream provides information about characteristic traits of the patient's personality, the nature and state of the transference, the patient's current problems which are uppermost, and the reciprocal relationships of his ego, superego, and id.

Special attention is directed to the logical meaning of the manifest dream for its value as a method of teaching dream interpretation to beginners and making note of the patient's current problems. The comprehension of the sense of the manifest dream must include the affect experienced in the dream. By constantly keeping it in mind as a guideline, it is useful in judging the relevance of the patient's associations to the dream and directing him to the essence of the latent dream content.

The manifest dream can be misused if interpretations are based on it solely without regard for the associations or a knowledge of the patient.

CHAPTER 4

Demonstration of a Supervisory Session

The bracketed portions are the author's observations. These are designed to illustrate how the analyst tries to understand in his own mind what the patient is saying. It indicates how the analyst's mind operates in making conjectures.

Dream C: The patient is at a scientific meeting—really a combination of a meeting and a party—and Kolmogorodm was there. Someone at the party said, "Did you know that Kolmogorodm is at the University of Khabarosk? Not only is he the outstanding probabilist but he is also an expert on meteorology." There was no affect.

Background: The patient was a thirty-seven-year-old mathematician who had been in analysis for two and one-half years and had shown considerable symptomatic improvement. For a number of months he had been talking about terminating treatment. When he returned from his vacation in September, he again brought up the question of termination. At that time the therapist had pointed out that even though he was symptomatically better, his basic problem had not yet been resolved. This seemed to make no impression on the patient.

The patient was born in Poland and at the age of eight was brought to this country by his mother when she escaped from the Nazis. They were later joined by the father. The latter had managed a successful business in Poland but found it difficult to adjust to conditions in America, and after a few years decided to return to

Europe in order to try to recoup his fortune. His wife objected to the move. The patient, who was fourteen at the time, sympathized with his mother and expressed his resentment toward his father by giving up his Orthodox religious practices. Many years later, however, he began to have compunctions about having left the synagogue when his ten-year-old daughter asked him, "What is Jewish?" He showed renewed interest in Judaism, but protested that it was not for religious reasons, but as a means of cultural identification. [I doubted this rationalization and considered the possibility that he had returned to religion out of guilt toward his father.] He later added that he felt guilty toward his father for having failed to pass on the tradition.

He became active in the synagogue, was elected president of the congregation, and as cantor conducted High Holiday services. When he started treatment, his father had been dead for four years as a result of uremia associated with an infection subsequent to a prostatectomy. Shortly after that the patient became ill with colitis and prostatitis. His reason for coming for treatment was that he became panicky when he discovered that his wife was having an affair with another man and was afraid that she would leave him. He had always suffered from occasional premature ejaculations, but following his father's death these became regular occurrences. When this change occurred, his wife told him she no longer loved him. They were divorced while his analysis was going on, but he later set up a satisfactory relationship with another woman.

[The patient identified with his father and out of guilt had to suffer in the same way his father had by developing a prostatic condition. Even though he said the resented his father for deserting the family, it is quite likely that he also admired him for refusing to accept defeat and striving to restore his self-esteem by wanting to become financially self-sufficient. His father could therefore have represented an acceptable ego ideal.]

Day Residue: During the previous hour the patient reported how much better he felt, but added that he thought there was no more to be gained from continuing the analysis, unless the therapist could point out some area that still needed to be analyzed. [By indicating

Demonstration of a Supervisory Session 57

that he was ready to abide by the therapist's judgment, the patient revealed his uncertainty about leaving.] The therapist replied that the patient had made much progress but that there was still more to be analyzed. [The therapist could have been more specific by pointing to the apparent discrepancy of the patient wanting to leave at a time when he was showing improvement. One could understand it if he wanted to leave when nothing was being accomplished, but why talk about leaving when he was doing well? Could his desire to leave at this time be a resistance? If so, it should be analyzed. Of course, it would have been more advisable if the patient's desire to leave had been taken up when he first spoke about it months earlier. By this time his determination to leave was probably fixed. There also seemed to be a similarity between the patient's desire to break away from the analysis and his break from orthodoxy, in that, in both, he asserted his independence. In the latter instance, the patient found an excuse in his father's desertion. Could he now be looking for some reason to blame the therapist?]

Associations: "Kolmogorodm" was the founder of the theory of probability. His monograph in 1933, incidentally the year of the patient's birth, laid down the basic principles of the probability theorem. The patient added that Kolmogorodm was to probability what Freud was to psychoanalysis. He said he himself once tried to extend some of Kolmogorodm's theories, and had his article published in the *Russian Journal of Probability*. He thought he had solved a problem and had contributed something to the literature.

"Khabarosk" was a Russian town near the spot where Francis Gary Powers was shot down in his U2 plane while spying for the United States during Eisenhower's administration.

The patient said he did not understand "meteorology." He had been asked the day before whether meteorology was a science, the instance cited being the credibility of the weatherman's prediction that there was a 30 percent chance of rain. He had replied that this implied that under prevailing conditions, there was a 30 percent possibility that it would rain. He added, "I think meteorology is not a science, but a lot of hot air." [He might really be expressing his opinion of analysis.]

I said the patient was indirectly bringing out negative feelings about the therapist which he might otherwise be too embarrassed to express. Frequently negative transference reactions first make their appearance in the manifest dream. The patient went on to say that a certain Applestan Spielhaus, a meteorologist, had been "thrown out" of a certain institute. The man was absolutely brilliant. It just showed how "crazy" the institute administration was. They didn't know what they were doing.

[Could Spielhaus refer to the analyst whom he was planning to "get rid of" by leaving? In that case, the use of the words "thrown out" instead of "dismissed" or "retired" might indicate the extent of his hostility to the therapist. His reference to the man's brilliance could then be an expression of his ambivalence toward the analyst.]

The patient continued, "Spielhaus—that's a peculiar name. *Spielhaus* in German is a playhouse or theatre. I wonder if meteorology refers to the analysis, because I have always wondered whether analysis was a science or not." There were no further associations.

[The patient's associations thus confirmed my empathic understanding of what he was thinking, either unconsciously or preconsciously. Being alert to the implications of the patient's associations, so that one can make logical deductions from them, helps one to understand the trend of the patient's mental processes and to keep on top of the material.]

Interpretation on a Superficial Level

At this point, the therapist told the patient that this was the first time he had expressed any overt criticism of the analysis. Hitherto his entire attitude had been one of respect and admiration for the therapist. His doubts must have existed for some time, but he had never expressed them.

[The therapist here properly interpreted the transference, drawing the patient's attention to something he might not have been fully aware of.] The patient replied that he had begun to have doubts recently. He did not consider analysis to be the answer to all of his problems. He had derived tremendous benefit from treatment, but he still had some questions. When the patient proceeded to associate to Spielhaus, a meteorologist who had been dropped by an institute, and spoke slightingly of analysis as being as little a science as meteorology, the therapist correctly pointed out that both Kolmogorodm and Spielhaus must refer to him.

[The therapist could have added that in placing Kolmogorodm in Khabarosk, the patient was implying that the therapist was a "spy" like Francis Gary Powers.]

It should be noted that these interpretations applied only to the current situation and therefore dealt with preconscious data that the patient could grasp as soon as he was made aware of it. Since the dream deals only incidentally with contemporary or surface problems, one must look for deeper meanings in the associations. So far, all we can conjecture about the dream is that the patient is mocking the therapist and his science, perhaps in order to bolster his determination to stop treatment. This is the superficial meaning of the dream.

Interpretation in Depth

I suggested that the therapist could have also included in his interpretation the fact that the change in the patient's overt attitude toward him took place after he was able to find fault with him. This paralleled the change of his attitude toward his father when he criticized him for leaving home.

I asked the therapist why he thought the patient needed further treatment. He replied that he was impressed by the abrupt manner in which the patient had announced his desire to leave. He thought that this represented a resistance, probably a reluctance to discuss his ambivalence toward the therapist. As a matter of fact, the patient had had a recurrence of anxiety and colitis when he returned from his vacation. He related it to an episode in which he had been dishonest. This reminded him that he had failed to tell the therapist about his recent increase in salary. [When he started the analysis he had agreed to an increase in fee when he received a raise in salary.]

He also recalled a memory of having stolen something during adolescence, soon after his father left for Europe.

[The patient had also had an attack of anxiety and colitis immediately following his father's death. Could his recent anxiety have had to do with his intention to leave the analysis, that is, "get rid" of the therapist? In other words, he could be repeating his relationship with his father in the transference, and feeling guilty for wanting to leave the analysis? This might account for the fact that he asked the therapist to provide reasons for him to remain, thus shifting the responsibility onto him. More remotely, could his stealing after his father's departure for Europe symbolize his unconscious desire to possess his mother, that is, steal her from his father? This behavior might have been unconsciously repeated when he failed to report his salary increase to the therapist; by not paying an increased fee he was also "stealing" from him. This might as yet be beyond the patient's ability to comprehend.]

At this point the patient became testy and said, "Look, I don't want to be dependent on you. I don't want to come here forever. I don't want you as a crutch. I'm doing well. What do I need you for at this point? The month of my vacation went nicely. My life is better than it has ever been before." He later added, "You know, there is one thing about this, you always turn out to be right. I can't stand the idea that you might be right about my needing to continue. I just want to be free, to be on my own."

The therapist replied that unless the patient understood why he felt the way he did, it was not a good enough reason for leaving.

I remarked that the patient was in effect saying, "I don't want to be subordinated to you." He no longer wanted to remain passive. He was in awe of the therapist's authority and in his desire to break away from him, he might also be struggling against latent homosexual tendencies. It would be premature to make this interpretation, but it should be filed away for future reference. His attention, however, could have been directed to his strong reaction against being subordinated.

At this point the therapist recalled the patient's relationship to his father. The latter was an erudite, self-educated man for whom the patient had great regard. He taught the patient mathematics and gave him shortcut methods which enabled him to add four or five columns of figures almost at a glance. The two often played chess together, but once when he beat his father, the latter was unable to acknowledge the defeat and said, "We'll change this into a session of instruction."

I remarked that the father was ungracious in defeat and revealed that he did not like to lose. This could have aroused guilt in the boy for beating him. Thereafter, in order to avoid his father's displeasure, he might have had difficulty in asserting himself, and he did not do so until he was able to point an accusing finger at him for abandoning his family. At the time the patient felt supported by his mother, who strongly opposed his father's leaving. In like manner, it was difficult for the patient to say anything uncomplimentary about the therapist. This could also have been interpreted.

Until now we had assumed that Kolmogorodm referred to the therapist. He could have also represented the patient's father, a mathematician whose teachings were extended by the patient, just as the latter had made a contribution to Kolmogorodm's work. The father had also been a successful businessman in Europe at one time, so that he was accomplished in two separate areas, business and mathematics. These resemblances could have been pointed out to the patient.

In the case of both father and therapist, the patient succeeded in denigrating the man to whom he was subordinated. In doing so, he could have felt liberated from someone else's control. Since he himself had said that he wanted to be free of the therapist, the reasons for his attitude could be pursued. On the other hand, it would be some time before he could accept his fear of homosexuality. An interpretation closer to his awareness would be that by not being dependent on his father or the therapist for approval, he no longer had to feel guilty toward them. He felt justified in leaving the analysis because he was not being permitted to grow up and become independent.

The patient terminated the analysis within a short time after he reported the dream.

Dream Wish

It should be noted that without the associations it would be difficult to ascertain what the wish in the dream was. It was only after his associations revealed his ambivalence toward the analyst and his desire to be rid of him that we recognized the wish, namely, to free himself from being subordinated to the analyst. Before he could do so, however, he had to debase the analyst as being the proponent of a mock science, under the guise of praising him as being another Kolmogorodm.

On a deeper level, we may assume that his break from Orthodox Judaism represented a similar attempt to throw off the shackles of his father and his oedipal guilt. The rebellion against the father could have been interpreted; this would have prepared the way for the interpretation of the oedipal guilt at some later time. Just as the attempt at solution in adolescence was not successful, it is likely that leaving the analysis would not be successful and that the patient would return. It was important, however, to let the patient know the nature of his resistance, so that if he did return for further analysis he would know with what problems he still had to contend.

The question was asked whether the case could have been managed differently so as to prevent the confrontation with the therapist. It was suggested that it would have been better to discuss the patient's reasons for wanting to stop treatment nine months previously, when he first mentioned his intention. By the time he brought it up in September, however, he already seemed to have a closed mind. On the other hand, since his guilt about leaving had not been fully analyzed, he would probably return for more analysis, just as he returned to the Orthodox tradition.

The dream wish becomes evident only after the associations have been related to details of the manifest dream and our knowledge of the patient's background and character structure. A definite pattern begins to emerge and we come to certain conclusions which are based on approximations of what the dream is saying. On the other hand, our conclusions are supported by clinical data. In these cases, we look for verification of our interpretations in further material provided by the patient.

Summary

The dream highlighted the patient's basic conflicts, namely, his desire to replace his father in his mother's affections, and to wish for his father's dethronement (i.e. death), on the one hand, and his defenses against his guilt by becoming homosexually attached to his father, on the other. This led to a struggle against his passive homosexuality and a need to punish himself by suffering in the same way that his father suffered (developing prostatitis and losing his wife's affection through his impotence). On the basis of this dream one may, therefore, draw tentative conclusions about his relationships to both his father and mother and the nature of his neurosis. One can also be fairly certain, on the basis of the repetition compulsion, that this pattern was repeated in other relationships throughout his life. The dream interpretation can thus give us an overall picture of the patient's character and motivations. The striking thing is that a dream, which seemed unpromising at first, turned out to reveal so much about the patient and his conflicts and motivations.

CHAPTER 5

The Dream Wish

According to Freud, the essence of the dream is the fulfillment of an unconscious wish originating in early childhood. There has been some controversy about this concept, but before getting involved in discussion, it is important to know what led Freud to this conclusion. His sense of conviction about dreams undoubtedly arose from his analyzing his own dreams; as anyone who has done similarly can attest, an unshakeable feeling of certainty is derived from these free and highly secret associations.

Freud correctly perceived that the purpose of the dream was to discharge inner tensions which tend to disturb sleep, and thus to permit sleep to continue. Inner tensions are caused by dammed-up instinctual drives which have originated during the day and have not been able to find expression. According to Freud, the dream wish represents the gratification of these drives. He distinguished four possible origins for such a wish:

(1) It may have been aroused during the day and for external reasons may not have been satisfied; in that case an acknowledged wish which has not been dealt with is left over for the night.... (2) It may have arisen during the day but been repudiated; in that case what is left over is a wish which has not been dealt with but has been suppressed. (3) It may have no connection with daytime life and be one of those wishes which only emerge from the suppressed part of the mind and become active in us at night.... A fourth source of dream-wishes... [is]

the current wishful impulses that arise during the night (e.g. those stimulated by thirst or sexual needs). [1900, p. 551]

He adds that preconscious wishes are not adequate for instigating dreams unless they are reinforced by wishes from the unconscious. "My supposition is that a conscious wish can only become a dream-instigator if it succeeds in awakening an unconscious wish with the same tenor and in obtaining reinforcement from it" (p. 553).

A positive statement of this kind should be supported by proof. Freud, however, did not offer such proof in the analyses of his own dreams in the *Interpretation of Dreams* (Jones, 1965), but this he himself freely acknowledged, adding, "I have probably been wise in not putting too much faith in my readers' discretion" (1900, p. 105n). He did, however, do so in "An Evidential Dream" (1913c) where he interpreted a woman's infantile wish to have intercourse with her father and have an anal child by him, and also in the case of the Wolf Man (1918). In the Irma dream (1900, pp. 106-120), which is discussed more fully below, he acknowledged that he did not carry the interpretation to its full extent, and that he did not pretend to have completely uncovered the meaning of the dream. He added that he had private reasons for being restrained from pursuing the interpretation any further, although he knew the points from which further trains of thought could be followed. We can surmise that further analysis might have brought out the resemblance of his reactions to the immediate problems of the day as well as to problems which had arisen in the past, and which might lead to painful misunderstandings if exposed to general view. In this connection Freud was inclined to say with Mephistopheles in Goethe's *Faust*, "After all, the best of what you know may not be told to boys" (1900, p. 142).

Assured in his own mind, however, Freud proceeded to explain the reasons for the wish-fulfilling purpose of the dream. It had to do with the nature of the unconscious. "The reason why dreams are invariably wish-fulfilments is that they are products of the system *Ucs.*, whose activity knows no other aim than the fulfilment of wishes and which has at its command no other forces than wishful

The Dream Wish

impulses" (1900, p. 568). He emphasized the fact that dreaming, like the unconscious, represented a regression to childhood modes of thinking, as evidenced by the fact that it is largely a visual phenomenon, which is characteristic of all primitive thought. It also showed the qualities which were peculiar to primary process thinking, namely, displacement, condensation, and the employment of symbols. This applied not only to infantile drive representations, but also to infantile modes of defense and punishment.

The dream is a compromise between the conflicting demands of the three psychic structures, id, ego, and superego. In dreams of a pleasurable nature the compromise has been acceptable to all "parties." Unpleasurable dreams result when a wish of one agency seeking gratification at the "expense" of another manages to upset the balance. If a forbidden instinctual drive arising in the id, for instance, succeeds in evading the censorship of the superego and threatens to erupt and make the meaning of the dream too plain, the ego resorts to emergency measures by producing anxiety. The sleeper wakes up, thus interrupting the dream before the wish fulfillment can take place. Anxiety dreams point to a failure of the defensive operations of the ego; the anxiety replaces the censor in preventing the forbidden wish from entering consciousness. The dreamer awakens before the wish is fulfilled.

On the other hand, if the need for punishment outweighs the desire for instinctual gratification, the result is also an unpleasurable dream. This takes the form of frustration, disappointment, remorse, fear, or depression. In such a case the aims of the superego appear paramount in the form of a wish that the dreamer be punished for his forbidden wishful impulses. The wish in punishment dreams, therefore, belongs to the ego (superego) and not to the id (Freud 1900, p. 557f.) The forbidden impulse can easily be inferred from the nature of the punishment, but at times it is expressed quite clearly in the dream. Such dreams often occur in obsessional neurotics who habitually reproach themselves for both real and imagined misdeeds.

In the following dream both instinctual gratification and punishment found expression, but it was clear that punishment was the dominant feature.

Case 1P: A man prominent in community affairs dreamt that he made sexual advances to a child and found it very exciting. He then feared that she would expose him to her parents, which in fact she did. The parents sued him in court and he was fined two thousand dollars. Greater distress resulted when the fact became generally known. His reputation was irreparably damaged and he had to move to another community. At the end of the dream he felt hopeless despair.

Those who have undergone a psychical trauma in early childhood, particularly of a sexual nature, tend to suffer from recurrent dreams which reproduce the original traumatic scene. The revival of these painful experiences in dreams may be an attempt to transform the memories of the earlier experience into the fulfillment of instinctual wishes connected with the unpleasant experience. Freud considered such dreams as efforts to restore an earlier state of things, a "compulsion to repeat," which expresses the conservative aspect of the instincts. Such "compulsion is supported by the wish ... to conjure up what has been forgotten and repressed" (1920, p. 32). Unpleasurable dreams of this type may also express a desire to be young once again or they may represent the fulfillment of masochistic wishes, a punishment for currently indulging in forbidden impulses.

The dreams of those who suffer from traumatic neurosis also repeat the terror of the original traumatic event. These dreams appear to be a delayed attempt to master the overpowering experience which caught the dreamer unaware, that is, before he could prepare himself for the shock, by generating the anxiety whose omission was the cause of the traumatic neurosis. These dreams were at first considered to be "beyond the pleasure principle" and not to express a wish. Freud later included them under the category of wish fulfillments by regarding them as *attempts* at wish fulfillment which had failed (1933, p. 29).

Experimental work on dreams has produced no evidence that would either prove or disprove the wish fulfillment theory. E. Hartmann (1973) believes that although various theories advanced by both experimentalists and clinicians that dreams have a function in discharging instinctual drives are plausible and contain some kernel of truth, the experimental evidence is not entirely convincing (pp. 15-17). Fisher (1974) stated that although in previous years he could have spoken with greater confidence about the implications of dream research for psychoanalysis, the contradictory findings that have more recently emerged make it almost impossible to synthesize findings from the basic sciences with the theories of psychiatry and psychoanalysis. His original suggestion (Dement and Fisher, 1960; Fisher, 1965) that REM sleep might be necessary for psychic health had not at that point been verified, although he still considered Freud's wish fulfillment theory a viable hypothesis.

In some dreams there is no resolution of conflict. The dream ends with the patient in a state of indecision, as if there were a balance between the desire to gratify an instinctual impulse and the prohibition against it, as frequently occurs in obsessional neurotics.

How does one determine the dream wish from the mass of data at hand? In this respect one must be guided by the general trend of the associations, their convergence upon a nodal point, and their relation to one's knowledge of the patient's background and current situation. To illustrate this we may again refer to the specimen dream of psychoanalysis, the Irma dream In the preamble to the dream, Freud states that he had psychoanalytically treated a young woman, a friend of the family, for hysterical anxiety. As a result of treatment the patient was relieved of her anxiety but did not lose all her somatic symptoms. Just before she left for her summer vacation Freud had proposed a solution, which the patient did not accept. The day prior to the dream he had spoken to a junior colleague, Otto, who was a friend of the patient's family, and who had just returned from a visit to their country resort. Freud asked him how he had found Irma. Otto answered, with what Freud perceived to be a tone of reproof, "She's better, but not quite well." In his mind it was as though Otto had said to him, "You don't take your medical duties seriously enough. You're not conscientious, you don't carry out what you've undertaken." Freud was disturbed and that evening he wrote out Irma's case history which he planned to give to a Dr. M. with the purpose of justifying himself.

I will not repeat the details of the dream since they are so readily available. After giving his associations, Freud came to certain conclusions. According to him, these fulfilled wishes which were set in motion by the events of the previous day, namely, the news given him by Otto and his writing of the case history. In general he felt that the wishes were: to be regarded as a good physician who was conscientiously concerned about his patients; to be acquitted of the responsibility for Irma's condition by showing that it was due to other factors:

1. Irma herself was to blame for her pains, since she refused to accept the solution offered by him.
2. Irma's pains were of an organic nature and therefore insusceptible to psychological treatment. Furthermore, Freud did not pretend to cure organic disease by psychoanalysis.
3. Irma's pains could be explained by her widowhood, that is, they were sexual in nature, and he had no means of altering them.
4. Otto himself caused Irma's pains by having given her an unsuitable drug without sufficient forethought; moreover, he had probably used a dirty syringe.

In this manner, Freud not only succeeded in vindicating himself, but also avenged himself on Otto for being against him. On the other hand, the dream evoked some disagreeable memories which supported Otto's "accusations" against him. (This presumably was the superego's contribution to the dream.) The dream was the direct result of Freud's preoccupations of the preceding day and no doubt helped to relieve the doubts and tensions which he experienced as a result of Otto's communication.

The dream wish is ascertained then by becoming aware of the *intention which is carried into effect by the dream.* This constitutes the motive for the dream. In this case the dreamer's associations were directed toward vindicating himself, so that we may conclude that this was the meaning or the wish of the dream. In other words, if the associations are in accord with the main trend and feeling tone of the manifest dream, the preconscious latent thoughts will disclose the dream wish, at least as it applies to the current situation.

The wish fulfillment in the Irma dream appears to be superficial, as I have already indicated. The wish was unconscious only in the sense of being preconscious and therefore intelligible. If Freud were only intent upon vindicating himself in the manner implied by the dream, he probably could have done just as well during the waking state. Aside from the fact that the ideas conveyed by the interpretation could be embarrassing to a mature and reasonable person, they were acceptable to one (the regressed) aspect of the dreamer's self, that is, they were ego-syntonic. To achieve this result, however, one need not dream. The interpretation of any manifest dream deals with the current preoccupations of waking life (wishes, anxieties, and unsolved problems). This material is all preconscious and is contained in the latent thoughts brought out by the associations. The dream, however, is supposed to tell us more about the patient than is already known; its dominant concern is not that which can easily be made self-evident. The work of dream interpretation must therefore proceed further and uncover the dynamically unconscious, or repressed, wish which provides the motive power for the dream.

Since the gates of the unconscious are opened up during sleep, the dreamer has access to the reservoir of repressed infantile memories, primitive defense mechanisms, and infantile forms of the superego. This is the result of the extensive regression that occurs in dreaming. Deeper exploration of dream material reveals a parallelism between one's reactions to current problems and those which have arisen in the past. This, in part, is the result of the compulsion to repeat previous experiences. As one follows one's associations back to an earlier, that is, more primitive, period of life, thoughts which are repugnant to the mature self make their appearance. These may consist of "immoral, incestuous and perverse impulses or of murderous and sadistic lusts" (Freud, 1925, p. 132), which are no longer in conformity with the adult ego—they are ego-dystonic—and must be repressed. They can appear in the dream only if they are disguised by the distortions produced by the dream work. It is when these deep memories have been reached that we can be certain of having arrived at the underlying meaning of the dream. Such complete interpretations are likely to be made only in the later course of an analysis when most resistances have been overcome, as is illustrated in the case reported in the chapter on Terminal Dreams.

The stimulus for a dream may be a concern that is currently preoccupying the dreamer as in the Irma dream, it may be something trivial or unimportant, or it may offer a solution to a problem that the dreamer has been wrestling with during the day. According to Freud, the so-called "problem-solving" dream is a misnomer since the unconscious, being involved with discharge of instinctual tensions, can do no intellectual work. Solutions to problems that appear in dreams are already present in the dreamer's preconscious, as is evidenced by the fact that they may be accomplished while the individual is awake, in a mood of revery or reflection. In these states of mind the restraint of directed attention is thrown off, thus facilitating the emergence of ideas "from below." A similar withdrawal of concentration from immediate problems is also operative in acts of creativity and in wit, as Reik (1949) has pointed out.

There has been a tendency among some psychoanalysts to play down the wish-fulfilling function of the dream and to regard the dream as a form of "thinking ahead" (Adler, 1911, p. 214) like a child's play, a preparation for serious activity later on (Maeder, 1912, p. 692), or "problem solving" (French, 1958 and French and Fromm, 1964). Each of these writers attribute main importance to the manifest dream. When closely examined such concepts reveal an inclination to deal with conscious and preconscious data, and to overlook the importance of the dynamic unconscious. They tend to devalue infantile data, to emphasize intellectual activity in contrast to affects, to deal primarily with secondary process thinking, and to focus their attention on preconscious processes, which are relatively free of anxiety. Such tendencies undercut the superstructure of psychoanalysis by disregarding the basic concept of conflict

The Dream Wish

between repressed and repressing forces. Although Freud agreed that some dreams contain attempts at solving problems, and also give indications of such intellectual operations as judgments and mathematical calculations, these are to be regarded as belonging to the preconscious latent dream thoughts which come up in free association. The dream-work, Freud says, "is not creative, ... makes no judgments and draws no conclusions" (1901, p. 667).

Case Reports

The following dreams will be considered elsewhere to emphasize other aspects. They are being presented here in abbreviated form in order to demonstrate what constitutes the dream wish. Dreams, as may be expected, cover many aspects of the patient's psychic activity. To obviate the need to refer back to the following reports of the dreams, the details of each dream will be repeated in its appropriate place. In discussing the following dream specimens the wishes described will refer mainly to the current situation of the dreamer; no attempt will be made to trace them back to their infantile roots or to reconstruct the patient's past history. In some instances, however, references will be made to the dreamer's past, but only in a broadly suggestive way without conclusive evidence. Ordinarily such associations direct attention to the paths to be followed for deeper analysis.

Case 2C: *Dream 1:* There were six bottles of orange juice on the back seat of a car. A woman was sitting next to them. I drank some of the juice and afterwards found that it contained LSD. I then ran around frantically trying to get some Thorazine.

Dream 2: A guy was checking and making comments about the shapes of men. Then someone threw up all over my pants. It was like "come" or paint. I was upset.

The day prior to the dream the patient became disturbed when a married woman with whom he had been having an affair became conscience-stricken and decided to break off the relationship. The therapist, a woman, expressed her sympathy for him. In the associations to the dream she was the woman sitting behind him who offered him the orange juice. In the dream he becomes frantic when he discovers that it contains LSD. The analyst, as it were, feeds him poison with her milk, that is, with her sympathy. The patient looks for *Thorazine* as an antidote. In the second dream a man vomits semen or paint on his trousers. It was felt that in accepting sympathy from the therapist, the patient was threatened by the danger of getting involved in a forbidden relationship with the maternal figure who feeds him. In addition he suspected her intentions, since women could not be trusted. The number *six* is a symbol for "sex." He is saved from his dilemma by turning to a homosexual relationship (presumably the *antidote* to incest, just as *Thorazine* is the antidote to LSD).

The main thought of the dream is that the patient seeks protection against his desire to return to a passive-dependent relationship with a mother figure, with its incestuous overtones, by turning to homosexuality. This is a well-known mechanism. We therefore take this to be the dream wish. In this manner the dream succeeds in relieving the patient's current tension. It is true that the patient is upset at the end of the second dream, which suggests that he is not completely reconciled to the homosexual solution of his problem, but the affect is much less upsetting than is his frantic state in the first dream. As a result his sleep is not disturbed. It may also be pointed out that the dreamer achieves partial gratification of his regressive preoedipal wish to be close to his mother in the act of drinking the orange juice.

Case 3C: The following is an example of the type of dream which ends in indecision. The dream consists of thought alone with no action and represents a modification of the pure wish fulfillment dream.

Dream: I was coming out of a subway. It was dark. I was carrying my older son, feeling that I knew where I was. It was a

The Dream Wish

familiar feeling. I thought I heard shots on the right and started to run in the opposite direction. Then shots rang out on the left and I ran back to the right. I felt very confused as to which way to go. At that moment I thought my wife and her father were across the street in the darkness. I thought I was being attacked by black revolutionaries and felt trapped and terrified. I was trying to decide where to go and which to save, my son or my wife and her father.

The patient had been having sexual problems with his wife, and in response to the therapist's encouragement, for the first time had succeeded in having intercourse with his wife by inserting his penis without her assistance. His wife expressed her appreciation and he felt very proud of himself. When he reported his success to the therapist the following day, however, he felt let down when the therapist said, "We still don't know what it is that you are afraid of. Putting it in yourself doesn't tell us what you are frightened of." To be criticized was like being shot at. The patient was confused by the therapist's apparent lack of appreciation of his achievement in having taken the initiative in intercourse. He felt he had been *entrapped* by the therapist's encouragement. In the dream, if he assumes his mature role as a husband he runs the risk of losing his *child* (penis); the alternative is to sacrifice his *wife*, that is, heterosexuality. He cannot make up his mind whether to assume the adult role (heterosexuality) or the dependent child relationship (homosexuality). This would fit in with the idea expressed in the dream of shots being fired both from the *right* and the *left* (symbols of hetero- and homosexuality.) His doubts remain unresolved.

The patient has always lived in a state of doubt and ambivalence; he is safe as long as he makes no decision, since any choice he makes may contain hidden dangers. The wish therefore is to maintain the status quo and to do nothing; in this situation he finds that he can satisfy the demands of both id and ego (superego).

Case 4P: *Dream:* I am driving a car in the wrong direction. The road is winding and curvy and I am going fast. There is danger of hitting a car coming in the opposite direction, especially on curves. As I come to an intersection at the end of the road I am afraid I will be stopped by a traffic cop, and although I am not caught, I wake up feeling worried and upset.

The patient suffered from high blood pressure and was constantly afraid of being brought low by a stroke. The dream was instigated by an event of the previous day—a minor automobile accident which the patient, out of guilt, blew up beyond all proportion. The guilt must therefore have referred to something else. According to his associations, it had to do with his sexual affair with a married woman (driving along the curvy road), the punishment for which was death (as indicated by the death on the same highway of a friend, who had been having an extramarital affair). In accord with the talion principle, the guilt must have been related to the wish to kill the father in the oedipal conflict. Despite the fact that he indulged his forbidden pleasure in the dream, the dominant mood was an unpleasant one—an ominous feeling that he would be caught by the traffic cop (father). When he woke up he felt that being caught was not the worst thing that could happen to him; he could succumb to a serious illness which might threaten his life. This was the dream wish; it satisfied the demand of the superego that he be punished. This was confirmed several days later, when he suffered a mild stroke. He reacted to his illness with a sense of relief and serenity, as if he were released from the feeling of doom which had encompassed him. It was as if, having received his punishment, he no longer had to feel guilty. Here again the severity of the patient's reactions pointed to the deeper origin of his guilt feelings, particularly since he was an obsessional person who repeatedly overreacted with guilt to his aggressive and sexual impulses.

Case 5C: The following was the dream of the phobic individual who experienced anxiety when he had to do night work and could overcome it only if his wife were present while he was working.

Dream: I walked into a bedroom. My father is lying on the bed covered by a sheet. He is dead. I begin to have difficulty in

The Dream Wish

breathing and go into the bathroom where my mother is. I open the window and start to breathe much better. My mother can always help me. I think what a wonderful wife I have.

The stimulus of the dream was the fact that the patient experienced anxiety while on night duty. He suddenly felt lonely for his wife and had an urgent desire to be near her. He then decided to go home and felt a sense of triumph in having the courage to defy his superior by leaving.

The thing that impressed us at first was the nature of the patient's reaction to the sight of his father lying dead. We would expect him to be affected by grief, but instead he has difficulty in breathing. He furthermore does not break the news of his father's death to his mother, who behaves as if she is not aware of it. We must therefore assume that the patient does not react as expected because his father has not really died. On the basis of previous experience, we make the assumption that breathing difficulty is an accompaniment of sexual excitement. That leads us to conclude that the patient is responding to a homosexual attraction for his father, in which case the rest of the dream becomes understandable. The fear of homosexuality can be overcome if one establishes a relationship with a woman. By juxtaposing his mother and wife, it is as if they are equated in his mind—they can both help him counteract his homosexual tendencies. The dream wish must therefore be to escape from homosexuality to heterosexuality. This interpretation succeeds in throwing light on his phobia of being alone with men, and his relief when he is accompanied by his wife.

The dream seemed to explain the nature of his phobia and his act of defiance of the previous night. It was as if his superior (father) was forcing him to submit to a homosexual act which the patient repudiated, both in the dream and actually, by leaving work. Although the dream succeeded in relieving the patient's immediate tension, his further associations indicated that similar tensions had been an ongoing problem with him since childhood, ostensibly as the result of his negative oedipal attachment to his father. The current dream wish was thus only a repetition of a much earlier wish.

Case 6P: *Dream:* I was putting on old clothes and shoes to do dirty work in the yard or cellar. I saw that my shoes had mud on them in the back. I was annoyed for having been so careless as to get mud on my shoes.

The patient tried to minimize the significance of the dream, but this only served to increase my curiosity. In the previous session I had pointed out to him that he almost routinely disregarded my questions, that his general thinking habits were undisciplined and confused, and that he often failed to complete his thoughts. He became very angry, but later agreed that his attitude toward the analysis had been a *careless* one.

In the dream, he continued with this careless attitude by having mud on his shoes. In reality, if he was planning to do dirty work in the garden or cellar there was no reason for him to be fastidious about his appearance. His concern could have meaning, however, if the dream were to refer to the analytic session. The wish seemed to be to show anal defiance against me ("mud on the back of his shoes"), as if he were expressing his contempt for me by showing me his dirty rear end. We are guided by the action in the manifest dream and must regard his dissatisfaction with himself as a deceptive attempt to appease both me and his superego. The dream wish thus represented an act of aggression.

Case 7C: This is the dream of a young man who was referred for analysis by a doctor who had been treating him by psychotherapy.

Dream: I moved to a new apartment. It was really a dump. It had only one small window, while my present apartment has three big windows. The whole apartment was dingy. It was in center city, somewhere on Spruce Street. I wondered why I moved when I already had a nice apartment.

In the dream the patient is comparing his former therapist to his present one, to the disadvantage of the latter. He had been transferred from a "plush" office to a more modest one, and also to a

The Dream Wish

man who charged him a lower fee than the other and therefore could not be as good. He is thus expressing his contempt for the therapist. Despite his feelings, the dreamer takes no action; the dream consists entirely of thoughts. We may ask why he does not decide to return to his former therapist if he has doubts about the present one. Since the dream ends in doubt we assume that the negative and positive aspects of the patient's ambivalence (i.e. his contradictory wishes) cancel each other out. It seems as if he will remain with the present doctor, probably because he is afraid of his own aggression and is not prepared to antagonize the therapist. The doctor thus receives a warning of the patient's ambivalence. In addition the patient may not be prepared to leave because he has been impressed by the therapist's integrity.

Case 8C: A woman, who was already living with one man, was contemplating affairs with two others. Both of them were in the process of breaking up their marriages and she hesitated to get involved with them inasmuch as her intentions were not serious and she was afraid she would only add to their confusion. She had recently thought of inviting one of the men to her apartment while her lover was at work. The day prior to the dream she was trying to decide how the meeting might be arranged.

Dream: She was in her apartment with her paramour. In the bed there were two men covered with a brown shiny plastic material as though they had been dipped in it. They were in agony. One could hear them screaming as they tried to free themselves. She was horrified and ran out of the room.

In the dream two men are being tortured. She is horrified, but instead of coming to their assistance, she escapes from the room. On the basis of the simple data of the dream we assume that the wish is anal-sadistic (the brown plastic). The dream suggests that the suffering she inflicts on the men is unacceptable to her adult ego; her affective response is a mature reaction to a more primitive tendency presumably dating back to early childhood. In order to come to terms with her superego and satisfy her conscience, the satisfaction she derives from hurting men must not be too obvious; she therefore experiences horror. From what we knew about the patient, the reason for her sadism toward men resulted from feelings of inferiority and competitiveness.

Case 9P: I include the following dream in order to elaborate on my discussion of the "problem-solving" function of the dream. In the dream the patient manages to deal with a disappointment of the previous day. He is depressed but indicates that he plans to overcome his immediate frustration in a regressive rather than constructive way, that is, one that might lead to productive results. It also points to the background of his method of resolving tensions, and particularly to its repetitive nature. If followed to its logical conclusion it would doubtless have led to the basic problems of his infancy. The patient's conviction about the validity of the interpretation was assured by his recognition that it faithfully represented his typical pattern of behavior throughout life.

Dream: The patient and a friend were walking along a railroad track in a bleak, unfamiliar countryside. He was in a solemn mood, somewhat depressed.

The day residue had to do with having been disappointed in a business deal. The friend was his associate in business and was therefore in the same boat with him. He recalled reading *With Napoleon in Russia* by Napoleon's aide, de Caulaincourt. The author, a member of the nobility, admired Napoleon but was also critically objective toward him. The bleak countryside reminded the patient of Napoleon's retreat from Moscow. While riding with de Caulaincourt in a sled, Napoleon reflected upon the reasons for the failure of the campaign and presented his general views of the European situation. Arriving in Paris late at night, he immediately went to his wife's apartment, where she had already retired, and dismissed everyone else. The dreamer understood this to indicate Napoleon's need for consolation. The situation reminded him of his

The Dream Wish

own need for the comfort of a woman after any disappointment and also of his belief that men, including his companion in the dream, were competitive and unfriendly. He then realized that he, like Napoleon, was an "upstart" who inwardly rebelled against being subordinated and who was inclined to challenge anyone in a superior position, ultimately hoping to replace him. In his business dealings he felt that his competitors regarded him as a newcomer out to destroy them. His fear of men's hostility was thus a projection of his own aggressive competitiveness. When defeated he turned to women (mother substitutes) upon whose reassurance and encouragement he could always rely. As a child he stood in awe of his father but was always able to discuss things with his mother, who served as an intermediary. His behavior throughout life was therefore a repetition of the oedipal struggle; he was the parvenu who sought to unseat the head of the household.

The dream wish, as indicated by the mood of the dream, was to be punished, but behind this lay the prospect of being consoled by his wife. This was no different from his behavior as a child. If the "focal conflict" (French, 1958) of the dream referred to the oedipal situation, as appears likely, the conflict can hardly be said to have been resolved. At most one could say that the patient's wounded feelings were relieved. The real solution of the problem, however, would depend upon clearing up his repetitious pattern of behavior through the analysis of the underlying oedipal conflict.

CHAPTER 6

Early Dreams and Premature Interpretations

It is not what the interpretation means to the analyst that is important, but what it means to the patient. An interpretation that does not touch on the patient's immediate problem and to which the patient has no affective response is bound to be ineffective. Before the patient can accept an interpretation it must be consonant with his *psychic reality,* that is, how the reality situation is seen through his eyes, taking into consideration the extent to which reality may be colored or distorted by his fantasies. The analyst cannot be rigidly reality-oriented but must be aware that reality may be a relative matter for the analysand. He must therefore show proper regard for the fact that reality may even be a source of anxiety to the latter. Interpretations must be presented cautiously. This is particularly true if the patient views reality as a repetition of a trauma which he has actually experienced in earlier life and which has become perpetuated in his fantasy world. The patient's conviction of the validity of his own views resembles the paranoid delusion which Freud explained by the element of historical truth which it contains. At times patients whose beliefs appear to be immune to reality testing may give the impression of being paranoid, without necessarily being so. The analyst, while recognizing the degree to which fantasies may dominate the patient's general attitude, must continue to represent reality. Only in this way can he hope to make the patient realize his distortions.

A patient, after fourteen years of married life, wanted to divorce his wife because she was not sufficiently affectionate. He insisted that she caress him openly, not only at home but also in public. He compared her unfavorably with his pretty secretary, with whom he was carrying on a dalliance, and who, according to him, was quite affectionate. He was literally blind to the fact that the two situations were not on equal footing. When he insisted that his wife hold hands with him or embrace him in public, he failed to realize that people were mocking him when they said, "Look at the two lovebirds." He thought that they were merely revealing their envy. His inability to recognize the objective reality when it was pointed out to him seemed to be related to his need to make up for his mother's lack of tenderness when he was a child, as well as his latent homosexuality.

Another man was ready to see the hand of fate in all his encounters, claiming that his pleasures were invariably spoiled and that he was constantly being victimized by others. He could not be convinced that his assessment of such situations did not accord with reality, even when it was possible to point out that in many instances he himself had unconsciously arranged to bring about the unhappy result. This pattern appeared to be related to his frustration at an early age (before two) when he was frequently left with relatives while his parents went away for long periods of time, in addition to experiences at the age of five with a seductive mother who often invited him into her bed and then failed to take his part when his father ordered him to leave. His feeling of being victimized also served to counteract his guilt which was generated by his ever-present hostility toward others. To have overlooked the impact of these early experiences, which had become part of the unconscious fantasy life of these two patients and had led to pathogenic conflicts, would have rendered the analyst totally ineffective (Arlow, 1969).

In brief, it is not only necessary to make certain that the patient at each stage of the analysis is fully prepared to understand the significance of an idea that has hitherto been repressed, but also to take account of the manner in which his life was affected by traumatic experiences in early childhood.

Interpretation of initial dreams is a special case of premature intervention. In these dreams, not only is the dreamer unprepared for the impact of the interpretation, but the dream itself may be so ingenuous and transparent as to disclose the patient's entire neurosis

Early Dreams and Premature Interpretations

in all its painful aspects and to expose the patient himself in his most vulnerable areas. Confronting the patient with his unflattering or painful unconscious impulses before he is prepared to face them may prove too traumatic. It is as if the analyst had barged in when the patient's defenses were down. Such confrontation may result in the patient's shoring up his defenses in order to protect himself against the repetition of such experiences. In other instances where the patient feels threatened he may, out of fear, suppress his symptoms and withdraw from treatment altogether (flight into health).

Although the meaning of many early dreams may be clear, they may also show ambivalent tendencies and be difficult to understand. At times their meaning may not become plain until the analysis approaches its end, as, for instance, in the case of the Wolf Man. Terminal dreams, namely, those that occur after most of the patient's conflicts have been resolved, are most likely to lend themselves to fuller interpretation.

If we consider the patient's state of mind when he enters treatment it is not difficult to understand his guardedness. Analysis represents a great unknown. The patient may come with the expectation that his problems will all be solved and that he will undergo a complete change of personality, as if he were to be born anew. According to Lewin (1954, p. 504) lying on the couch represents sleep with its maternal overtones, but it may also remind the patient of death. The patient may idealize the analyst but in his ambivalence he often regards him with both awe and distrust. At best he believes that his analyst is competent as well as a benign, all-knowing and forgiving parent who will be concerned about his welfare and will protect him. Under these circumstances, he is usually prepared to disclose all his thoughts freely. Even a skeptical individual may be quite open, particularly if his skepticism is a mask for a passive, receptive attitude. On the other hand, the patient may fear that in disclosing his innermost self he will become totally uninhibited and lose self-control. He may also be afraid that uncovering the layers of his mind will bring to light an underlying psychosis.

What then should be the analyst's attitude toward dreams that are reported early in the analysis? If the dream reveals no anxiety, perhaps nothing need be done. If the patient feels anxious he can be reassured by being told that he is reacting to a new and unaccustomed situation. The analyst may also anticipate the patient's reaction to his silence early in the analysis by describing his role and what the patient is to expect. The patient may thus be advised that analysis differs from the psychotherapeutic situation in that there is no regular give-and-take between patient and doctor. On the contrary, he should be told that it is essential for the analyst to find out as much as possible about him from his associations before he is in a position to say anything meaningful. When the doctor has something to say, the patient can be assured that he will do so.

When should the doctor intervene and begin to translate to the patient his unconscious thoughts? First of all, the patient's confidence in the analyst's good intentions must be built up, so that he comes to regard the analyst's interventions as being helpful. The analyst's attitude should be that of a sympathetic listener who shows concern for the patient and takes a serious interest in his productions. Under such circumstances, the patient is likely to identify the analyst with the affectionate parents of his childhood. This type of relationship should lead to the establishment of a positive transference. Only then will the patient willingly cooperate with the analyst by following the fundamental rule of free association. Until this development occurs, the patient is likely to be unduly sensitive to criticism. A young man, who disclosed his masturbatory habits with much embarrassment and chargrin, was greatly relieved by the analyst's comment that he must have been laboring under intolerable sexual tension and had to find an outlet. Any indication that the analyst was judgmental would have had a deadening and inhibiting effect upon the patient.

The positive transference itself, however, may become a resistance, if the transference is eroticized or if the analysand wants to retain the analyst's good opinion of him. Under such circumstance he may report only those things that are likely to win the analyst's approval. On the other hand, he may resent his posture of subservience by becoming critical of the analyst. When such

Early Dreams and Premature Interpretations

resistances appear the analyst may intervene in order to learn what is interrupting the progress of the analysis and the flow of new material. In this endeavor he may fall back on his knowledge of the patient; this is further reason for delaying interpretation of dreams until the analysis is more advanced. Such interventions should be limited to uncovering the cause of the resistance. It will be found that it most often has to do with the patient's attitude to the analyst. The investigation of the resistance is in accord with the basic tenet that one analyzes defenses before interpreting id content. Moreover, since defense is an ego function, it is more likely to be recognized by the patient than is the instinctual drive.

It is at this point, namely, when the transference becomes a resistance, that one may begin to offer interpretations, including the interpretation of dreams. The interpretations most likely to be accepted are those "from above," that is, those that consist of ideas that exist in the waking state and of which the patient can be made aware (Freud, 1923b, p. 111). By working with a recent pathogenic conflict, one avoids dealing with regressive material (Loewenstein, 1951, p. 10).

For instance, if the patient's dream about the death of a close relative were to be interpreted as a wish, he would necessarily find it unacceptable; he would not only reject the interpretation, but would in all likelihood express resentment against the analyst and become less cooperative. One rather seeks to relate the dream to a current situation which is intolerable and which could be cleared up by the removal of the offending person. A frankly incestuous dream might likewise be referred to a current fascination or one that existed in the past. In other words, in offering interpretations of early dreams, it is generally appropriate to confine them to surface material and to what is acceptable by the conscious ego. At any time in the analysis, however, an interpretation that is too disturbing to the patient may increase his resistance so that the ultimate acceptance of the interpretation may be delayed for months. This is well illustrated by the fourth case reported in this section, where the patient's desire to be free of the analyst's surveillance was prematurely interpreted as a wish for the analyst's death. In any event a wish of this type must be regarded as being too deepseated to be readily acceptable early in the analysis and without adequate preparation. Generally speaking, interpretations which are unacceptable to the conscious ego can be made more palatable if the patient is told that the wish exists in the unconscious—the repository of all infantile memories—and thus represents a thought that may have been present at the time when he was a guileless child, but is certainly not the way he thinks at the present time.

According to Bornstein (1949) the value of an interpretation "from above" is based on the fact that an emotion consists of both ego and id derivatives, and thus gives access to roads leading in both directions. She illustrates this by the case of a small boy who suffered from severe phobic states related to the birth of a sibling. The child presented aggressive and tyrannical behavior which in the author's opinion replaced feelings of sadness and loneliness. In order to be able to interpret his conflicts to him, she felt it was important to bring the warded-off affect into consciousness without arousing undue resistance. On one occasion he presented a fantasy of a lonely boy, sitting on an elevated chair in a hospital that had been destroyed by a fire in which all the babies and most of the mothers had burned to death. After considering a number of alternative interpretations, such as his resentment against his mother for giving birth to a sibling, Bornstein expressed sympathy for the lonely child who was barred from the room where his mother had given birth to his sister and who was too little to understand why his father was admitted and not he. The boy responded to her sympathy with growing sadness which until then had been covered up (p. 186).

It is a sound rule to remain silent if one does not fully understand what is going on. This is particularly true in dealing with initial dreams. A woman reported the following dream in the fourteenth hour of her analysis:

Dream (C): I am not sure it was B. [her fiancé]. Maybe it wasn't. We had to go through a maze. He blindfolded me so I wouldn't get upset seeing what was in there. There were things we had to carry through. We had to keep coming back and making more trips. My grandma was there. I was trying to remind her I was me, but her memory was bad. I thought a monster was there and some people said, "He won't hurt you." I said, "I have to seem afraid to make sure he won't hurt me." I think water was also there. At one point, I lost the person I was with and ended with my grandmother, but I'm not sure about that.

On the surface the dream disclosed some anxiety about moving around in a maze which contained an unknown danger, namely, a monster. The patient loses touch with the man who leads her into the maze and ends up with her grandmother. This was understood to refer both to her forthcoming marriage about which she entertained doubts and also to the analysis, which was terra incognita to her. According to the dream, she prefers to lose her guide (her fiancé and probably also the therapist) and to return to the security of her grandmother. Since her anxiety was apparently relieved in the dream, no further reassurance was deemed necessary, although it would have been appropriate for the therapist to tell her that it was naturally upsetting for her to start the analysis, which to her may have appeared as a maze.

Dream (P): In another case, a man dreamt that he was in a barber chair. The barber behind him held a razor in his hand and the patient was afraid he would be stabbed in the back. He woke up in alarm.

The dream seemed to reflect the patient's homosexual and castration fears. He was a querulous person and reacted to the analyst's comments with a characteristically disputatious form of skepticism. In the course of the analysis he gradually became more suspicious and paranoid. Within a short time he terminated the analysis of his own accord. In this case it would have been foolhardy to offer any interpretation before one knew how stable the patient's ego was and what it could tolerate.

Greenson (1970) reported a dream which he analyzed when the patient was in the sixth week of analysis:

> The patient was arguing with a clothing salesman over the phone, refusing to pay for clothes he had bought. He said the clothes did not fit, as if they had just been taken from the rack. At this point he began to vomit.

In his associations the patient connected vomiting with free association. Shortly before the dream, he had expressed considerable skepticism about pat psychoanalytic phrases which were easily bandied around in social situations by friends who were in psychoanalytic treatment. Greenson made the interpretation that the patient was reluctant to accept the analyst's interpretations which did not seem to fit him and were just taken off the analyst's "psychoanalytic rack" (pp. 534–536).

Greenson uses this example to demonstrate that it is possible to work productively with a first dream. He goes on to say that avoidance of dream interpretation by the analyst can frighten the patient, because the patient may sense the analyst's fear of the dream contents. (I myself have not had this experience.) He adds, however, that one must assess carefully with each patient how much and how little one can do with early dreams and with early material in general.

Here the impression is given that although the dream was reported during the sixth week of analysis, the patient already had a good working relationship with the analyst and was free to express his doubts about him. This suggests that Greenson was analyzing a piece of the patient's transference resistance and felt fairly confident in doing so.

Case Reports

Early dreams, even when the analyst does not offer an interpretation, will frequently reveal much about the patient. Such information can be filed away for future reference.

Early Dreams and Premature Interpretations

Case 1C: A young professional woman who had recently married a lawyer, reported the following dream in the ninth week of her analysis:

> Her husband, the therapist, and the patient were looking over an apartment where she was to move. The rooms were all open so that anyone could see everything that was taking place. In one room there was a young woman with her breasts exposed. In another there was a sick woman. The patient thought to herself anyone would have to be crazy to move into such an apartment.

Day Residue: The patient had assumed a challenging attitude toward the therapist from the very beginning of the analysis. During the session prior to the dream, she had broken down and confessed that she had had an affair with a co-worker before she was married. She felt guilty about it and wondered whether she should tell her husband. She was afraid she might talk about it in her sleep. This need to confess was increased when her husband asked her how the analysis was going. The therapist responded by asking her why she felt she had to tell her husband anything that took place in the analysis.

Association: The patient reported the dream the following day, after arriving twenty minutes late. In associating to the dream she said that the apartment in the dream reminded her of the analysis where everything was laid open. She wondered why anyone would want to undergo an analysis. She said she felt let down after the previous session, because the therapist had little to say, so that she did not know where she stood with him, that is, what he thought of her after she told him of her premarital affair. She said she did not know whether or not to continue with the analysis, and then added she would like to leave ten minutes early, so that she would not miss her lunch hour.

[The patient's understanding of the dream was undoubtedly correct and followed close upon her confession of guilt about her premarital liaison. One might hazard the guess that the girl of the dream with exposed breasts represented the patient herself and that she had fantasies of seducing the therapist. The fact that she expressed lack of security with the therapist suggests that a positive transference had not yet been established and that she was not yet ready to accept an interpretation of the dream. She obviously needed reassurance after her confession. The therapist's question about her need to confess to her husband, which was intended to reassure her, actually failed to do so. She apparently still needed his approval.

Could the situation have been handled differently? The therapist might have told her that since she felt guilty about her misdeed, it was evident that she herself did not approve of it: one could, then, not really condemn her. Perhaps she was being too harsh with herself. Such comments would have conveyed the reassurance she sought. In addition, instead of asking her why she felt compelled to confess to her husband, a question which may have appeared to her as a reproach or (if she unconsciously intended to be seductive) as an added danger, the therapist might have advised her not to discuss her analysis with anyone, her husband included. He could have added that she might not be able to see the reason for such advice at present, but she would become aware of it as the analysis proceeded. Others were not privileged to know what was going on in her unconscious; the unconscious was her own private preserve that outsiders could not fully understand and could only use against her. In this manner the therapist could preserve his objectivity and also convey his concern about her welfare and his desire to protect her. In saying this, however, he would have been doing nothing to remove her feelings of guilt; these had still to be ananlyzed. An approach of such directness should increase the patient's confidence in the therapist and promote the development of a positive transference and a working alliance.]

Comment: We learn from the dream that the patient has a severe superego, probably associated with an obsessional character. As she had a tendency to react with anger to any criticism, as evidenced by her remark about wanting to give up treatment, we may expect her to be rather rigid, but probably a good candidate for analysis.

Early Dreams and Premature Interpretations

Case 2C: A man who was in analysis for about four months, introduced the following dream with the remark that it was a "funny" dream.

> In it he went to visit his mother who had been raped two days previously. She was very angry with him, as if he were the one who had raped her. His sister, who was present, was also angry with him.

Associations: The patient said he found the dream "funny" because it was the sort of thing one heard in jokes about analysis, namely, that one can have sexual feelings for one's mother and "stuff like that." Nevertheless when he began to associate to the dream he felt quite uncomfortable. This was not surprising, since his comment about the dream indicated that he was disturbed by it and wanted to minimize its significance.

The therapist correctly understood that it was much too early in the analysis to try to interpret the dream. As a matter of fact, he was unable to see the connection between the dream and the patient's current situation. He was nevertheless perplexed because he did not know how to handle the matter of incest.

Comment: We ordinarily assume that the dreams are disguised or distorted so that the dreamer will not recognize tendencies in himself that are alien to his moral standards. When the dream threatens to reveal the raw forbidden wish underlying it, the censor causes the dreamer to awake in a state of anxiety, so as to prevent the unconscious wish from becoming conscious. The same holds true of dreams involving the death of a close relative. Although the dream represents an infantile wish, the frank appearance of such wishes in adult life, if unaccompanied by anxiety, must refer to something relatively harmless in his current life. When a patient once recounted to Freud that in his puberty he had dreamed of having intercourse with both his mother and sister, Freud remarked that the patient must have been very much in love with a girl at the time (quoted by Loewenstein, 1951, p. 10). This is an example of interpretation "from above."

Although no specific accusation has been leveled at the dreamer, he interprets the anger of his mother and sister as being an indictment. This may be construed as a commentary on the reaction of his superego to something he has recently contemplated or actually done.

Early in the analysis one is frequently at a loss to know what a dream which contains potentially inflammable material refers to. Unless one can relate it to some current situation which is relatively harmless, it is advisable to remain silent. The fact that the patient referred to it as a "funny" dream indicated that he did not want the therapist to take it seriously. At a later stage of the analysis one might make such a comment, but at this point it would be best to leave the dream alone.

Case 3C: A young social worker reported the following dream in her twenty-first session. The dream obviously had a strong effect on her, as manifested by the disjointed manner in which it was reported. There were frequent interruptions in which the patient commented on her reactions.

> This dream—it was the weirdest feeling—I woke up and thought, "Oh, my God!" It wasn't one I want to talk about at all, but I know I just have to say whatever comes to my mind. In the dream there was some man who was making love to me and it wasn't my husband. It looked like him but I just know it wasn't him. I was all involved. It was a complete sharing and I woke up all in a sweat. It made me feel that I had never met the man who I instinctively felt was ideal for me. It's like part of myself was asking to be expressed. The feeling was so strong. In the dream I was euphoric; it was not a very sensual feeling. It was a complete loving of someone else.

After relating the dream, she added, "Either I have no one in mind or I do have someone in mind and don't want to let it out. I don't remember what we were lying on. It was just a pillow. I felt as if I really wanted to be engulfed by this feeling, but I was afraid of it. It

Early Dreams and Premature Interpretations 99

left me feeling strange. But I felt very, very feminine all day afterward, as if I wanted to feel my feminine qualities more than usual. I really felt like a woman. It reawakened my drives and I don't want that to happen. I want to suppress my drives. I don't want to feel feminine. I guess I'm in conflict. One part of me wishes to express my drives, but another part is afraid."

[The dream apparently touched upon some current situation which evoked the memory of strong conflicts. This in itself indicated that the dream dealt with sensitive material which might be upsetting to the patient were it to be interpreted. Such excessive reactions to a dream should caution the therapist about offering a premature interpretation, although, in the absence of external factors, he should be alerted to the possibility that it might be a reaction to an eroticized transference.]

Day Residue: The dream occurred on a Sunday night and was reported the following day. The patient recalled that during the previous session on Friday she had been quite agitated but did not know why. The following day she was annoyed by the bickering of her children. She went to the grocery store and was agitated about everything. She was irritated by other drivers on the road and felt like running someone down with her car. When she returned home from shopping she "ripped" into her husband and "tore him to shreds," so that he finally left the house. She then felt she had to get rid of her excess energy by performing physical jobs that were usually her husband's. On Sunday she again started on him with her "sarcastic" tongue. Although she was remorseful and felt like cutting out her tongue, she was unable to stop herself. She related her anger toward him with the anger she used to feel toward her mother. She added that she also went out of her way to appear unattractive and unfeminine.

The patient stated that she married her husband in order to escape from her sexual attraction to a co-worker. She had tried to encourage a relationship with the latter, but he reacted as if he were afraid of becoming involved with her. She said she felt better after the dream and was less grumpy and irritable. Nothing was said by the therapist. When the session was over she arose from the couch and said, "I'd better get out of here or I'll seduce you—or you'll think I will. No, I didn't mean that, I didn't say that." As she walked out of the office, she turned with a flushed face and said, "Now, don't write that down."

[The patient was obviously having fantasies about the therapist. He seemed to be the man in the dream who was making love to her. The question may be asked why she was so afraid of her emotional response in the dream, when she was obviously enjoying it. Since in the associations she joined her husband with her mother, it could be that she felt guilty for having sexual fantasies about the therapist. But how can one account for the appearance of sexual feelings for the therapist so early in the analysis? Women patients, as a rule, are reserved in expressing positive feelings toward the therapist. The patient's attraction to the latter seems to have resembled her seductive attitude toward her fellow worker. One surmises that she had an impulsive need to become involved with men, either as a defense against something else (homosexuality?) or because of overstimulation in early life (by her father?)]

Background: The patient was an attractive woman in her early thirties, who came from a well-to-do family. She spoke of her "absolutely perfect" early relationship with her mother. In her adolescence she became aware that her mother had a drinking problem. Her parents were separated when she was twelve or thirteen. She and her younger sister remained with the mother. The latter, however, did not want to keep them and they went to live with the maternal grandmother. There were frequent quarrels between the patient and her mother over the latter's drinking, and after a year the girls returned to their father. The patient then lost contact with her mother, except for occasional visits. While the patient was at college she learned of her mother's death which resulted from hepatic cirrhosis complicated by pneumonia. At the time she did not seem to be much affected by the news.

At eighteen the patient married her first husband after a short courtship. He worked in the same field as her father. After a daughter was born she began to feel that her husband did not understand her, and she refused to have sexual relations with him. She then went into psychotherapy. Shortly thereafter a violent scene with her husband ensued, in the course of which he struck her. A little later they were divorced, and she terminated her therapy and returned to college. She taught school for a while and while there met a man whom she married after a whirlwind courtship, like the previous one. After six years of marriage, during which she had two more daughters, she again began to complain that her husband did not understand her or recognize her needs. She refused to have sexual relations with him and returned for more therapy. After several months her husband demanded to have intercourse with her and struck her when she refused. This terminated the marriage.

The patient thus followed a similar pattern in both marriages. Although she described both husbands as being inadequate, it later turned out that they appealed to her because they were much more aggressive in pursuing her than the other men she knew. The patient was playfully seductive and flirtatious. During the first interview, for instance, she said, "I know analysts don't say much, but I'll find out what you're thinking, you wait and see!"

[The patient's early strong positive feelings toward the therapist seemed to resemble her "whirlwind" courtships. She apparently had a drive to establish this type of relationship with men quickly. What could have motivated her?]

Sense of the Dream: At this point in the seminar I suggested that we review the manifest dream in order to determine what the sense of the dream was. It amounted to the following: the patient has a wondrous, beautiful sexual experience with a man other than her husband. She describes him as her ideal man and falls in love with him. But the dream also frightens her and she awakens.

Comment: The patient is thinking of leaving her husband and falls in love with the therapist. She could either be afraid of her aggression or of her mother's disapproval, or perhaps both. She reacted impulsively in marrying twice after whirlwind courtships and then rejected each husband after giving birth to children. She is now ready to repeat the pattern with the therapist. Flirtatiousness is often a way of gaining control over men, and from her past behavior and her attitude toward the therapist ("I know analysts don't say much, but I'll find out what you're thinking, you wait and see"), one might assume that this is the thing that motivates her. She apparently regards sex as a controlling thing; she uses it as a weapon. To yield to sex frightens her; she says she doesn't want to have her sexual drives reawakened because it emphasizes her femininity, probably referring to her passive tendencies. With her husbands, she managed to gain control in the end by forcing them to leave. She may be afraid that if the therapist responds to her, she may also hurt him. We must find out what lies behind this.

The point to remember is that a rapidly developing transference usually has a defensive purpose. There was no need to say anything to the patient at this time since she seemed to be able to deal with her anxiety and was not too upset, nor did she seem to expect a response from the therapist. On the contrary, it might have been hazardous for the therapist to say anything. Were he to offer her reassurance, for instance, he might have caused her to become inhibited, since she might take it as encouragement to become more bold.

Case 4P: The following dream illustrates a situation of conflict over destructive drives resulting in inhibition which prevented the acting out of the impulse. It must be classified as a punishment dream. It is reported here, however, as an illustration of a premature interpretation.

> I was driving a Cadillac in a lot of traffic, like a funeral procession, trying to keep up with the other drivers. Suddenly the motor stopped. I pushed down on the pedal and nothing happened. The dashboard lights did not turn on red, that would show that the motor was off. The car slowed to a halt, but it was still going. I knew that it was going to stop but I woke up with anxiety because I could not keep up with the other cars.

Background: The patient was a businessman who came for treatment because of a poor marriage and disappointment with his accomplishments at work, even though others considered him to be quite successful. In early life he was close to his mother. He often expressed contempt for his father's lack of culture and was determined to outstrip him. Nevertheless, he repeatedly sought out father figures toward whom he was quite deferential. His urge to discuss his marital difficulties with various men seemed to stem from an unconscious need to bring his failure with women to their attention. When I informed him that I would be moving to another state within a few months, he thought that he might turn to his older son as a confidant. He was thus clearly unable to assume the role of a father figure himself.

Day Residue: In the hour prior to the dream he had discussed his reserve and inability to demonstrate feelings for others which interfered with his social contacts, his relations with his three children, and his work. He was also unhappy with his slow progress in the analysis. He felt that at his age it was difficult to change a lifelong pattern of behavior. During the previous week he again began to complain of his failure to progress in treatment. He said, "I have stopped short," as if he were grinding to a halt in the analysis. This seemed to match the thought in the dream that his car was coming to a halt. It was beyond his control so that he was not the master of the situation. He said he felt helpless and incompetent when anything went wrong with the car, since he was not mechanically minded and could not figure out what the trouble was.

Cadillacs are expensive cars and to the patient represented self-sufficiency, power, and success, and thus masculinity. When the patient drove his car he could let out his frustrations by expressing his impatience with other drivers. A car also represented freedom and independence. Without it he felt immobilized and dependent on others for lifts.

At this point he said he had no more comments to make. I pointed out that he had said nothing about the funeral procession. He replied rather sharply that he was not sure it was one. His irritation indicated that he was reluctant to discuss the subject. I said, "Whether it was a funeral procession or not, the important thing is that you said it was one." He thought I was angry with him and was rebuking him. When I assured him that this was not so, he went on to say that the funeral procession referred to my funeral. He wanted to free himself from the analysis. He didn't want to do it on his own, but if I were to die he would have a perfectly good excuse. In that case he wouldn't want to start with anyone else. He wanted me to be punished, he said, for making him talk about things he would rather not discuss. He added that he envied me because he did not possess my capacity for understanding and directing people. This was the first time he had ever expressed hostility toward me; previously he had only words of appreciation and praise for me. Here, too, he coupled his anger with praise.

I asked him if he had been thinking of my death recently. He replied that the possibility of my death had been in his mind for some time. He was frightened recently when I had occasion to tell him that I didn't go out much at night. Ever since he started the analysis he had thought of me as a frail person. When I was hospitalized some time before, he was afraid I might be taken away from him. He wondered how I could listen to discussions of this kind.

I pointed out to him that I could understand his feeling of frustration and helplessness in the dream when his car stalled, but not why he became so anxious. He said he too could not account for it. I suggested that he couldn't allow the dream to finish, that is, to show off his superiority, as symbolized by driving a Cadillac—a distinctive car—to attend my funeral.

[I had arrived at this conjecture by asking myself under what circumstances one might feel similarly anxious, that is, as a result of trying to keep up or compete with others. Such a reaction might occur in acting or public speaking—situations in which an individual seeks the approbation of others, as a means of confirming and maintaining his self-esteem. If he is uncertain of receiving such approval he may have a phobic reaction such as stage fright.] According to Fenichel (1945b, 1946) stage fright results from the threat of punishment both for unconscious sexual tendencies (displaying sexual excitement) and for destructive drives in the attempt to obtain gratification of narcissistic demands. It is as if the performer intends to force his audience to grant him recognition or to impress it with his superiority. Ferenczi (1923) was also of the opinion that stage fright resulted from excessive self-consciousness in people whose narcissism required them to impress others, especially if they had reason to doubt their inner motives. The thing feared is that instead of receiving approval, they will be snubbed or ridiculed. In the dream, then, it was as if he were flexing his muscles on my grave, exhilarated by his freedom and boasting of his own survival. Because of his superego he was not permitted to enjoy his triumph; he was unable to "keep up" with the others or to be present at my "interment." The anxiety could then have resulted from his fear of retribution which, in line with the law of the talion, would be castration. The inhibition (the car coming to a halt) not only prevents the fulfillment of the wish, but also emphasizes the patient's weakness. If the threat of punishment were carried to its logical conclusion (castration) it would lead to intolerable fear and the patient would wake up before he could fully enjoy his new-found freedom.

There was support for this interpretation in the fact that only after he left home for college and was free of his father's surveillance, was he able to assert himself by masturbating and visiting prostitutes. He was a very talented individual and had achieved considerable success in his career, but no amount of success could satisfy his apparently insatiable need for approval and acceptance. The only thing that provided him any degree of reassurance was to have his work favorably received by men who served in the role of father substitutes. I was one of these. His need for fresh achievements to prove himself ever anew resulted no doubt from the sense of unworthiness imposed on him by unconscious guilt and invidious comparison with father figures. He was envious of any of his associates who appeared self-confident or who received recognition for their work. At such times he became depressed and unsure of himself. Although on the surface he appeared forceful and well-spoken, he was unable to assert himself or demand his just dues when facing his superiors. In the transference he suppressed all his aggressive strivings and was inclined to be self-effacing and ingratiating. It seemed to be a full-time job for him to remain on friendly terms with me, by behaving in accordance with what he thought I expected of him.

He stated that he wanted to be free of me so that he could impress me by his reputation. I said, "If I died you wouldn't have to envy me or feel inferior by comparing yourself with me. But then you would have to punish yourself by appearing helpless and incompetent. Grinding to a halt in the analysis could be regarded as a form of self-punishment."

His reply was that he did not recognize this as a consious thought. He then said that he would like to deliver the eulogy at my funeral. In it he would say how absolutely masterful I was and what incredible perception and insight I had. This seemed an attempt to make amends for his repressed hostility, which had become conscious only as an association to the dream. He was unable, however, to recognize this as a death wish. It is true that he had expressed a wish for my death in his associations, but this seemed largely an intellectual exercise which he treated in a detached manner as a philosophical fantasy. In other words, my interpretation of the dream as being a wish for my death fell flat as far as he was concerned. One would have to assume that to accept the interpretation would have been too traumatic for him; he had to reject it. Could this premature interpretation have increased his resistance? On the other hand, could the suggestion have "gotten across to the jury," as it were, and have started to incubate in the patient's mind so that he could be more ready to accept it later on?

In retrospect, the patient's statement that he could not feel the death wish against me consciously should have been an indication that I had overlooked an intermediate step, namely, that the grinding to a halt of the analysis could have been a form of self-punishment, a paralysis resulting from his envy and hostility toward me. This would have constituted an interpretation of the defense rather than of the wish. After the hour I continued to think of it and presented the revised interpretation to him the following day. It had no effect. Despite our discussion of the previous day he could not grasp it; according to him, he did not know what guilt was, since he had never experienced it. Obviously the resistance had set in. Not until several months later could he recognize the existence of death wishes against me, and even then he could do so only haltingly and with much discomfiture.

CHAPTER 7

Transference Dreams

Transference and dreams have one thing in common: they both deal with infantile memories and experiences; one by attempting to relive them through object relationships and the other through wishful thinking. They thus reinforce each other in recalling memories of the past which cannot be summoned in any other way. Transference phenomena in dreams are indicators of the patient's current attitude toward the analyst, as a result of which the analyst can be alerted to the patient's ongoing problems and the role he himself is playing in the patient's mind at the moment. It is therefore of singular importance that the problems of both transference and dreams should come together at a common point.

If we agree with Ferenczi (1912, p. 349) that one feels impelled to relate one's dreams to the very person to whom the content relates, we may assume that the analyst will appear in one guise or another in every one of the patient's dreams. He will essentially take on the characteristics of the significant figures of the dreamer's infancy, such as his parents and siblings, or their surrogates. In this sense every dream is a transference dream. Why then emphasize the transference character of dreams? Perhaps a review of the nature of transference and the part it plays in analysis may contribute to an understanding of its particular significance in dreams.

Transference phenomena, as indicated, deal with infantile experiences and wishes that have been kept alive and active in the unconscious, where they have been influencing the individual's behavior, thought, and desires, as well as creating conflicts. If we take a longitudinal view of a person's life, it becomes clear that he has repeatedly sought to obtain the gratifications that he enjoyed in early childhood, and to overcome frustrations by resorting to the same defense mechanisms. In forming a new relationship he has a compulsion to repeat his relationships to infantile objects, seeking fulfillment of his ungratified desire for love, or a more satisfactory solution to his frustrations. Since these desires by their very nature cannot be attained now, they have led to the current disappointments and maladjustments which have brought him to the analyst's couch. In suitable cases analysis can succeed in breaking the repetitive cycle by providing more realistic substitutes for the patient's infantile wishes. It accomplishes this by helping the patient in two ways: by getting him to recognize his unconscious reactions, and thus to view them more objectively; and, secondly, by helping him to achieve mastery over his desires through understanding, so that he can become more mature.

The patient naturally relates to the analyst in the identical way in which he has related to those from whom he was once accustomed to receive affection and gratification of his needs. This outcome is facilitated by the regression which characterizes the analytic situation. Because of his need for love, the patient transfers the feelings which originally applied to the infantile object onto the analyst, just as he has always replaced former persons by contemporary objects.

In the state of positive transference, the patient's confidence in the analyst's good will and his dependency upon him for help, enables him to discuss aspects of his life that are unsavory, and to accept unpleasant truths about himself. This feeling of trust in the analyst protects the patient's narcissism from the unconscious affects which threaten it (Tausk, 1924, p. 140). This is the compensation for the acceptance of something unpleasant. The patient "finds in the feeling of pleasure accompanying the transference love a consolation for the pain that this acceptance [of unpleasant affects] would otherwise have cost him" (Ferenczi, 1926, p. 369). The analyst becomes the subject of the patient's fantasies, both of love and hate. The analyst, on the other hand, strives to remain emotionally

Transference Dreams

uninvolved, by not allowing his biases and positive or negative feelings for the patient to influence his judgment. He must also be sufficiently sure of himself so that his narcissism does not suffer when his interventions are rejected. He can then view the situation dispassionately and objectively and observe the patient's conflict being unfolded in situ as it were.

We have spoken of the beneficial effects of the positive transference. The positive transference of repressed erotic impulses as well as the negative (hostile) transference can, however, become resistances to treatment (Freud, 1912a, p. 105). The negative transference results from the inevitable frustrations that occur in the course of analysis, whenever the patient's infantile needs come up against stark reality. Another factor that tends to give rise to hostile reactions against the analyst, is the fact that he represents an authority figure whom the patient fears and from whom he would rather withdraw than express disagreement. Persons who have to acquiesce out of fear usually resent having to do so. Such resentment sooner or later comes out into the open.

Resistance is more likely to occur when the patient can no longer rely on his previous defenses. He is then inclined to distort the transference by projecting his hostility onto the analyst, as a means of not having to face his own instinctual drives. In time the patient's entire conflict centers around the transference. His behavior in the analysis is an example of his customary method of relating to people and characterizes his personality. We first aim at uncovering the patient's defense mechanisms before dealing with the id content, since an understanding of the patient's typical defenses will give us a clue to his resistance in analysis. The earliest interpretations should show the patient the connection between his defenses and his resistance in treatment. When the patient reports his disturbed relations with other people, the analyst cannot be certain to what extent the patient has contributed to the problem. The transference, however, puts him in a position to know both sides of the equation, and determine the true state of affairs. He is then able to point out that the patient's behavior has no foundation in the actual relationship with the analyst, and must therefore be a fantasied replica of the patient's actual relationships with others in the past. The patient's capacity to accept the likelihood of his feelings about someone else being his own unconscious distortions rather than the reality of the situation, is a large step toward distinguishing between fantasy and objective reality, and accepting the connection between the present and the past.

The transference gives rise to the most obstinate resistances of the analysis. The patient then substitutes acting out for remembering. This may appear as an eroticized transference in which the analysand's feelings for the analyst are taken to be real and not imagined. Under the cover of complete dedication to the analyst, on the other hand, the patient may repress his hostile feelings. An illustration of this occurred when a patient who was inclined to idealize his analyst, heard the latter use a word incorrectly at a conference. Another conferee corrected the speaker in a friendly manner, upon which the patient became indignant at the other man for his "presumptuousness." In this fashion he managed to gloss over his own critical attitude toward the doctor. Unless the analyst pays heed to the patient's progress in the analysis, and bears in mind the nature and state of the transference, he may find that the analysis is unduly prolonged, or even brought to an abrupt close by the patient.

Although one looks for evidences of transference in all dreams, their particular significance is that they anticipate the manifest appearance of transference phenomena in the analytic situation. One is therefore alerted to the possibility of things to come, or one may succeed in bringing to the surface ideas that are still only amorphous or half-formed in the patient's awareness.

Since the purpose of the dream is to gratify infantile wishes, an understanding of the transference also provides a clue to the nature and intensity of the patient's infantile relationships, and to the pattern of his behavior throughout life. If the transference is successfully interpreted, the patient is frequently enabled to overcome his repressions and to recapture early memories that have never crystallized or have been forgotten, either because the events occurred during the preverbal period and prior to the final

Transference Dreams

consolidation of the psychic structure, or during the oedipal period. We are also prepared to reconstruct the patient's childhood, with its gratifications and disappointments, and to understand the subsequent vicissitudes of his life. The pictorial nature of the dream, being on a more primitive level than intellectual comprehension, may assist the patient emotionally to relive his early experiences so that they have more meaning for him.

An understanding of the transference also enables the analyst to keep his finger on the patient's pulse, as it were, and to recognize the level of the analysis at any given moment. It prepares him to be on the lookout for the patient's reactions and to deal with them. Since the dream frequently imparts information before it becomes clinically manifest, it enables the analyst to work toward uncovering repressions without permitting them to smolder in the dark, only to appear later in an explosive form which may be difficult to control. It also guides the analyst in selecting the appropriate interpretation from among the several possible. When the dream discloses the patient's displeasure with the analyst, the possibility opens of forestalling the development of resistance in the form of the negative transference. Since the interpretation of transference resistance is fundamental in analysis, no opportunity to analyze it must be overlooked. The dream, in large measure, can prove that the elements of infantile development are being worked out in the transference. By means of it "we can see what is being transferred, what situation is being enacted, what role is being thrust on the analyst, what past affective situation is being restaged" (Sharpe, 1949, p. 74).

The case reports which follow are designed to indicate the various ways in which transference resistance manifests itself, and how it may be dealt with. Some of the dreams reported elsewhere are included here to emphasize this aspect.

Case Reports

Case 1C: The following is Case 2C in Chapter 5. In addition to being a transference dream, it suggests how one may understand a dream to which the patient gave practically no associations. Although one ordinarily avoids trying to make conjectures on the basis of the manifest dream alone, the justification for it in this case lay in the fact that one's previous knowledge of the patient could be utilized, as well as in the fact that the precipitating components of the dream drew attention to the patient's current problem and how the dream attempted to find a solution in order to relieve the patient's tension. Some light could also be cast on the nature of the transference situation and the life pattern of the patient. The dream, which is divided in two parts, happily lends itself to our purpose because it is short and fairly clear.

Background: The patient, a man, had been having an affair with a married co-worker. He had come to realize that the situation was a potentially dangerous one, and he was planning to put an end to it. Before he could do so, however, the woman announced that she had decided to break off the relationship, because of her own guilt. He took this as a rejection and felt crushed. He went on to say that he was ill-at-ease with women unless he could have sexual relations with them. Otherwise he had a constant fear of being rejected as a "shmuck." On the other hand, if he had sexual relations with a woman he felt master of the situation.

When he first began the analysis, he repeatedly made lewd, suggestive remarks to the female therapist. Since it is highly unusual for a patient to address a therapist in this manner, especially at the start of analysis, it was difficult to understand the meaning of his behavior. On the day of the dream he said he felt ill-at-ease with his paramour after she had rejected him, and he was cautious about getting involved with anyone else.

Dream 1: There were six bottles of orange juice on the back seat of a car. A woman was sitting next to them. I drank some of the juice and afterwards found that it contained LSD. I then ran around frantically trying to get some Thorazine.

Dream 2: A guy was checking and making comments about the shapes of men. Then someone threw up all over my pants. It was like "come" or paint. I was upset.

Transference Dreams

Comment: The dream was presented to me during a supervisory hour. The patient had given no associations. This was one of the few dreams reported by the patient, and since the material he was producing in the analysis was more or less repetitious, it seemed important to try to understand the meaning of the dream, to see if any underlying trend could be detected. The problem was to discover whether it could provide an insight into the patient's current state of mind, the unconscious problems with which he was contending and the nature of the transference. In cases such as this, one must rely upon the sense of the dream, one's previous knowledge of the patient, the day residue, and a knowledge of dream mechanisms, as well as upon the therapist's empathy and intuition.

One could start out with the assumption that the woman in the back seat represented the therapist, who in reality sat behind the patient. She was the one in charge of the orange juice, and when he took a drink it was presumably with her consent. In this sense one could conceive of her as being concerned for him, like a mother who feeds liquids to her infant. But what could LSD refer to? LSD, in part, produces a modification of the ego by removing repressions, thus placing the ego in an unguarded state in which the unconscious has full sway. This partially accounts for the bizarre psychological phenomena which are experienced under its influence. By the same token, LSD lowers inhibitions so that impulses become unrestrained. The number *six* symbolically represents sex. This then might be the danger which confronts the patient in the dream, so that he rushes frantically to find the antidote, Thorazine. What impulses could he be afraid of? The therapist had been sympathetic when he reported being rebuffed by his paramour. Could he have regarded her attitude as being seductive, and then been afraid that his sexual desires for her might be aroused? But then why should he be so frantic? This seemed to be an exaggerated reaction, particularly since he had already expressed his sexual fantasies about her. There could be two reasons for his disturbance at the present time. When he had freely expressed his fantasies about the therapist early in the analysis, he apparently did not mean them to be taken literally, but was probably using them in a provocative way, designed to make her feel uncomfortable and to put her on the defensive, which he could equate with overcoming her sexually. His feelings toward her now, however, would have been more real, so that he might be afraid of being rejected if he were to express them. On a deeper level, he might have thought of such feelings as being incestuous, since the therapist represented a mother figure.

To what could Thorazine refer? The first dream stopped at the moment of his frantic search. We know that all dreams occurring in one night are part of the same dream. Subsequent dreams usually either supplement, confirm, or clarify the first dream, or offer alternate solutions to the problems with which the dream is dealing.

The sense of the second dream is that someone (a man) is making comments about the shapes of men. Someone then throws up something white on the patient's pants, like semen or paint. What sort of man is usually interested in the shapes of other men? Is he not likely to be a homosexual? This is confirmed when the patient says his pants were stained with semen, as if he had been having a homosexual relationship with a man. Homosexuality could be the antidote (Thorazine) to incestuous desires. Although the patient was upset at the close of the second dream, the reaction was much less drastic than his frantic state at the end of the first dream.

What have we accomplished thus far? We have made certain assumptions that do not seem to be far-fetched, namely, that the patient felt drawn to the therapist when she was sympathetic toward him. This, however, constituted a danger for which he had to seek an antidote, namely, homosexuality. We cannot, of course, be certain of either of these suppositions. We have worked with certain probabilities, assisted by our knowledge of the patient and of dream mechanisms. Our conjectures provide us with clues about what may be going on in the patient's unconscious. Such clues can serve as guidelines for the further conduct of the case, but they must be confirmed by clinical evidence. We are not bound by them. If they turn out to be wrong, they will be discarded for more likely ideas. In this case, at least, we can say that we have a working basis for understanding several things: the nature of the transference; the patient's uneasiness with women (if women represent his mother he

Transference Dreams

runs the risk of being told he is a "shmuck," that is, his penis is smaller than his father's); his ease with women once he has had sexual relations with them (intercourse is a sadistic act which reduces the woman's status by demonstrating that she has a vagina, or is proof of his masculinity); the reason for his current depression (being rejected by his paramour emphasizes his feeling of inadequacy); and that homosexuality represents his defense against incest. If our interpretations turn out to be correct, we may thus have acquired an insight into the patient's neurosis and life pattern. The more immediate lesson to be learned from the dream is that the therapist could become aware of the impact she was having on the patient; this could guide her in relating to him.

What could the patient be told? It would obviously be premature to discuss incest or homosexuality with him. One could, however, mention the possibility that he sought to overcome his disappointment in his paramour by turning to the therapist. One could also ask him whether he had any uneasiness about coming to the therapist for reassurance.

Case 2C: This case was briefly discussed in Chapter 5 (Case 3).

Background: The patient was a married man of thirty-one who had been in analysis two years. Until recently the analysis had been "fluffing" along, that is, whenever the therapist made an interpretation or attempted to clarify something, the patient became confused and began to daydream. He himself described his state of mind as being "screwed up in a piece of wood, looking down two pipes and not knowing which to choose," and also "as if it were whirling or spinning around." It was, therefore, difficult to know what was going on within him.

The patient came for analysis because of depression and anxiety. He was having trouble in his work, which consisted of selling money orders from house to house in impoverished areas of the city. He was terrified of entering homes and talking to prospective customers. Because of these fears he frequently left off work in the middle of the day and returned home.

He was the second son in a family of five. His brother, two years his senior, was a successful physician. As the second son, the patient felt that he got short shrift in his parents' affections; his older brother was given "everything," while he felt he was left out in the cold. He was naturally jealous and envious of his brother, regarded as the bright and successful son while he was the "stupid" one. On one occasion, in the sixth grade, when he tied for top grades in the class, he came home feeling exhilarated, but when he announced it to his father, the latter received the news in a matter-of-fact manner. The patient was crestfallen. He was very sensitive and if criticized by a teacher would go into a tailspin and remain confused for several days. At eighteen or nineteen, after being spurned by a girl, he made a half-hearted suicidal attempt by taking sleeping pills. During the analysis he was able to obtain a good job in a bank, at which he did very well; this increased his self-confidence.

The patient had a peculiar pattern of masturbation which began during adolescence. In bed he kept his hands above the sheets, raised his buttocks and by pelvic movements managed to rub his penis against the sheets until he had an ejaculation, thus soiling the sheets. His father once said to him, "Cut that out. Only queers do that." After this experience, he continued to masturbate, but ejaculated into a towel. In having intercourse with his wife he kept his hands up and felt around for the vagina with his erect penis, trying to insert it without using his hands. His wife would then take hold of his penis and insert it for him. Recently, for the first time, he had used his hands in masturbating while taking a shower.

The patient's relationship with the therapist and others was characterized by similar passivity. The therapist, for instance, had to be specific and literally guide him at every step before he could accept any explanation, just as his father and wife had to show him what to do. At work, too, he could make no decision on his own. When frightened he needed the reassurance of others. When his father died, eight months before the beginning of the analysis, he felt lost, since he had no one to whom he could turn for advice.

[To make a decision on his own would be to behave like a competent male, a role which frightened him. He needed someone to assume responsibility, as when he had his wife insert his penis into her vagina. By not using his hands in masturbating he was likewise avoiding responsibility. But what could responsibility mean to him? Could it be equated with committing a hostile or forbidden act? In view of his deference to superiors, could it refer to his unconscious hostility toward them? In coming for analysis shortly after his father died, he may have been seeking a replacement for his father. Once before, the patient had gone into psychotherapy in opposition to his father's wishes, because of intense anxiety and a feeling of falling apart after his first son was born.]

Day Residue: The patient felt reassured after an analytic hour in which the therapist had interpreted his fear of inserting his penis during intercourse as a fear of assuming responsibility. He seemed to have reacted to the interpretation as if the therapist had given him permission to become more active. He felt more confident and on the following night for the first time he inserted his penis without his wife's assistance. His wife expressed her appreciation and he felt very proud of himself. When he reported his success on the day prior to the dream, however, the therapist said to him, "We still don't know what it is that you are afraid of. Putting it in yourself does not yet tell us what you are frightened of." The patient replied, "I had been feeling so good about the way I had sex the night before, and then was dismayed when I found that it didn't solve the entire problem." He said he believed the dream had to do with the analysis.

Dream: I was coming out of a subway. It was dark, I was carrying my older son, feeling that I knew where I was. It was a familiar feeling. I thought I heard shots on the right and I started to run in the opposite direction. Then shots rang out on the left and I ran back to the right. I felt very confused as to which way to go. At that moment I thought my wife and her father were across the street in the darkness. I thought I was being attacked by black revolutionaries, and felt trapped and terrified. I was trying to decide where to go and whether to save either my son or my wife and her father.

Associations: The therapist asked the patient what impressed him most about the dream. He replied that it was the feeling of being trapped and confused, as if black revolutionaries were taking over, so that he did not know which way to turn. It was like being trapped in his work at the bank, where he felt he would be criticized if anything went wrong. Whenever he was criticized at work or by his wife he felt as if he were being shot at. The therapist asked how he felt during the previous hour when he was told that being successful in intercourse did not solve the underlying problem. He replied he had come away thinking that his success meant he had finally gotten over his difficulty, and that he could now wash his hands of the whole matter. ["Wash his hands" could mean that he no longer had to feel guilty about sex.] He went on to say that his older son was presenting a problem; he was getting out of hand and the patient and his wife could not handle him anymore. The therapist repeated the words, "Getting out of hand?" The patient said, "That's my penis. I don't handle it. I never handled it all my life. I don't handle anything right. I'm always fumbling with balls, dribbling in the back court. When I played basketball I fumbled around when it came time to shoot the ball into the basket, so that I never managed to score any points."

[It is clear that the patient was confused and unsettled by the therapist's apparent lack of appreciation of his success in taking the initiative during intercourse. He felt he was being criticized, as if he were being "shot at." It should have reminded the therapist of the incident when the patient returned from school in the sixth grade proud of his high marks, expecting to be praised by his father, and then was disappointed by his father's indifference. The patient might have concluded that any success on his part was wrong and therefore not acceptable either to his father or the therapist. The "black revolutionaries" may have thus represented both his father and the therapist.]

I remarked that the patient seemed to be frightened of holes (vagina and basketball nets). The presenter recalled one of the patient's adolescent fantasies, namely, that the woman's vagina was like a big hole into which the penis could fall. He believed that the

Transference Dreams

urethra, vagina, and rectum were all one. In another fantasy, he was in bed with his mother who had her back to him while he played with her genitals. He reacted to this fantasy with disgust and said, "I don't believe it is true; this didn't happen to me. It is disgusting; it isn't my mother." There was a subsequent elaboration of the fantasy: he was in bed with his mother, his legs dangling over the side of the bed, and his back up against his mother's back. She was playing checkers and suddenly called out. His father came crashing through the door and the patient became very frightened. He attributed his fear of sex to this fantasy.

[The presenter's recollection of these details was really an association to my comment about the patient's fear of holes. It demonstrates the value of being on top of the material at all times. Similarly, if the therapist offers his intuitive reactions to the material, he can frequently evoke meaningful associations from the patient. The therapist did this when he repeated the patient's words "getting out of hand" to which the patient immediately responded, "That's my penis."]

Discussion: There were no further associations. The main thought of the manifest dream was that the patient found himself in a dangerous situation and did not know whom to save—his son or his wife and her father. The decision was left up in the air and the patient experienced extreme terror.

I asked if the patient's wife had ever expressed dissatisfaction with his method of having intercourse. The reply was that she was very unhappy about it. She was always impatient with him during intercourse and would say, "Come on, let's go." His father-in-law was a domineering, opinionated person who liked to order people around. The patient felt indebted to him because he had loaned him money for the down payment on his home and he felt uncomfortable in his presence. This was a repetition of his attitude toward his own father. I suggested that the patient might also be afraid his wife would leave him. "Coming up out of the subway and into the light" (i.e. moving up from the subterranean unconscious) could refer to the idea of being confronted by the responsibilities of adult reality. In the manifest dream the patient was coming up from the subway, carrying his son in his arms. Suddenly he heard shots from the right and from the left. He was afraid of thugs and did not know whom to save, his son or his wife and her father. I said it was necessary to fit this in with what he knew about the patient and with what had been happening lately. The patient felt he had accepted the therapist's suggestion to become more active in sexual relations with his wife, and was let down by the therapist's failure to compliment him when he succeeded in doing so. He was obviously proud of his achievement but the therapist's comment may have seemed to him to express disapproval. This seemed to be the precipitating cause of the dream.

We know that the patient reacted to criticism with terror, as if he were being shot at. This recalls how he reacted in his fantasy of being with his mother when his father came "crashing" into the room. Could success as a man be related to impressing his mother, or perhaps to incest? In the dream, he was apparently afraid that someone would be killed. It would be natural to ask why the patient felt endangered and developed anxiety in the dream. Could it be related to his fear of assuming responsibility in the act of intercourse? This might just as likely have given rise to depression or guilt, however, and not terror. What could have caused him to become terrified? He had associated that holding his son was like holding his penis in his hand; could the danger be that in becoming a man, a competent male, he was endangering the intactness of his penis? In the dream he could not rescue both his son and his wife and her father. This was his dilemma. Should he save his penis by not behaving like a man in the marriage, and run the risk of having the marriage break up? Or should he save the marriage at the risk of displeasing his father and losing his penis? The dream does not come to a conclusion, but ends with the patient in a state of indecision, as if he, as yet, has not made up his mind about which course to take.

The dream could then explain the patient's life pattern of being subordinate and dependent without accepting responsibility; to be otherwise would have meant that he had replaced his father or his superiors, in which case he could be the object of their retaliation. Since he was really a capable individual, it is likely that guilt over

Transference Dreams

competitiveness with his brother and father was responsible for his inhibitions and early lack of success.

What could be communicated to the patient in connection with the dream, keeping in mind that one first deals with the surface of the patient's life? One could say, "When you told me of your successful intercourse yesterday, you may have expected to be praised, and so you may have been hurt and disappointed when I said there was more work to be done. That would be like being shot at." Since he had always been afraid to assume responsibility or behave in a self-sufficient manner, did he think that the therapist disapproved of him for assuming the responsibility of inserting his penis into his wife's vagina? In other words, instead of bringing up the question of castration, the patient's more immediate fear is mentioned first, namely, fear of the therapist's disapproval. This is in accord with the principle of first considering the state of the patient's ego when offering interpretations, that is, the patient's ability to understand the interpretations in terms nearest to his awareness ("from above"). If the patient recognized the validity of this interpretation, one could have gone further and suggested that his reaction of the previous day seemed to resemble his feeling at the time when he came home from school with high marks and his father failed to appreciate his achievement. This could have given him the idea that his father was not interested in his success. The additional interpretation would include elements of the past that he was not aware of at the moment. It would thus demonstrate the effectiveness of the transference interpretation in connecting the patient's present with his past and emphasizing the repetitive nature of his behavior.

The main point to be considered in these comments is that we first deal with surface phenomena—in this case by drawing attention to the patient's fear and annoyance with the therapist. If the situation is properly handled, the patient should be sufficiently reassured by the therapist's solicitude and understanding to venture further toward making independent decisions. Otherwise he could readily fall back into the resistance of a negative transference.

Another factor in this approach is that the therapist aims to break the unconscious chain that links him to the patient's father. One attempt in this direction will usually be insufficient; the patient tests the doctor in many ways before he can finally be convinced and alter his pattern (working through). In this instance, the process may have already begun, to judge from the fact that the patient felt free enough to report his success to the therapist. At this point in the analysis it may be sufficient merely to encourage the patient to give up some of his defenses. It will be observed that the therapist is advised not to be arbitrary and authoritarian but, by putting his interpretation in the form of questions to which no one as yet has positive answers, to stress the cooperative nature of the relationship between the patient and the doctor (Freud, 1937, pp. 261–262).

Case 3P: A male patient presented the following dream:

> It was about my father and a horse. I don't remember if my father gave me the horse, but, in any event, it was mine and I had personal and affectionate feelings for it. At one point, it turned briefly into a man and embraced me—hugged me close to him. I was surprised and a little embarrassed at the thought that he was being affectionate. He was wearing black clothes. Then he turned back into a horse.

[The partial vagueness of the dream suggests the presence of resistance due to repression.]

Associations: The patient's father loved horses and even owned one. He rode the horses often.

The patient said the man in the dream did not look like me, but then added that if he put it in the negative it must refer to me. The man appeared to be a working man who looked familiar to him. He was formerly an employee in the printing plant where the patient worked, and operated a sort of guillotine that was used to cut large masses of paper. He was considered an excellent worker. The patient recalled vaguely that he did something else on the side that was degrading, like running a whorehouse or a cheap dance studio.

The black clothes reminded him of death. He had checked with my secretary to find out what the last appointment hour before the

Transference Dreams 125

Christmas holiday would be. The idea of a last hour made him think of my death, a thought that had occurred to him frequently in the past.

In the previous analytic hour he had reported a dream but was unable to do anything with it. I had remarked that he appeared to be in resistance. According to him, I was not annoyed but rather sympathetic and trying to be helpful (in the dream he was embraced by the man). He was surprised by my attitude and felt warmly toward me. This was the direct stimulus for the dream. I asked why I should be represented by the particular man in the dream. He replied that he had always wanted to think of me as being tops in my field, but he had recently begun to have doubts about me. This reminded him of a man who once induced him to make a bad investment in a scheme in which he had lost a good deal of money. He was resentful toward me because of the size of my fee, which he thought was excessive. He wondered if I was worth it. In that sense I resembled the man in the dream who, despite the fact that he was a good worker, was engaged in a questionable side business.

The man's job was to operate a guillotine. These machines are very frightening because, if one isn't careful, one can have one's hand or finger cut off. The French guillotine was used to execute people by decapitation. According to the patient, I frequently pointed out things to him that he felt were belittling, in other words, I cut him down to size. It was as if I were beheading or castrating him.

He then recalled that once he had lost his cap while riding a horse. He tried to get the horse to turn back, but the horse refused to obey him and insisted on going its own way, until he finally succeeded in making it turn back. When he dismounted in order to retrieve his hat, he found that the saddle had twisted around the horse's belly, and he was afraid to set it aright lest the horse bite him. Someone else had to straighten the saddle for him. I was like the horse, in that I insisted on directing his thoughts. He often wanted to talk in technical and sophisticated analytic terms while I brought him back to the specific situation that was under consideration. Recently, for instance, he provoked a quarrel with his wife and later blamed her for his lack of sexual interest in her. At the time I interpreted his provocative behavior as an excuse for refusing to have intercourse with her. He was annoyed with me, although he recognized the appropriateness of my observation.

Comment: The dream revealed the patient's ambivalence toward me. During the previous hour he felt drawn to me because I was sympathetic to him. In the dream this was represented by the fact that the man hugged him in an affectionate embrace. This was countered, however, by the transformation of the man once more into a horse. This seemed to be a defense against the patient's homosexual attachment. The horse is an animal for which one can have personal and affectionate feelings, but which can also be dangerous if he bites. It is more acceptable to have such feelings for an animal than for a man. The patient's ambivalence toward me thus represented both passive homosexual feelings and resentment at the thought of being subordinated to me, which he equated with being castrated. By denigrating me, he succeeded in overcoming his awe of me. This was a paradigm of his habitual attitude in the analysis, which was characterized by general disregard of my comments, repetitious acting out which retarded the analysis, and almost regular attempts to challenge my remarks in an obsessive, quibbling sort of way. Whenever positive feelings for me appeared, he had to guard himself by thinking of me as both an inferior and dangerous person. The horse also represented his father as well as me, since we were equated. The dream thus brought to light both the nature of the patient's current resistance and the meaning of his negative transference.

In the interpretation, the patient was told that on the previous day he felt warmly toward me, but since this was too close for comfort as well as being dangerous (fear of castration), he had to fend me off by thinking of my death. This was an unacceptable idea, and he had to belittle me and transform me into someone who could be controlled and directed (by his intellectualizations). In that sense, I was like a horse who could usually be controlled and toward whom one could allow oneself to be affectionate. His intellectualizations in the analysis were not always effective, however, so that he was in danger of being called to account (fear of being bitten). This time he was able to accept my interpretation.

It will be observed that I spoke only of things that were part of his conscious experience. It was felt that he was not yet ready to deal with deeper problems, such as homosexuality.

Case 4P: A social worker had the following dream:

> I called up my hairdresser and asked to have Ann get breakfast or lunch ready when I come, or perhaps it's something in between, like brunch.

Associations: At her hairdresser's, customers frequently ordered lunch while they were waiting to be taken care of. Ann was the girl who took the orders. The patient felt that Ann was a sour, bitchy kind of person who did not like her and always served her reluctantly. She thought that she herself might have been responsible for Ann's attitude because she never tipped her well.

Calling on the phone was a way of making sure that the food would be delivered by the time the patient arrived for her appointment. The phone could also refer to the analysis (in that one hears the doctor without seeing him). When she woke up in the morning she felt fresh and on the go. She had felt good after the last two sessions because she had just accepted a new position and was impatient to get started on it.

I pointed out that she had seemed more friendly toward me lately, after having resented my criticism of one of her friends, who seemed to be interested in her welfare but who had later let her down. I suggested that it resembled her resentment against me once when she thought I was being critical of her mother. This could be a projection of her own anger against her mother. In addition, I had observed that lately she was more punctual in coming for her appointments. Did she possibly regard me as being interested in her welfare, since I had advised her to select a particular area of endeavor and not flit from one thing to another? In this respect I could be Ann, a mother substitute, who provided her with food.

She replied that she herself was not really a good mother. Her children often said, "Why don't you be a mother and prepare breakfast for us?" She had recently given a party but let her husband and maid make all the preparation. At the time I had remarked that she seemed to expect everything to be done for her by mother figures.

Even though I was "sour and bitchy" in refusing to satisfy her need for plaudits, I might still be a good mother, since I was concerned that she be successful in her career. This ended the hour.

The day after reporting the dream, the patient had difficulty in starting to talk. She then said, "It's not that I am depressed," which immediately suggested that she was indeed depressed. She then went on to say that shortly after leaving the previous session she suddenly felt ravenously hungry. She went to a restaurant and ate a conglomeration of foods which she afterwards vomited up. She also stole a pair of sunglasses at the hairdresser's, justifying herself by saying that Ann was a bitch anyway. Following this she had an intense desire to sleep, and took a fifteen-minute nap in her car. She realized that her behavior was infantile. I suggested that in eating ravenously she seemed for some reason to have a need to regress to feeding at her mother's breast. Her response was negative, as if to say that I was talking nonsense and that she didn't see how that helped her in any way. I pointed out that she was apparently hostile to me and wondered why, particularly in view of the fact that on the previous day she felt I had been so helpful. She replied that as she walked out of my office she saw an attractive young woman sitting in the waiting room. She thought I would naturally be more attracted to the latter than to her, but then comforted herself by thinking she was preparing herself for more important things by becoming seriously involved in her work. Although she felt that she had dealt with the episode in a mature way, it was shortly thereafter that she felt the desire to eat. She recalled a dream of the previous night in which it turned out that a semipsychotic boy, who was one of her clients, had an organic brain disease. She had been reading about a boy who had stuffed himself into a trash can and was sent to the acute ward of a mental hospital. It later turned out that he had witnessed a policeman club a woman, who screamed out that he had kicked her in the stomach and killed her unborn child. The boy identified himself with the policeman. He felt he was responsible for the death of his foster mother several weeks earlier, because he had disobeyed her. The patient thought he was punishing himself by treating himself as a piece of trash. I said this might be true, but why did he choose to do it in just this way? In view of the subject we were discussing, I suggested that by getting into a closed container he could be making atonement by returning to his mother's womb, in addition to proving himself unworthy. The patient, in effect, had confirmed my interpretation of the meaning of her sudden hunger after having dismissed it. This happens not infrequently (Freud, 1937, p. 263).

I remarked that if the boy of whom she dreamt and who was causing her much frustration turned out to have an organic brain syndrome, he could not be held accountable for his continued misbehavior. Could the boy represent herself? We knew from the past that she could not tolerate success, because she felt guilty for surpassing her mother. She would thus allow her mother to defeat her in tennis even though she was the better player. The day before she had said how well she felt about finally being settled on the proper course in life. Upon leaving the session she automatically assumed that I would prefer the other patient to her, and to make sure that I would consider her unworthy, she proceeded to behave regressively. She did not reject the interpretation but instead recalled that when she became depressed at times she insisted that her condition was organic in nature and she reproached me for not prescribing medication for her.

Comment: We seem to have wandered from the original dream and taken up a number of side issues. In a sense, however, the entire discussion may be regarded as a whole. The patient was ambivalent toward me because, although I was helpful, I was also "sour and bitchy" like Ann. This presumably referred to the fact that I did not join others in giving her accolades, but insisted that she be realistic. When she made a serious choice in life she had then to regress. The dream seemed to express a desire to be taken care of by a mother figure, instead of becoming self-sufficient. In other words, out of guilt she could not tolerate the rarefied atmosphere of being successful and had to punish herself by appearing infantile and therefore unworthy in my eyes.

By means of the dream we were able to clarify many aspects of the transference which threw light upon much of the patient's behavior throughout life.

Case 5C: The following dream of a sadomasochistic individual was reported at an advanced stage of her analysis. As a result, it was possible to point out the oedipal nature of the transference and the regressive (anal-sadomasochistic) form it took.

Dream: The patient and a man were riding in a car and had to stop for a red light. A man in a truck in front of them also stopped and unloaded an old beat-up sofa from his dump truck and left it in the street, thus blocking the patient's car with the trash from his truck. The man beside her said, "Well, shove it out of the way over to the curb and then you can drive on your way." She did so. The truck driver, who appeared to be drunk, started yelling and then drove off. He stopped again. She found herself bent over as if to tie her shoelaces; she felt the man was approaching her from the back and felt nervous. A hand grasped her hand and tugged it, and a voice said, "Come along with me." It was the sheriff. She yelled to her companion in the car, "We have to go to the sheriff's office." They went to a storefront police station and she was afraid she would be abused, although she thought it wasn't her fault; her companion had told her to move the sofa to the curb, although she didn't want to do it. She could have driven around the obstacle. The drunken truck driver was also in jail. The patient felt she had been victimized and was very anxious.

The patient added that she had another dream the same night, which she remembered only vaguely. It also had to do with the fact that she got into trouble by listening to a man.

While giving her associations she added several details to the first dream.

She thought her companion in the car was annoyed with her. He wanted her to move the sofa closer to the curb or sewer, and although she was afraid to do so, she did it to please him. She was indignant at being collared by the sheriff, but felt too intimidated to protest. He was handling her roughly, but out of guilt she was afraid to remonstrate with him. She was too embarrassed to tell her companion that the policeman pulled her hair. No man should have taken that liberty with her; she felt insulted and hurt. When she was treated that way it made her feel degraded and unworthy. She was afraid her companion would create a scene if he knew of it.

Background: The patient was a social worker who had been having an extramarital affair for a number of years. Her husband knew about the relationship and tried to regain her affection, but after a few years, when he realized that her mind was set, he agreed to grant her a divorce. She was given custody of her two daughters and had been living with her lover for three years. At first there had been much friction between them, but things then settled down. Her friend was aware of her immaturity and had urged her to enter analysis. She was now in the third year of treatment.

Day Residue: The day before the dream she and her lover had visited her brother. The two men spent most of the time conversing with each other and she felt left out. On their return home she was depressed and wanted her friend to embrace her, but felt uncomfortable about asking him to do so. She felt sorry for herself and did not want to come to the analytic hour the next day. She said that she wanted to remain the way she was, and no one was going to make her change. The analysis was a yoke around her neck because it made her feel "maligned." She had arrived several minutes late for the session.

Associations: While she was still living with her husband she had wanted to dispose of an old sofa. Her friend, who was represented by her companion in the car, said that he could use it and she gave it to him. Later she felt guilty toward her husband for giving away something that he had worked for. After the divorce, her husband became bitter and depressed and said he would never marry again. This increased her feeling of guilt. In the dream she was sympathetic toward the drunken truck driver, whom she identified with her husband. She could not tell her companion of the sheriff's rough handling of her because it would degrade her in his eyes. Likewise she could never tell her mother about her disappointments because it would be admitting that there was something wrong with her. She said, "I was confused in the dream. I shouldn't have moved the sofa. This happens all the time in real life. I'm always getting into trouble for doing the wrong thing or for being negligent." For instance, she would put off paying bills or summonses for traffic violations until she received threatening notices. She thought the sheriff represented the therapist.

She again discussed her visit to her brother's home and the feeling of being left out. It recalled how she felt left out as a child by the close relationship between her two older brothers. It was also typical of her to feel uneasy about expressing affection for anyone, although she had no difficulty in expressing hostility. She could readily quarrel with others and torment them, but she felt uncomfortable when it came to demonstrating tenderness or warmth. The patient spoke of her almost constant feeling of guilt. If she took a day off from work, even though it was part of her vacation, she felt apologetic toward her supervisor.

When asked what she thought the main theme of the dream was, she said, "I commit actions about which I am not clear, and get into trouble for them. I wind up feeling guilty." She went on to say that she had a tendency to make other people responsible when things went wrong. In the dream, for instance, she could have gone around the obstacle and thus avoided any problem, and even though she failed to do so, she wanted her companion to share the blame with her. She often picked quarrels with her lover so as to make him suffer. He was prepared to marry her and wanted her to set a wedding date, but she kept finding reasons for postponing it. In this way her passive aggressive attitude was making life difficult for him. It carried its own punishment, however, since it gave him ground for criticizing her as an irresponsible child. The patient added that her "crazy behavior," that is, getting into trouble by not meeting her responsibilities, produced a voluptuous feeling of excitement in her which she enjoyed. She said that nothing gave her greater pleasure than to nail someone to the wall. She was afraid of doing so openly with the therapist, however, since he might become angry and terminate the treatment. She was provocative merely to the point of having people strike back at her, without abandoning her altogether. [The patient's sadism toward others was thus accompanied by her masochism in so arranging her life as to feel guilty and be punished. Her sadomasochism was eroticized, which obviously complicated the prognosis.]

She was embarrassed whenever she felt close to a man, and in attempting to cover up her feelings, she would become derisive and hostile toward him. In this connection she associated memories of having frequently witnessed the primal scene between the ages of two and a half and six. She later felt angry at her parents for having exposed her to this, although she "would not have missed it for the world!" At the age of seventy-seven her father was still interested in looking at *Playboy* magazine.

[To love a man or be loved by him reminded her of the oedipal situation, so that she had to deny all tender or affectionate feelings. We might therefore assume that on the previous day she was trying to repudiate her positive feelings for the therapist by expressing dissatisfaction with the analysis. In the dream the positive feelings were replaced by a sense of being insulted and debased by the sheriff. Could the dream be expressing a wish to be abused, that is, to gain masochistic gratification which would serve both self-punitive and sexual aims? This would resemble her characteristic way of dealing with tender affection for a man, namely, by transforming it into a sadomasochistic relationship. Being approached "from the rear" in the dream also pointed to the anal character of her sadomasochism.]

In response to my inquiry about the patient's recent attitude toward the therapist, the latter replied that for a week before the dream she had been speaking of her reluctance to come to the analytic hour. On one occasion he had to cancel a session, following which the patient quarreled with her lover. She said she missed the opportunity of talking to the therapist; if she could have done so, the quarrel might not have taken place. After saying this she was struck by the realization that she was attached to the therapist. Later that day she had a fantasy that a car crashed into hers while she was on the way to treatment. In the fantasy she asked a policeman to notify her office that she couldn't come to work that day, but she failed to ask him to call the therapist. The latter would be angry at not being notified, and she could then say, "I've got you now. You thought I was really irresponsible, but I had a good reason for not coming—I was in an accident."

[The patient wanted to withdraw from treatment because of her awareness of being attached to the therapist. Instead of acknowledging her fondness for him, however, she reacted with a hostile fantasy in which he had occasion to accuse her wrongfully, so that she could turn the tables on him and make him appear ridiculous.]

Comment: How could the dream be interpreted to the patient? We attempt, first of all, to relate the patient's associations to the current situation. According to her, the therapist was represented by both the truck driver and the sheriff. The truck driver dropping trash (the sofa or couch) in front of her car suggested that she regarded the analysis as trash. Since the sofa was also her husband's, it could mean that she degraded him by having an affair with his knowledge. She then added insult to injury by giving the sofa to her lover. On the other hand, her recent remark that she had a need to see the therapist on the day when he had to cancel, would suggest that the analysis was important to her. It was as if she had to deny his importance to her by denigrating both him (the drunken truck driver) and the analysis.

The other interesting thing about the dream was that she could have avoided the obstacle by driving around it, but instead she followed her companion's advice and pushed it away. In other words, she did not have to do anything wrong if she did not want to; she was under no external compulsion. Her lover had asked for the sofa that belonged to her husband, and she gave it to him, although she sensed that it was the "wrong" thing to do. He had also urged her to go into analysis. Was that also "wrong?" It could be something for which she deserved punishment at the therapist's hands, namely, that she did something to provoke him. She indicated that she would like to "nail him to the wall," but she was afraid of his reaction. She also expressed dissatisfaction with the treatment. In the dream, the language used in regard to the sofa (couch; analysis), "shove it," suggests that it was an anal product, of little value. In this fashion, she equated the therapist with her husband, whose sofa she treated as "trash." The intent of the dream would then appear to be a wish to be punished by having the therapist (sheriff) humiliate her, just as she sought to humiliate him in her fantasy. She thus felt guilty about her fondness for the therapist and had to deny it by turning it into hostility and inviting punishment. This was also what she did in her relationships with her father, husband, and lover.

In the dream she wanted her companion (lover) to share the blame with her. This would fit in with her tendency to do "forbidden things" and then seek to project blame onto someone else. It was thus his fault for putting her in a situation where she could become attracted to the therapist. This was reminiscent of the way she blamed her father for exposing her to the primal scene, even though she said she "wouldn't have missed it for the world."

The above conjectures dealt mainly with material of which the patient was fully aware. In this way one can make the interpretation more meaningful, and therefore more convincing and acceptable to the patient. A limited interpretation is preferable to one that tries to cover too much ground. Interpretation of defense precedes interpretation of id content, in this case, the masochistic punishment instead of the responsibility for her own aggression. The patient's reaction to the therapist was not new, but was one of a series of similar reactions to significant men in her past. In this way her repetitious behavior pattern could be interpreted. The patient's oedipal attachment and sadistic-anal regression were merely hinted at rather than explicitly spelled out. The interpretation of this could come later.

Case 6C: The following dream of a patient with preoedipal problems was presented at a seminar.

> I am a nurse in an intensive-care unit. The patient was supposed to be a boy four or five days old, but he was like a little old man. People treated him like a little old man at times and like a baby at other times. They were giving him very tiny doses of Digoxin. A female resident came by. She was really concerned and stayed three hours longer to talk to me. I said to her, "You know, you are treating him like an old man but he is really a baby. He has an infant's needs." At the end of the dream I take a bus.

Background: The patient was a twenty-five-year-old married nurse who had entered analysis because of chronic depression. This had recently been aggravated when her mother was hospitalized for involutional melancholia. The analysis was soon to be interrupted because the patient's husband was being transferred to a post in a distant city. She had known for several months that she would be leaving and she was planning to continue her analysis after she moved. The dream occurred during the last week of the present analysis.

A few days prior to the dream the therapist's office had been moved to another room further down the hall. The therapist worked in a hospital and was not responsible for the move. When the patient was directed to the new office, she became very anxious because she had not been previously informed of the move. She thought the therapist might have moved deliberately in order to provoke a reaction in her. She had heard of psychiatrists doing such things to patients and wondered how she could ever trust anyone who played "games" and was so unreliable. She could not think of him as remaining in one place for any length of time.

[The patient's reaction to a minor change in routine suggests that she was the neglected baby in the dream.]

The therapist asked her why she reacted so strongly to the move, since it was only a short distance from his former office. She then realized that her reaction was that of a child. This led to a flood of

Transference Dreams

associations about her family. Her father had been a career officer in the army and was shifted from post to post, so that the family was constantly on the move. Her mother invariably became depressed when her husband left home. The patient's older brothers would begin to act up at such times so that her mother's attention was taken up with them, and the patient felt entirely left out. The patient was wondering what her next analyst would be like. She said, "He'll probably be an old bald-headed man with a smelly cigar, who won't be interested in me. I bet as soon as I start with him, he will be going away on his winter vacation. I really want a caring person, someone who will be very understanding and sensitive to my needs."

Day Residue: In the hospital, the patient was nursing an old man toward whom she felt very maternal.

At this point in the seminar a student remarked, "I understand the day residue is that which stimulates the dream, but I don't get the impression that she was really emotionally involved with the old man." I replied that any occurrence of the previous day, however indifferent, which evokes a responsive note from the patient's unconscious, may serve as a stimulus for a dream. It does not have to agree in all details. In this case, the patient said that she treated the old man in a maternal manner, which is presumably how she herself would like to be treated; the day residue therefore may not have been altogether indifferent. Since the identical emotional involvement referred to herself, it is probable that she identified with the old man. This could have been sufficient to stimulate the dream.

Another candidate commented that the dream ended abruptly when she took the bus. This might refer to her desire to terminate the analysis abruptly. I said this was very likely, but since we were not prepared to draw any conclusions, it would be better at this time to continue with the patient's further associations.

Associations: The dream led the patient to talk of the turmoil that she was undergoing. She said she must be the old man in the dream. There were times when she wanted to be treated like an old man and times when she wanted to be treated like a baby. The dream, according to her, had to do with her problems in analysis; she wanted a doctor who would care for her and gratify her needs. On the other hand, she wanted to be regarded as an adult. She realized that her childish needs at times took over without her awareness. She connected the part of the dream in which she took the bus with leaving the analysis. The three hours which the resident spent with her referred to the three analytic hours that still remained before she would be leaving.

Discussion: I suggested that leaving the analysis could have stirred up memories of the traumatic experience of observing her mother's depression whenever the patient's father left home, with the result that the patient felt entirely alone and neglected. She wanted the therapist to be sufficiently concerned about her to allow her to stay longer. The dream recapitulated experiences that she underwent many times in childhood. It was thus a repetition of a childhood trauma, with the wish that she find a better resolution of it than the one she had previously experienced. When the wish was not fulfilled in the dream, she left abruptly.

The presenter then recalled that when the patient's father was at home, he spent his time going fishing and hiking with the patient's two older brothers, while she was left home. She held her husband responsible for the interruption of the analysis, even though he had put in a request for the transfer long before she began the analysis. When she learned that he was to be transferred, she was reminded of the time as a child when her parents decided to move without telling her about it.

I recalled her remark to the woman resident (i.e., a mother figure) in the dream, "You are treating him like an old man, but he is really a baby." She herself was showing separation anxiety and wanted to be treated like a baby and have her mother stay with her. I asked if she had ever manifested feelings of clinging dependency toward the analyst. The presenter replied that she once became upset when he announced that he was taking a vacation. At that time, she dreamt that she had prepared a banquet for President Nixon at his home in the country. She was part of the entertainment committee, but she was also involved in a plot to assassinate him. Her associations were Nixon-President-authority figures-analyst. She expressed her annoyance at the latter's planning to leave her. She pictured him

Transference Dreams

vacationing with his children at the shore, and hoped it would rain so that he would be stuck in the house with the kids.

A student questioned whether Digoxin would be given to a baby. I pointed out that it was more important to deal first with the main thought of the dream. Was the main issue the medical treatment of the person, or the fact that the dreamer was upset because the resident was treating the patient like an old man instead of like a baby? One should direct attention to the obvious sense of the dream before proceeding to other aspects. In the current situation the patient was behaving like a clinging child who resented change because of separation anxiety. She was angry with her husband because he was taking her away from the therapist, that is, mother. She was also angry with the therapist for being unreliable, and probably also for allowing her husband to take her away. She may have wanted him to tell her husband that the analysis was more important than his job. In effect, it was the therapist who was treating the patient as if she were an adult and not a child. It was as if he were saying to her, "You are a big girl now." She was upset by the fact that she was moving away from him, and that he did not really care enough for her to want her to stay. It would be more fruitful to keep an eye on the ball and pay attention to the facts we already knew about the patient, than resort to theoretical speculations. To judge from the fact that she was working effectively as a nurse and had made a fairly good adjustment in her marriage, one could assume that she had reached the genital level and then regressed, rather than having been arrested at an earlier level. There were evidences of an effectively functioning ego. We could ask what level of regression she had reached. Was it to the level of object constancy or further back than that? Object constancy means that the child feels sufficiently secure to tolerate the mother's absence for progressively longer periods. In such cases, we assume that the child has received adequate love and reassurance from the mother. Here, however, the patient behaved as though she was not sure of her mother, so she may not have reached the level of object constancy. This could be related to the mother's repeated depressions, during which the patient felt abandoned.

A student commented about the part of the dream in which the patient took a bus. It was, he said, as if she marched off and left.

I again referred them to the current situation. The patient expressed her anger toward the therapist when his office was moved down the hall, charging him with being "provocative and unstable." This was clearly an infantile reaction. She was also angry with him for failing to urge her husband to remain in town, so that she could continue with the analysis. Taking the bus meant that she walked off and left the analysis in anger. What could the dream wish be? Could it be that she wanted to leave the analysis as a means of revenge for being let down?

I suggested that the anger could represent a death wish toward the therapist, analogous to the dream of plotting to kill Nixon. In that case her anger would be an expression of her desire to kill or destroy. Instead of doing that, however, she left abruptly. Her abrupt departure could also be a way of substituting activity for passive dependency. By assuming an active role she managed to overcome her feeling of helplessness and dependency, so that she was no longer subject to the whims of others. This also built up her self-esteem and helped her feel self-sufficient. Had she repressed her anger and redirected it toward herself, she might have become depressed and perhaps suicidal. Her ability to express anger, therefore, was probably self-protective and quite salutary.

A student asked why the patient herself had not asked her husband to remain in Philadelphia until she completed her analysis. Furthermore, the therapist might have said to her, "What about the possibility of remaining here?" Another student objected that by indicating that he wanted her to stay, the therapist would be tipping his hand and compromising his objectivity. The other student replied that it would be rather like approaching her on a preoedipal level, so that she could get some reassurance from the therapist.

I agreed that to treat a patient of this type altogether as an adult, by getting her to face stark reality, could be traumatic, since her infantile needs might make it difficult or impossible for her to accept reality at this point. It is often too much to expect this type of person to deal with reality as long as her fundamental needs have not been met. Such support need not imply abandonment of the analytic stance, but may help to build up a positive feeling for the therapist. This could facilitate the changeover to her next analyst. One must be more outgoing and relaxed with patients whose infantile needs require partial gratification before they are ready to accept reality. The preoedipally deprived patient must be reassured that the therapist is constant and reliable. One does not actually have to take the role of the mother and treat the patient like an infant. One need merely indicate that one understands her problem. For instance, one might have asked her, "Have you discussed with your husband the problem of deferring the date of your moving? Could he get a deferment so that you could remain here longer?" In doing so one would not be directly advising the patient, or indicating that one would intervene with her husband. On the contrary, one would be treating her like an adult and also showing that he was sympathetic and understanding. If the patient was sufficiently mature, the added assurance might enable her to deal with the situation more adequately, or at least to view it realistically. If, on the other hand, this degree of reassurance did not suffice and it became evident that the patient required constant and repeated support, it would be questionable whether classical psychoanalytic technique could be maintained, or whether the patient was analyzable. In that case one might have to be content with a limited therapeutic result. To take this patient as a paradigm, interpretation of the type of modus operandi of her defenses could conceivably protect her from future depressions and help her make a better adjustment. In her case, however, it is more likely that her ability to express anger may have enabled her to release herself from her bondage to her mother earlier in life, as well as from the therapist in the present situation.

Summary and Conclusions: In the dream the infantile trauma of having been abandoned is repeated, but the ending differs. Instead of being abandoned, the patient leaves of her own accord. The dream wish appears to be a desire to express her anger actively instead of by playing the helpless victim. By being self-assertive she regains her self-esteem and also protects herself from becoming depressed. This recalls the sense of loneliness and abandonment she suffered as a child when her mother became depressed. The aggravation of her depression which brought her to treatment occurred when her mother was hospitalized for involutional melancholia. She may have sought to find a replacement for her mother in the therapist, but when he "failed" her, she reacted not by becoming depressed, but by expressing her anger against him.

In reviewing the patient's transference situation we become aware that it was not the type of transference found in the usual psychoneurotic patient, but was characterized by a clinging infantile quality. The patient was unable to tolerate ordinary frustrations, as evidenced by her unusual reaction of anger when the therapist's office was moved a short distance down the hall. At the time she called him "provocative and unstable." Any change from the usual routine gave rise to separation anxiety. According to the dream, the patient regarded herself as a newborn infant, namely, four or five days old. We can assume that there was some developmental disturbance in the preverbal period. At this level the individual's conflicts are related to the external world, that is, they are linked up with adaptation to the environment. This sets the patient apart from the neurotic patient who suffers largely from intrapsychic conflicts, that is, conflicts between drive and defense. If this type of patient is unable to recognize the infantile quality of her behavior or to regard it as ego-alien, the therapeutic goal must be different from that aimed at in treating the psychoneurotic patient, whose personality is structuralized. The situation in the case of the patient under consideration is confused, because she seems to have made a good outward adjustment by becoming an efficient nurse and relating fairly well in her marriage.

As is often the case, the pathology resulting from disturbances of development may not be evident at first, and may appear only later in the course of treatment. Even when the facts of a patient's past are known, it may not be possible to predict the future outcome, because of the effect of later life experiences. It is therefore only when the total effect of past experiences becomes manifest in the transference that one can determine whether the classical analytic technique must be modified. Where the effects of impaired

Transference Dreams 143

psychosexual and ego development persist, we should be prepared to accept a partial issue, since the patient cannot endure the frustrations and narcissistic hurts that adaptation to reality entails. Such patients require much support in the form of libidinal and narcissistic gratifications. It is in this area that an understanding of the transference, particularly as it manifests itself in dreams, can be most helpful.

When a patient changes from one analyst to another, it is important for the new person to know the nature of the previous transference, since this provides him with guidelines for the further conduct of the case. The first therapist is in a position to facilitate the change by his skillful management of the transference.

CHAPTER 8

Resistance and Dreams

General Consideration of Resistance

Psychologically speaking, sleep represents a retreat from the unpleasant aspects of life and from external stimuli which require constant readjustment on the part of the individual. In sleep one regresses to the Nirvana of the mother's womb, to a state of narcissism where one is protected from the demands of reality. As the ego's alertness is diminished in sleep, unconscious wishes, which never rest, press toward consciousness and threaten to awaken the sleeper. The censorship of the ego is not entirely relaxed, however, and proceeds to control the unconscious drives and wishes from entering the preconscious and giving rise to distressing affects. The latent dream thoughts are first required to undergo distortion by the dream work (condensation, displacement, and plastic, mainly pictorial, representation) and only when they are sufficiently disguised can they be linked with preconscious wishes. The manifest dream which results is an amalgam of the derivatives of infantile drives and the defenses against them, and constitutes an attempt to resolve the conflict between the two by means of a compromise. As a result the dreamer is protected against an outbreak of anxiety and can continue to sleep undisturbed.

The defensive activity of the dream censorship, however, does not cease with the successful preservation of sleep, but continues after waking in the form of resistance. Both the censorship and resistance are thus aspects of the ego's defensive apparatus, which includes all processes designed to protect the ego against instinctual demands.

Since the aim of free association is to circumvent the repressions imposed by the ego, it is not surprising that it is opposed by obstacles placed in its path by resistances. The effect of the resistance is to clamp down on the inflow of the id into the ego, thus interrupting the progress of analytic work (Freud, 1900, p. 517). At the beginning of treatment, the patient, under the stress of his neurotic suffering and with the encouragement and protection of the analyst, is ready to discuss freely many topics which are ordinarily distasteful to him. As the urgency is reduced, however, the patient becomes increasingly aware of the disagreeable nature of his confessions and is reluctant to continue. He holds the analyst responsible for advising him to drop his guard and he begins to rebel against the analysis. His associations come haltingly or cease altogether and are replaced by long silences. The patient has a feeling of emptiness when he has nothing to say and looks to the analyst to carry on the analytic work. Resistance is thus inherent in the very nature of analysis and cannot be avoided if the ego is intact. As a matter of fact it becomes more pronounced as the analysis deepens and approaches the crucial intrapsychic conflicts. If the patient intuitively understands the deeper implications of his dreams or accepts them too readily, we begin to suspect that there is a serious breakdown of ego boundaries.

When resistaneces appear our attention is turned away from a study of the id and is directed to the ego's defensive operations. We are then in a position to learn something about the patient's character structure, since character traits, insofar as they participate in maintaining repression and thereby protecting the ego against instinctual demands, are really mechanisms of defense. Resistances thus serve a double purpose: they are not only obstacles to the flow of information about the id and protect the ego from anxiety, but they also provide information about the ego (Anna Freud, 1937).

Resistance may appear in dreams either in the latent content or in the form in which the dream is reported or dealt with in the analytic session. Resistance may be reflected in the latent dream content in several guises: as a wish for the analyst's death or degradation; as an intention to terminate the treatment as a flight into health or to express dissatisfaction with the analyst or the treatment, as a desire to give in to the id and continue acting out; and as an intention to commit suicide. These forms of resistance usually become evident from the patient's associations or the disinterested or hostile manner in which he discusses the dream. Occasionally the analyst can detect the presence of resistance from the content of the manifest dream itself. If it has to do with erotic feelings, hostility toward, or death wishes against the analyst, it may be difficult to obtain confirmation from the patient. Indeed his overt attitude toward the analyst may show just the opposite tendencies, namely, those of frank hostility or contempt, on the one hand, or adulation and dedication, on the other. One must be on the alert for the appearance of negative feelings in dreams when the patient's general attitude is consistently bland.

Formally, resistances may take on many guises. There may be fogginess on recalling the dream, with expressions of uncertainty about its contents. The dream may be reported at great length with a wealth of detail. Its recital may consume much of the hour, or may come toward the end of the hour so that little time is left for discussion. If the patient believes that the analyst is interested in dreams, he may bring in a plethora of dreams as "gifts" or as acts of appeasement, without attempting to work on them. He may try to divert the analyst's attention from the dream by minimizing its importance. ("It's a crazy dream," "It doesn't seem to be worth working on," or "It can't have much meaning"), or he may habitually forget his dreams. Lewin deals with the forgetting of dreams and reports several cases where the forgetting was associated with oral fantasies which he attributed to the infant's desire for the breast. He described a patient whose chief neurotic problem was a continuous struggle against a wish to remain asleep. The patient would bring many unanalyzable dreams into one analytic hour, apparently enjoying the mere reporting of them. Telling his dreams turned out to be a form of acting out: he was literally repeating his sleep of the previous night, as if he did not want to have that sleep disturbed. Lewin interpreted to the patient the wish to sleep as a resistance (1948, p. 227).

When his thoughts run dry the patient may bring in dreams simply to have "something" to talk about and thus avoid a sterile hour. In this way he manages to bypass the resistance when he may have something unpleasant to report. If he is asked to repeat a dream which was unclear on the first telling, he may add some details or delete others that he has already mentioned. In such case, the parts deleted may be the most important aspects of the dream, although the new aspects may also be meaningful, since they may have been repressed during the first account. Writing down dreams in order to counteract the tendency to forget them does not really succeed in overcoming the resistance; the writing is often illegible or uninformative, and even if not, the associations fail (Freud, 1911, p. 95; Abraham, 1913).

It often happens that after a weekend or a long holiday the patient brings in several dreams that occurred on different nights. Instead of discussing the most recent dream, however, he will choose to work on one of the earlier dreams. It will then be found that the day residues of the previous days are no longer fresh in his mind, so that he can give only few associations. On the other hand, dreams that have occurred many years previously may be successfully interpreted, since the conflicts that gave rise to them have long been overcome and no longer exist.

Method of Dealing with Resistance

The presence of resistance is indicated by the fact that the progress of the analysis is impeded. The patient is at first unaware that he is in resistance and must be confronted with the fact. Merely to tell him that he is in resistance, however, may appear to him to be a reproach, as if he were doing something willfully. It is therefore important to let him know that resistance is not an intentional act or the result of conscious opposition. He may be withholding his associations because he has something on his mind that he is reluctant to discuss.. By means of such explanations he comes to learn that the word "resistance" does not have critical implications.

Resistance and Dreams 151

On the contrary, resistance is an inevitable part of the analytic process, and as such requires joint participation both by him and by the analyst in order to study and understand the reason for its appearance at a specific time. Resistances are handled by first understanding them and then trying to resolve them so that the analysis can proceed.

Resistances may appear to be annoying interferences with the smooth progress of analysis just when the patient seems to be doing so well. It is inherent in the analytic process, however, that resistances are most likely to arise precisely when the patient is making progress, that is, coming closer to the core of the pathogenic conflict. Far from being a distracting intrusion, resistances can tell us much about the ego's habitual unconscious defensive operations against the emergence of instinctual impulses and disagreeable affects.

The patient in the process of being analyzed cannot be expected to take such a detached view of the situation. He is only aware that confrontation with his reprehensible affects and drives threatens to upset his equilibrium and generate anxiety. He regards the analyst as a disturber of the peace because he favors the undoing of repressions. The patient's resistances are premarily directed against the analyst. All the forces that maintained the repression are now turned in oppostition to the analyst. In the presence of resistance the transference inevitably comes up for consideration. The transference is under the influence of the repetition complulsion and may belong either to the id or to the ego. When it becames a resistance it may take the form of libidinal attachment to, or aggression against, the analyst according to previous patterns. Transference resistance thus differs from ego resistance. The patient relates to teh analyst by strong emotions of love and hate and finds it embarrassing and distressing to express them. Until he does so, however, he cannot deal with other problems. It becomes easier for him to discuss these affects if he can be shown that they have their source in earlier relationships and that the analyst serves only as a convenient object onto which to transfer them. Such explanations get him off the hook, as it were. In this way we can learn a great deal about the patient's early affective life and object relations.

As a defensive measure against the instincts the transference adopts the ego's defense mechanisms of the past. It is difficult, however, to convince the patient that his hostility to the analyst is not justified by the current situation, and is merely a replica of past reactions. In other words, the transference pattern has become imbedded in his character structure and is not regarded as a foreign body inherited from the past.

Acting out is another form of transference resistance. This is a particularly difficult type of resistance to overcome since the ego allies itself with the id and is ready to accept the inconveniences resulting from acting out for the satisfactions derived from it. As a result the patient is likely to be little influenced by the analyst, who is left with the alternative of either analyzing the acting out or suggesting that the patient restrain his behavior. As a rule the patient is not ready to give up his acting out until he no longer obtains satisfaction from it or finds that it creates too many problems for him in real life. We can, however, learn much about the ego and the id, as well as the superego, by observing the acting-out pattern.

In the presence of resistance it is natural to inquire, first of all, about the transference. The analyst may look for evidences of transference changes that have occurred in recent analytic sessions or in his acting out, both in and out of the analytic situation. He may ask the patient directly what thoughts he has been having about the analyst. If he is empathically identified with the patient, he may be able to come upon the specific cause of the resistance or even anticipate it, without having to interrogate the patient. By being in a position to point out the patient's attitude in the transference and to connect with it a recent or ongoing situation, he may succeed in overcoming the resistance before it becomes firmly fixed. This is illustrated by the following incident, although it was based on a reality, rather than on a transference, situation. When a patient who had been cooperative suddenly became silent and withdrawn, I asked myself what could account for the abrupt change. It then occurred to me that on the previous day I had failed to give him credit for something he had accomplished and instead had stressed

Resistance and Dreams 153

the fact that he might have done better. Since he was a sensitive person he could very well have experienced this as a narcissistic hurt, and was probably afraid to express himself lest he reveal the degree of his anger. I then remarked that he must be angry because of what I had said the day before. He immediately replied how chagrined he had been by my remark. It seemed that by meeting him halfway and inviting him to express his resentment, I had helped him overcome his inhibition. I then apologized for not giving him the credit he deserved. This was intended to let him realize that he was not always wrong and that I, too, could make mistakes. It also supported his sense of reality, in that his reactions were not all necessarily rooted in the unconscious and therefore subject to analysis.

Another patient's reluctance to reveal an embarrassing fact about himself appeared to be an acting out of his hostility, until the situation was cleared up. The patient reported that he had engaged in a conversation concerning me with someone who he knew was not well disposed toward me. From the way he spoke I assumed that he had initiated the conversation, perhaps from a hostile motive, and I asked him what had induced him to do so. It turned out later, however, that the other man had started the conversation, but the patient made no attempt to correct me. Instead he permitted me to continue talking for a while about it as an expression of his hostility, and then disclosed the fact that it was not he who had approached the man but the other way around. I was naturally taken aback, since his failure to correct my initial impression appeared to be a hostile thing in itself. I asked him why he had not told me this at the beginning. He replied that he felt guilty about having masturbated the night before and felt that he deserved to be criticized! It was as if he had welcomed punishment. What seemed to be an acting out of hostility was therefore really a reaction to the demands of his superego. The patient's resistance consisted in his reluctance to confess his act of masturbation. Instead he acted out by "inviting" the punishment. One, however, cannot altogether dismiss the likelihood that, under cover of his masochistic attitude, he was giving vent to his resentment against me by causing me to appear "foolish" in having falsely accused him. From this point of view I represented his punitive superego, and ultimately his father. In such cases one's spontaneous reactions often accurately reflect the patient's unconscious intentions. One must keep this fact in mind. For instance, if one begins to feel bored by a patient's report of seemingly endless dreams, one may assume that one's reaction is in accord with what the patient unconsciously planned. It is important not to allow such occasions to pass but to make the patient aware of the situation. I have said to a patient at such times, "I wonder if you realize how tiresome it might be for me to listen to your long detailed dreams. Is it possible that you unconsciously want to produce this effect in me, perhaps in order to divert my attention from something you would rather not talk about?"

The general rule is to interpret the resistance before interpreting the id content. To carry out the intentions of the superego is more acceptable to the ego than is giving in to the warded-off drives. The ego can better tolerate the idea that it is *repelled* by antisocial acts and fantasies, or that it is *fighting off* certain temptations, than that it *wishes* to indulge in them. As a consequence such tendencies are closer to consciousness. It is important, however, that in confronting the patient with his inner struggle he should be made aware of the specific temptation or desire that he is fending off. The rationale behind this is to get the thought across to the jury, as it were, where it can incubate and begin to set up connections with related ideas in the unconscious. Ultimately it is hoped that the repressions will be lifted, and that the patient can deal directly with the repudiated drives.

Case Reports

Case 1P: A man whose mother died suddenly when he was three years old was characterized mainly by his distrust of others. He reacted as if his mother had left him deliberately. In speaking of her he expressed real grief, repeatedly breaking down in tears and asking, "How could she do this to me?" His constant fear of being abandoned was manifested by his need to be in control at all times.

Resistance and Dreams

In the analysis, for instance, he habitually refused to take my statements at face value but insisted on trying to second guess me, that is, look for hidden meanings, as if on guard against being caught unawares. He would then proceed to reverse the roles of analyst and patient by analyzing what I said. When confronted with his attitude he explained that he was afraid of being stripped of his defenses and appearing as a helpless child lying in his urine and feces. He behaved as if his self-esteem were constantly being threatened and often found it necessary to prove his competence even in areas where it was not called for. For instance, when among those skilled in fields not his own, he would venture nonetheless to demonstrate his knowledge in those areas. He said he preferred to do all the talking in the analysis so that way he could be in control. He became anxious when someone else was in charge; he was like a child who didn't know what was going on and was afraid of what might happen. He could not trust others to tell him honestly why certain things were happening, because in his mind they were unconcerned about his welfare.

The patient was ever on the lookout for evidences of my vulnerability. If I expressed impatience he would regard it as a victory for himself, as if he had broken through my facade of impenetrability and proved that I was no better than he. He was envious of me and considered having to lie on the couch and submit to the analytic rules as a humbling blow to his pride. He was also pleased to hear anything derogatory about me from others. These persistent character traits could presumably be traced to his feelings of impotence and anger when his mother "deserted" him, since it is well-known that the loss of a parent in early childhood is experienced not only as the loss of a love-object but also as a narcissistic injury, like castration. Playmates often reinforce such feelings of degradation by pitilessly mocking the unfortunate child. In addition, since the patient's mother was a depressive individual, it is likely that his sense of frustration was reinforced by her earlier neglect of him (Jacobson, 1971).

The patient was easily won over by women who admired him and thus supported his inflated image of himself. His resistance to any interpretation I gave him seemed to stem from the fact that he would feel diminished if he accepted anything from me. Often when I ventured to call some aspect of his behavior into question, he would protest indignantly, "Who are you to pass judgment on me?," as if it were an impertinence on my part.

External relationships with people were characterized by a superficiality and a tendency to devaluate others. People were valuable to him only insofar as they could contribute to his sense of self-importance. When called to account for his aggressiveness and lack of regard for the sensitivities of others, however, he would become apologetic. This, however, did not denote a basic change of attitude. In the analytic situation, for instance, if I pointed out that he was talking at length without being relevant to the subject at hand, he would stop short as if he had offended me. He would then, without real comprehension, make an anxious show of paying close attention to my every word. It was as if he were reacting to discipline by appearing the over-obedient child. His self-inflating and controlling behavior could be regarded only as an attempt to cover up and compensate for his underlying feeling of worthlessness.

On one occasion he brought in the following dream:

> Rabbi B. is delivering a sermon from the pulpit to a large congregation of worshipers. While he is speaking, a young man begins to talk out loud, and it strikes me that he is interrupting the sermon. I tell him to keep quiet. His attitude is one of total absolute lack of respect for a religious leader; he has no feeling for synagogue decorum. He shows no regard for what I'm saying. I grapple or wrestle with him. I yell at him or use physical force to get him to conform. He still doesn't respond to me at all; he's not at all affected. Finally, for the third time, I grab him and smash his head against a pole, almost killing him. I begin to feel guilty about the violence I've employed.

Associations: At first he thought I might be the rabbi and he the troublemaker, since he was the one who usually rebelled against any kind of control. But then he recalled that he never interrupted me;

on the contrary, he was always careful to maintain an appearance of compliance and of being attentive when I spoke. Beyond that, however, he was inclined to intellectualize and talk incessantly in a rambling manner. It was really I who interrupted him. In other words he was the rabbi who didn't like to be interrupted or told what to do. He felt like killing me when I pointed out his errors. "Who was I to talk to him that way?" he asked. He described Rabbi B. as a pompous, arrogant person.

Comment: The dream masked the patient's hostility to me by means of a reversal of persons. Ordinarily the one in authority in a dream would be equated with the analyst, as the patient himself understood, but it turned out *I* was the rebel who challenged *him*, while he was the one to be respected. He thus externalized his own aggression while I became the personification of his aggressive self. By means of this externalization or projection he succeeded in denying his aggression (projective identification). It was as if he looked into the mirror and instead of seeing himself saw me, created in his own image. The dream also revealed the murderous rage of the patient when he was thwarted or frustrated. One could imagine that he managed to check his destructive anger by maintaining a feeling of superiority and authority. The dream suggests that following the trauma of his mother's death he attempted both to repair his injured self-esteem and to control his anger against her by retreating to the fantasy of narcissistic omnipotence. It thus revealed the patient's central defense against narcissistic injury and provided a key to his character structure. By maintaining control over others he could protect himself against a repetition of the original trauma.

What can this dream teach us? In analyzing the resistance as we did, we were able to open the door to a knowledge of the patient's ego defenses against internal and external dangers. The striking resemblance between the patient's behavior in the dream and his acting out in the transference threw light upon the latter, insofar as it indirectly helped to recapture early experiences. According to Anna Freud (1968, p. 167) such repetition or reliving of behavior may be the only way of recapturing the "forgotten past," especially so far as it refers to the preverbal period, before it has undergone secondary repression and become part of the ego organization. She adds that such acting out or reliving has to do with the aggressive drives rather than with the sexual urges, which are more likely to be repressed. When the patient interpreted the rebellious attitude in the dream as an affront to the deference due him, he was also expressing his outrage in submitting to the analyst's judgment of him; presumably he felt similarly when rejected as a child. Instead of recalling an actual memory which had been repressed, the dream could have been reliving the past by mirroring the patient's recurrent behavior in the transference.

We might assume that the transference reproduced the defiant feelings of the patient's infantile attitude toward his mother, now redirected against the analyst. The patient's persistent tendency to challenge the analyst's authority, almost from the very beginning of treatment, indicates that the transference reaction was set in motion not by loosening of repression as occurs with neurotic patients, but as an expression of unrepressed hostility resulting from the excessive strength of early emotional experiences. It was obvious that we were dealing with a character structure with excessive narcissistic elements. In such cases the question always arises whether the patient is analyzable by classical technique or whether the introduction of parameters should be considered (Eissler, 1953; Stone, 1954). We must realize, however, that narcissistic problems exist in varying degrees in all neurotic patients and that the final diagnosis rests upon quantitative factors. Furthermore, in stressing very early phases of development we always run the risk of underestimating the later libidinal and ego phases of development. We must keep in mind that internalization of object representations are not confined exclusively to early object relationships. The oedipal situation, later associations with individuals serving as ego ideals, and the vicissitudes of life must also be taken into consideration.

There is no doubt that the patient's ego suffered a serious trauma at the time of his mother's death. The first question we must ask ourselves is whether the patient's ego development at the age of three was sufficiently advanced to cope successfully with the overwhelming ambivalence conflicts released by her death. If the ego were underdeveloped at the time, the release of great amounts of free aggression could be responsible for the breakdown of ego and superego functions. Since psychoanalytic technique relies on a relatively intact ego which can respond appropriately to interpretation, we must determine to what extent the ego was damaged before we can decide whether the situation can be dealt with by analysis. If the patient's resistances are mobilized against any alteration of his character, as evidenced by a persistent inability to accept interpretations of his defensive mechanisms, one may finally assume that psychoanalysis is not the treatment of choice and one may have to be content with something less than an analytic cure (Frank, 1955; Kernberg, 1975). Although interpretation cannot undo the early damage, such patients can frequently be helped in other ways, mainly by establishing a good transference relationship from which the patient can derive the sense of security he lacked in early life and by establishing an identification with a new superego and new ego-ideals. In the present case there were a number of factors which favored the continuance of analytic treatment, namely, the fact that the patient showed genuine grief in discussing his mother's death (indicating that he had established internalized object relationships), that he had fairly good impulse control, and that he was dissatisfied with his life situation.

Case 2P: A young woman student announced that she had had a dream about the therapist. Upon awakening, she was told by her lover, with whom she was living, that she had called out in her sleep, "You're the only one in Philadelphia who loves me." She did not know who was being addressed in the dream.

The dream, in three parts as narrated, was as follows:

1. She was walking with her friends, Bill and Jane. She saw Norman Mailer, the author, who greeted her. This pleased her. They all went up to Bill and Jane's apartment. There seemed to be two Bills and two Janes and the apartment looked like her own. Norman Mailer came in and became sexually aggressive

toward her. They were lying on the bed and he was giving her a lot of "come on" with his eyes and smile. He kissed her and she experienced a thrill but was also frightened. Her friend was there but he did not interfere.

2. She was with Professor C., who was talking to her about one of her classmates, a woman or girl, who was either threatening the patient or had assaulted her in class.

3. She was at home preparing dinner. She was killing flies who were dying slowly. There was also something about some ladies who were coming to her home.

Associations: One of her instructors, who resembled Norman Mailer, was known to be "cheating" on his wife. She hesitated to mention the instructor's name since the therapist might know him. Recently she had seen him outside the therapist's office buying flowers for his wife. She felt uncomfortable lest people know that she and her friend were living together. Beyond this she produced no further associations.

The therapist asked why she supposed the dream referred to him. She replied that she thought Professor C., who was a protective person, represented him. The therapist remarked that *Norman Mailer* could also refer to him, because the patient had often said she could not understand why he was always smiling. She usually held her head down as she walked into the office in order to avoid eye contact with him. [In the dream Norman Mailer smiles and establishes sexual contact with her through his eyes.]

The patient's responses to the dream were typical of her general reluctance to reveal her thoughts to the therapist. She consciously withheld data by giving little information about herself and by leaving many things unsaid. The therapist stated that he was bringing these dreams to the technical seminar because he was at a loss to know how to proceed with a patient who gave only limited associations.

With this type of patient it is clear that one must be more active in eliciting data.

I inquired about the circumstances surrounding the analysis. The patient had previously been in analysis with another doctor who had

Resistance and Dreams

the same name as her present therapist. The former therapist had died while he was on vacation. The present man had worked under him in a hospital and felt inhibited in discussing the patient's problems with her lest she discover that he was less competent than his predecessor. She apparently sensed his uneasiness and this in turn made her more inhibited.

The few associations indicated what the nature of the patient's transference reactions to the therapist were. Professor C. was a protective type of person, while the unnamed instructor was a philanderer and Norman Mailer was an aggressive man who seduced women with his eyes and smile. These seemed to represent various aspects of the therapist. The central idea of the first dream was that someone was making forbidden love to her.

I suggested that the first question was whether she had ever been in a situation similar to the one in the dream. The presenter stated that the patient was angry with her friend because he spoke openly of the fact that they were sleeping together. She felt guilty about the relationship and wanted to keep it concealed. Bill and Jane knew of the relationship, but did not question it.

In the dream, Norman Mailer was the man making love to her and she was both thrilled and frightened. Norman Mailer makes love to her and like her instructor has "cheated," according to her. Was it possible that she was also curious about the therapist's married life and, in particular, did she want to know if he "cheated?" Such questions could yield additional information about the content of the transference.

The presenter in reply to these questions recalled that several weeks prior to the dream, the patient had expressed a wish that he might love her, take care of her, and put her head in his lap and stroke it.

Day residue: The presenter was asked what had happened during the previous session. He said that the patient was self-conscious about the length of her abbreviated skirt and repeatedly sat up on the couch to make certain that it had not slipped up too high. He had commented that she was apparently worried about exposing something. She acknowledged this but did not know what it could be. She then recalled as a child sitting with her dress lifted and finding the touch of her underpants on the chair exciting. After saying this she became angry with him and felt like saying, "Leave me alone. I'm not going to tell you something." In reply to his question, she said that she had no idea what the "something" referred to. She then connected it with the recollection of an older uncle who used to tease her by holding her at arm's length while she tried to hit him, so that she could not reach him. She also spoke about having made love to her friend the night before. At this point she complained of dryness of her throat, as though something was stuck there.

[The therapist connected the pulling down of her skirt with a fear of exposing *something*, without being more specific. Her anger against him suggested that he had touched upon a delicate subject which she wanted to conceal. By the same token, however, he had caused the repression to be lifted, so that she was able to recall related memories from childhood.]

[The patient had worn a short skirt on coming to the previous session, probably with the unconscious intent of seducing the therapist. Her concern about her skirt slipping up and her sitting up on the couch were reactions to the wish. This was related to the sexual excitement she experienced as a child when she felt her panties next to the chair. She became angry with the therapist for bringing this to her attention and also for "teasing" her the way her uncle used to do, by maintaining the analytic stance of non-involvement. She probably also felt frustrated because of her fantasies about him. That the associations referred to sexual feelings was confirmed by her statement that she had had sexual relations the previous night. This was followed by the sudden dryness of her throat, as if something was stuck there that she could not get out. This could refer both to saying something compromising or to a fellatio fantasy. All the possibilities of the interpretation of the transference were not exhausted, however. According to the presenter, the patient repeatedly expressed guilt about her sexual relations with her friend, even though she had often defied her parents during her teenage years by her promiscuity and despite the fact that she and her friend were planning to get married shortly.

Resistance and Dreams

This pointed up a discrepancy in her attitude and led to the natural question why and towards whom she felt guilty.]

When these questions were raised in the seminar, the therapist remarked that the patient did not have much feeling for her friend and had become engaged to him while the therapist was away on vacation. Upon resuming the analysis after the therapist returned, she said she did not want to analyze her motivation for becoming engaged, since she might discover something about her fiancé that she did not like.

[This suggested that her guilt had to do with fear of the therapist's disapproval. The patient was probably unaware of her reasons for suddenly deciding to become engaged and would, therefore, be in no position to explain her behavior. In such instances we are justified in forming our own conjectures. It would not be far-fetched to suppose that when the therapist left for his vacation it reminded her of the fact that her former therapist had "abandoned" her by dying while he was away on vacation. She might have thought unconsciously, "I'm not going to put myself in the same position of helpless dependency again," and, in her resentment, became engaged. Her fiancé could then be a substitute for the therapist whom she loved. Her guilt toward the therapist could also be the result of her anger and her wish that *he* would also die while he was on vacation.]

In the conference I made the following observations: The patient said that she did not want to discuss her reasons for becoming engaged. Since she had said this several months previously when the therapist returned from his vacation, her attitude could have changed since then and she might feel differently now. The first dream, in which she practically acknowledged her fantasies about the therapist, suggested that this was so. How could the question be reopened at this time? Being mindful of the patient's sensitivity, the therapist could ask, "Why should you have guilt about going to bed with your friend when you are planning to marry him soon?" In this manner he would be indicating that he was not taking sides with her superego by passing moral judgment on her. Depending on the patient's reaction, subsequent comments could proceed as follows: "When we resumed the analysis after I returned from my vacation you said you didn't want to discuss your reasons for becoming engaged because you might discover something about your fiancé that you didn't like. Perhaps you are more ready to do so now. We might then learn why you feel guilty about having intercourse with him." By the use of the word "we" the analysis could be regarded as a collaborative enterprise. This would support the therapeutic alliance. If the patient responded favorably she could be led to discuss the reason for her anger against the therapist when he returned from his vacation and whether this had any connection with her decision to become engaged. In that case her doubts about being in love with her fiancé and her guilt for having intercourse with him could both be explained. One would hesitate to bring up the question of death wishes against the therapist at this time. It should be noted that all the interpretations suggested were from the surface, in keeping with what was in the patient's preconscious, the intensity of the current conflicts, and the capacity of the patient's ego to assimilate the interpretations. The interpretations were also designed to support the patient's ego (Loewenstein, 1954, p. 189).

Comment: In instances where the patient's associations to the dream are meager, the therapist is warranted in asking questions designed to clear up discrepancies or paradoxes both in the dream and in the patient's behavior. In making his inquiries he is guided by the central thought of the manifest dream, his empathic inferences from available data, and the need to protect the patient against narcissistic injury by discussing her defense against affects before discussing her defenses against instinctual drives (Bornstein, 1949, p. 187). The readiness with which the patient was able to reveal her erotic feelings for the therapist (by identifying him with the seductive *Norman Mailer* of the dream) suggests that the real drive which was being warded off was not entirely erotic in nature but also one of hostility, as implied in the subsequent dreams.

It is important at all times, but particularly with the resistant patient, to keep in mind the proper timing and the amount and depth of interpretation offered. One continually asks oneself how much the patient can accept at one time. In the present instance the questions raised were closely related to the material produced by the patient and dealt with the current situation.

The patient's second dream could be understood as being related to the criticism of her mother (girl classmates) for oedipal wishes and her desire to be protected by her father (Professor C). It may therefore be a punishment dream. In the third dream she is killing flies. Could this be related to death wishes against the therapist, both for his rejection of her and as a protection against her erotic attachment to him? [She had been embarrassed and angry with the therapist in the previous session for drawing attention to her preoccupation with her short skirt. This led to repressed sexual memories and fantasies.]

The above understanding of multiple dreams is in accord with Freud (1923b, p. 113) who points out that during a conflict arising from ambivalence, there are often two dreams every night, each of them representing a different attitude. He considers this an indication of progress in that isolation of the two contrasted impulses has been achieved. Hendrick (1958, p. 677) discusses resistance dreams in which the sexual content of the associations serves to conceal the hostility that dominates the transference situation. He regards "dream resistance" as a special form of "transference resistance." We know from Freud (1914c, pp. 163 & 167) that one of the distinctions between the positive eroticized transference and true love is that the former has an unconscious content of a hostile nature and that the ambivalence of neurotic patients best explains their ability to enlist their transferences in the service of resistance (1912a, p. 107).

Multiple dreams may, of course, have other meanings. Alexander (1925, p. 449), for instance, writes about two dreams in one night which produce a wish fulfillment in two stages if they are taken together. One dream may represent a punishment and the other the sinful wish fulfillment. If one accepts the punishment, that is, the moral demands of the superego, he can then allow himself to transgress again. In other instances of multiple dreams, the same thought which is concealed in the first dream becomes more openly expressed in subsequent dreams (Freud, 1911, p. 94). It may also happen that subsequent dreams show alternate ways of achieving relief of tension and of "solving" problems.

One conclusion to be drawn from the above dream specimen is that resistances in dreams can be understood by inferences based on the sense of the manifest dream. Such inferences are supported by the patient's associations, our familiarity with the patient's background, and our intuition. In the present case, the patient's resistance seemed to represent the hostile aspect of the positive (erotic) transference. It thus informed the therapist that he first had to analyze the meaning of her hostility. In the long run it could conceivably lead to the patient's oedipal problem.

Case 3P: This is the dream of an obsessional patient who acted out his hostility under the guise of being compliant. He would thus arrive at my office breathlessly after rushing up the stairs lest he be a fraction of a minute late, but would then proceed to express his scorn for me by criticizing me in a mocking tone. (See Case 6, Ch. 5)

Dream: I was putting on old clothes and shoes to do dirty work in the yard or cellar. I saw that my shoes had mud on them in the back. I was annoyed for having been so careless as to get mud on my shoes.

Associations: The patient tried to minimize the significance of the dream by stating that it did not seem to mean anything. This, however, only served to increase my curiosity. He added that there was more to the dream but he did not remember it. He did not think he could make anything of it. (These are all common expressions of resistance.) I said nothing and of his own accord he related the word *careless* in the dream to his attitude in the analysis. He kept on talking at random without bringing up any further relevant associations.

In attempting to discover some point of entry in order to clarify the dream in my own mind, I thought of the previous session. At that time I told the patient that he almost routinely disregarded my questions, that his thinking habits in general were undisciplined, confused and hazy, and that he often failed to complete his thoughts. He became very angry and said that he was merely following instructions, namely saying whatever came to his mind—the one defense that obsessional patients cling to and consider irrefutable. I remarked that it was also necessary at intervals to stand off and reflect on what one has said. When I reminded him of what had occurred the previous session, he replied that his anger had subsided following the hour and he was able to acknowledge to himself that he had been *careless* in the session.

[In the dream he continued with this *careless* attitude by having mud on his shoes. In reality, if he was planning to do dirty work in the garden or cellar, there was no reason for him to be fastidious about his appearance. His concern could have meaning, however, if the dream were to refer to the analytic session. The wish seemed to be to show anal defiance of me ("mud on the back of his shoes"), as if he were expressing his contempt for me by turning his dirty rear end on me. Although the patient had declared his agreement with me about his *carelessness* in the session, the dream not only revealed his continued anger toward me, but also compounded the injury by displaying his anal aggression.]

I asked, "Why should your carelessness be represented in the dream by getting mud on your shoes?" He replied that he was always a tidy kid. His mother scolded him whenever he dirtied his clothes; as a result he became scrupulously clean as far as his body was concerned. He thus showered once or twice a day, a practice which his wife recognized as being compulsive. In addition, he could not tolerate untidiness in his son.

Since this seemed to direct attention to his anality, I asked him, "Why *mud*?" In his characteristic manner he disregarded my question until I returned to it. He then thought of making mud pies and of slinging mud. This, he added, could refer to his tendency to scoff at all authority figures. I related this to his attitude in the analytic situation. Was he in effect making a caricature of the analysis by assuming no responsibility for what he said and by disregarding my comments? Perhaps this was his way of slinging mud at me.

It will be noted that my comments were concrete and specific. I avoided generalizations, anticipating the patient's tendency to becloud the issue. Parenthetically, it should be added that the analyst must be aware of a tendency in this type of person to regard all comments and interpretations as punitive. In this way he manages to obtain both masochistic gratification and relief from guilt. The negative therapeutic reaction thrives on this sort of fare, so that interpretations or confrontations frequently produce no lasting effect.

The patient's compulsive cleanliness made it appear likely that he resented his domineering mother and inwardly rebelled against her. His rebelliousness toward superiors manifested itself in his disregard of their instructions, his slovenly appearance and work habits, his habitual laziness, and the fuzziness of his thinking processes.

I asked the patient whether he recognized the paradox that from having been an obedient child he had become negativistic, often looking for rationalizations as excuses for breaking rules. He said that although he recognized these things he could not explain them. (Treatment had at least succeeded in making these tendencies ego-alien.) I suggested that his attitude could have provided an outlet for his resentment against his mother's strict control over him. He agreed. I wondered whether he had not placed all authority figures, including me, in the same category as his mother. I left it at that in order to give him an opportunity to digest my interpretation. It will be noted that in so doing, I interpreted his attitude not as an expression of hostility but as a defensive maneuver. He was able to accept it with no difficulty.

Case 4P: The following example of technique illustrates how a patient's particular form of resistance to dream interpretation was treated and what it revealed about the patient's personality.

An obsessional man related a dream and after giving a few desultory and unenlightening associations said, "No more comes to me." Since this was not an uncommon response from him, I decided to make a test of it and selected a part of the dream which represented a fairly common experience. I said, "Some time in your life you must have had an experience similar to this. What could it have been?" He replied that he could not recall. I then suggested that he must be in resistance and asked him if there were something on his mind he did not want to say. He admitted that he consciously

Resistance and Dreams

tried to control his associations lest they reveal something unpleasant. He did not want anything to get out of the bag before he knew what it was; he had to be in control. He was, therefore, on guard about anything he said.

I remarked that in view of his fear of talking freely, no progress could be made until we understood the meaning of his resistance. He replied that he did not want to appear "idiotic" by sprouting off everything that came to his mind. I might tell him that he was talking nonsense and he would then feel humiliated. In addition, he did not want me to find out anything about himself before he did; he wanted to avoid surprises. He realized that this was his usual way of reacting; he tried to plan everything in his life beforehand and became upset if things did not work out as he wished. At work, for instance, he raised hell if anyone disturbed the arrangement of his desk, even though it was disordered. Everything had to remain exactly where he had put it.

How was one to understand the patient's problem? His need to manage things in his own way and his intemperate anger when his arrangements were disturbed suggested that he had an anal problem, perhaps a fear of loss of sphincter control. His refusal to take orders or instruction from others or to be dependent on them suggested a homosexual conflict, while his fear of talking nonsense and being humiliated represented castration anxiety.

Since it was impossible to deal with all of these possibilities at once, I decided to take up one he had evidenced in the past. I said, "You seem afraid of losing control. What might you be afraid of?" He was unable to say. I then reminded him that when he was a boy of nine he was ridiculed at camp by the other boys in his bunk for bedwetting. This, I pointed out, was an example of loss of control resulting in humiliation; it perhaps resembled his fear of being humiliated by me if I were to say he spoke nonsense. At this point he recalled how his family ridiculed him whenever they showed movies taken of him at the age of two: "There he goes running around with his wet pants."

I further recalled an incident that had occurred when he was between the ages of six and eight. On that occasion he had lost control of his bowels while at school and some of the bowel movement dropped on the floor. He had come in from recess before any of the other children returned, and when he realized that he could not restrain himself, he was careful to drop his feces near another boy's seat. When the latter was accused of soiling, the patient joined in with the others in mocking him. [Incidentally, this episode directed attention to another of the patient's characteristic traits. Whenever he felt guilty or found himself at fault, he would invariably criticize someone else and work himself into a state of indignation. He thus used the defense of identification with the aggressor.] The patient said he had an aversion to using the boys' toilet at school because it was "dirty" and he always tried to control his bowel movements until he reached home.

Comment: The patient's resistance in this instance was part of a general character trait, of which his reluctance to give associations to dreams was only one facet. His dreams were of great length and contained a wealth of detail, so that their meaning was invariably unclear. As a result of my intervention he could discuss some of his personal idiosyncrasies objectively and recognize that they colored his conception of reality. Many more confrontations of a similar nature are usually required, however, before such tendencies become entirely ego-dystonic, and the patient can be brought to the point where he wants to change.

CHAPTER 9

Dreams With Unpleasurable Affects

In listening to dreams it is important to take cognizance of the feeling tone of the manifest dream if one is to understand the meaning of the latent dream and the nature of the wish fulfillment. In addition, the affects felt after awaking must be considered as part of the latent dream content. In the following instance, the affect which occurred after sleep succeeded in negating the attempt at cover-up in the dream.

Dream (P): A physician dreamt that in examining a patient who had been referred to him for consultation, he criticized the way the case had been handled by the referring doctor, and indicated that he would have done things differently. A colleague who was present commented that his remark was indiscreet. He then had the uncomfortable feeling that the referring physician would hear of it.

When he awoke from the dream he became depressed and had a foreboding that something ominous would happen. The depression was much stronger than the affect of the dream. He immediately recalled that on the previous day he had felt that he was being suspected by a friend of having an affair with the latter's wife. This led to a fear of a showdown between them (*something ominous.*) The connection with the dream was the fear of being exposed. The depression felt upon awaking led to his recall of the day residue which instigated the dream. The patient had tried to suppress his fear of exposure before falling asleep and the intent of the dream, which continued to minimize the fear by reducing it to a feeling of mild uneasiness, was subsequently amended by the appearance of the postwaking depression (Freud, 1900, pp. 467–69).

The affects of dreams are in general either pleasurable or unpleasurable, but there are also dreams in which the affect is one of indifference or in which it may be entirely absent. The reduction or absence of affect may be regarded either as a defensive measure against an affect that is really overwhelming, or as an expression of doubt or indecision on the part of the dreamer. In the latter case the dream is often characterized by the presence of ideas rather than of action. If we were to consider only the latent content of dreams, we would find that all dreams contain elements which are unflattering to the dreamer's ethical or moral standards and which he is reluctant to divulge. These consist of unconscious fantasies which have been distorted and made unrecognizable by the dream work (condensation, displacement) and symbolic representations. The distortion is accomplished by the ego under the influence of the superego in order to prevent the generation of anxiety (using anxiety as a generic term for all forms of unpleasurable affects). If the watchfulness of the ego relaxes or is overwhelmed by the strength of the instinctual drive, the dreamer may be threatened by the emergence of the unadorned impulse. A state of exigency arises and the ego is suddenly jogged into activity by the pressure of the superego, and mobilizes the very anxiety whose appearance the distortion was meant to prevent. The dreamer then wakes up before the wish can be gratified. By means of its synthetic function the ego thus succeeds in maintaining the psychic equilibrium (Nunberg, 1931). In effect the anxiety replaces the dream work as a defense against the repudiated wish. In other cases, however, the ego may permit the dream to end unhappily, if it serves the purposes of the punitive superego.

Those with unpleasurable affects may be classified as anxiety dreams, punishment dreams, and recurrent dreams accompanying traumatic neurosis or resulting from the traumata of early childhood. They range from the inexpressible terror of nightmares, the night terrors of children (*pavor nocturnus*), the more usual forms of moderate anxiety: embarrassment, inhibited motility, frustration, depression, guilt, remorse, humiliation, and disgust, among others. The intensity of the reaction and the fear of its repetition may lead to difficulty in falling asleep.

The absence of appropriate affect, as may occur for instance in dreams of the death of a loved relative, usually means that what seems to have happened in the dream is not to be taken literally. In other words, the death refers to something else to which the affect is appropriate, or it is only incidental to some other wish which is not repugnant (Freud, 1900, pp. 462f). Likewise dreams in which a judgment appears ("after all, this is only a dream") or the "dream within a dream" is designed to deny the significance of the dream (Freud, 1900, p. 338 and pp. 499ff). In some dreams where there is a reversal of affect, the real meaning can be decided only by the context or by the associations. Such dreams emphasize the importance of the affect in casting light on the meaning of the dream.

Typical dreams, so-called because they are universal and are assumed to have a uniform meaning, are very often associated with disturbing affects. Among these are dreams of the death of close relatives, of appearing nude or partially undressed in public, of performing natural functions in the presence of others, of taking examinations, of flying, of falling, of drowning, of swimming, of passing through narrow spaces, of being pursued by dangerous characters or threatened by sharp weapons, of inhibition of movement, of respiratory difficulties, and of frustration in reaching a destination, or arriving on time for train departures. Many of these dreams deal with forbidden or unacceptable sexual and aggressive fantasies such as incest, homosexuality, rape, exhibitionism, and death of people of whom we are fond. In some cases where the dream has to do with striving for success in an endeavor, it may end in failure or humiliation (punishment dreams). In the patient's associations the endeavor turns out to be a forbidden one, and the failure is acceptable to the ego because it is in accord with the wish of the superego. In such instances sleep is usually not interrupted.

Recurrent dreams are those which first appeared in childhood as a result of a traumatic experience. They are repeated subsequently on appropriate occasions with some variations introduced by the current situation. In traumatic neurosis a special form of recurrent dream occurs in which the dreamer relives the experience of the original accident and wakes up in a state of acute anxiety. At the time of the accident it seems that the ego was taken unaware by the trauma, and was therefore unable to mobilize its defenses and meet the danger with purposeful actions. In reexperiencing the accident in the dream, it is as if the ego is attempting to master the trauma under more favorable circumstances. It is thus provided with a second chance to undo the effects of the shock. This is an aspect of the repetition compulsion, the aim of which is to maintain old, familiar patterns of reaction as a conservative and reassuring measure. The same is true for recurrent dreams following a childhood trauma. The mechanism calls to mind the image of the child who listens in terror to a chilling mystery tale on the radio or television, and yet refuses to leave it. One can understand this as an antiphobic reaction designed to counteract the fear. If, in addition, the fear has been sexualized it may provide an extra bonus in the form of pleasurable effect. Freud stated that recurrent dreams in older people may represent a wish to return to one's youth (1900, p. 476).

Inhibited motility in dreams indicates the presence of an inner conflict between the desire for gratification and the prohibition of it. The inhibition succeeds in interfering with the gratification so that the dreamer is awakened. It is as if the anxiety induced by the dream is increased by the feeling of helplessness in the face of danger. This is particularly evident in situations where the dreamer tries to call for help. If the scream is stifled the sleeper awakens, whereas if he succeeds in letting out the scream he can go on sleeping. According to Deutsch (1965, p. 31) the scream represents the child's call for the parent to prevent him from masturbating.

The practical significance of dreams with unpleasurable affects lies in their coherence, and in the fact that the wish fulfillment, having evaded the censorship of the ego and undergone compara-

Dreams with Unpleasurable Affects 177

tively little distortion, is often transparent. As a result one may be tempted to interpret the instinctual content of the dream directly, without paying regard to the fact that the distressing affect constitutes the patient's defense mechanism. Such dreams must be dealt with circumspectly if the patient is not to become too upset and his resistance increased. In this respect one should be guided by the nature and intensity of the anxiety and be prepared to give greater support to the patient's ego. One must not be misled by the frankness of the dream into assuming that the patient's ego can deal directly with its content.

The following vignette (P) illustrates how an attack of acute anxiety was managed. The incident occurred during the waking state and its cause was relatively undisguised. It may serve as a general model for treating anxiety in dreams.

The patient, an alcoholic, was being seen in psychotherapy. She was married to a sadistic man who repeatedly tormented her by threatening to have her institutionalized. After one of their violent quarrels her husband went into the bathroom. A few minutes later the patient heard a heavy thud and rushing into the bathroom found him lying unconscious on the floor, bleeding from the forehead. He had evidently slipped and struck his head against the porcelain bathtub. The patient's immediate thought was that he was dead and she became frantic. Although he regained consciousness within a few moments and soon recovered completely, her anxiety persisted. She called me on the telephone and asked if I could see her. She sounded so panicky that I told her to come over at once. As she told her story it seemed obvious that her anxiety resulted from an unconscious or preconscious wish for her husband's death. I tried to allay her fears by pointing out that her husband had apparently suffered a mild concussion, and that it was nothing really serious or anything to be concerned about. I then went on to say that one could understand her disturbed frame of mind at the time, because it happened so soon after a bitter quarrel. It was not unusual in the heat of such quarrels to have hostile thoughts about the other person and even to wish that something should happen to them. If such a thought had occurred to her, she might be holding herself responsible for her husband's accident, and her anxiety was merely the result of her guilt.

The patient was immediately relieved and became calmer. She undoubtedly felt supported and perhaps forgiven by my reassurance. This was obviously her reason for wanting to see me in the first place, and on that account she was ready to respond as she did. The point I want to make is that I confronted her with the possible cause of her guilt, although in such a way as to modify its impact and not allow it to be overwhelming. Such confrontation of one's wrongdoing renders confessions more effective in alleviating guilt.

The therapist should not be led astray by a dream in which an undisguised impulse is completely gratified, while the dreamer stands off and regards it objectively. Objective judgments of this kind are intended to disengage the ego from its natural reaction to the situation depicted in the dream, and to render the dream more palatable. This is illustrated by Dream No. 2 in the chapter on "Corroborative Dreams and Validation."

Case Reports

Case 1P: The patient was a homosexual man of thirty-one, intelligent and quite perceptive. I had seen him from time to time over a period of seven years, primarily because he was having disagreements with his mother over his homosexuality. He returned now because of a depression which had come on acutely after his lover left him. Although he knew that the latter was a psychopath who had exploited him, he was nevertheless strongly attached to him. The patient had been deserted by other lovers in the past, but he had never reacted as strongly as now. He had known the man for several years but had become intimate with him only after the death of his own father, five months previously. Following his father's death, his mother reproached him for not coming to see her more often. I remarked that one would ordinarily expect a son, after the death of a parent, to try to overcome his feeling of loneliness by becoming closer to other members of his family. He replied that he

Dreams with Unpleasurable Affects

avoided his mother because she was too domineering. She also bored him by wanting to discuss her problems with him, just as she had done with his father. It seemed that she wanted him to take his father's place. He added that he also felt some physical aversion to her when he was in her company.

Day Residue: The day before the dream, the patient had driven back to his home town, and on the way had developed a severe headache which continued until he arrived at his destination. There he met a homosexual friend, with whom he smoked marijuana and then arranged to have sexual relations. At this point the headache cleared up completely.

Dream: I'm on a beach with my mother and Aunt May. Suddenly the tide comes in and I find that we are really on a long sandbar which has a somewhat oval shape. The waves are very high and I'm afraid we'll be caught in them. Finally I see one wave that is extremely high and I'm sure we are all going to be drowned. I wake up with anxiety.

Associations: The dream, the patient said, was a variant of a recurrent dream which he had been having for the last five or six years.

He recalled one such dream in which he was swimming in the ocean. A big wave came up and he was caught in the undertow. He was afraid of being dashed against some pilings and being cut up by the sharp barnacles which covered them. He woke up in a state of anxiety.

He remembered that at the age of five or six he enjoyed going to the beach with his mother. He was close to his mother and her sister May until the age of fifteen, at which time he became a confirmed homosexual. He used to spend much time with his Aunt May, often staying overnight and sleeping in her room, even though he was aware of her husband's disapproval.

The patient said that the dream could be interpreted in any way one wanted to. I replied that it would be advisable to defer to the main thought of the dream, namely, that he, his mother, and his aunt were in danger of being overwhelmed and swept away by a big wave. Did that remind him of anything? He replied that he once had a frightening experience at Acapulco when he was knocked down by a ten-foot wave and then caught in the undertow. He said the wave could refer to an "it" or to a "person." The "it" could be the problems of living, specifically his desire to meet wealthy homosexuals who would take care of him, despite the fact that he felt ill-at-ease when he was entertained in their luxurious homes. He realized at once, however, that this would not fit in with the sense of the dream in which his mother, aunt, and he were all endangered. The "person" might be his mother, whose overpowering domination he feared. He recognized, however, that in the dream she was also one of the victims.

I repeated his associations to the dream: the pleasant memories of spending time with his mother at the beach as a child, his close attachment to both his mother and his Aunt May until the age of fifteen, and the disapproval of his uncle. The associations as well as the oval (phallic) shape of the sandbar could suggest that the dream had a sexual significance. Could the threatening wave refer to an elemental force like sex? In that case, all three—he, his mother, and his aunt—might be endangered if their sexual drives were to become unrestrained. The danger would be the fear of uncle's (or father's) anger. This could also be the meaning of the previous dream in which he was afraid of being dashed against the pilings and being cut by the sharp barnacles (phallic symbols).

The patient went on to say that when he became an overt homosexual at fifteen, his father was more tolerant of his homosexuality than his mother was. Nevertheless he was afraid of his father until he was twenty-six, that is, five years ago. At that time he became financially independent and began to have less to do with his mother. During those five years he felt that his father had become more friendly toward him. I reminded him that his recurrent anxiety dreams of being engulfed by water also started about five years ago. I suggested that when he drew away from his mother he felt less guilty toward his father, and was thus able to overcome his fear of him. The recurrent dreams indicated that he might still be afraid of his attraction to his mother. I pointed out that in speaking about his mother he said he felt a physical "aversion" to her. This carried a different connotation than saying that he avoided her because she was domineering or boring. The word "aversion" conveyed the sense of disgust or distaste. Why would he feel that way about her? Could the feeling of aversion be designed to counteract his attachment to her?

The patient stated that he accepted my interpretation intellectually, but he failed to be convinced by it, since he was not aware of having any sexual interest in his mother or his aunt. I agreed with him and said that I was probably saying more than he could comprehend at the moment.

Comment: This is a typical instance of where the analyst can overlook the rules of interpretation in dealing with apparently obvious material. I committed at least two errors: I tried to explain too much at one time and gave deeper interpretations (i.e., interpretations "from below") than the patient was able to assimilate. I was misled by the clarity of the dream, the appropriateness of the patient's associations, and his readiness to discuss the dream on an intellectual level without much affect. Ideally an interpretation close to home would have been more effective. For instance, it might have been more productive to have discussed the immediate precipitants of the dream. The thing that stood out most prominently in the day residue was the onset of the severe headache and its abrupt disappearance when he met his homosexual friend. From these circumstances it would be reasonable to surmise that the headache was the result of an inner conflict. Returning home meant returning to his mother, with all the unconscious implications this might have for him. The fact that the headache cleared up after he had contacted his homosexual friend and looked forward to having intimate relations with him, suggests that the conflict had to do with unconscious incestuous fantasies which he managed successfully to repress by means of homosexuality.

Bearing these thoughts in mind, one could have asked how he accounted for the sudden clearing up of his headache when he reached home. This could lead to the fact that he turned to homosexuality as a means of overcoming a conflict concerning his mother. This might then be connected with his feeling of "aversion" when he was in her company. In this manner this attention could be directed to his attachment to her. The other implications of the dream could have been held in reserve for future consideration.

The same patient later reported another dream in which he was being defrauded. This was regarded as a punishment dream.

Dream: I sell a vacuum cleaner to some Jewish people who own a motel. It is done in an underhanded way. The cleaner is put in a bunker. When I ask for the money they don't give it to me.

Day Residue: The patient had asked me to fill out an insurance form for him which would have required me to make a false statement. When I told him that I could not fill out the form, he accepted my refusal nonchalantly, and gave the impression that he minimized the incident and held no grievance against me. It was as if to say, no one could be blamed for trying to get away with something.

It was characteristic of the patient to avoid asserting himself with men for fear of alienating them. His aggression was therefore never overt but took the form of outwitting others in an "underhanded" way while appearing to be friendly. In his business dealings he sought to gain his ends by shrewdness, even discussing his purposes with a disarming candor which made it difficult to take offense.

When the patient came to Philadelphia, he had arranged to stay at a motel owned by a friend of his who, on the basis of their friendship, charged him only a nominal rate.

Associations: The patient discussed his reluctance to assume the masculine role in his sexual relations with men. He preferred to be penetrated by "strong" men, and although he felt the need to prove his masculinity by entering them in turn, he derived little or no

Dreams with Unpleasurable Affects

satisfaction from doing so. He was never successful in maintaining relationships with his homosexual partners, because he antagonized them by his insistence on being in control after having submitted to them. He thus tried to obligate them by showering them with gifts and favors, and then expecting them to be completely devoted. This was his way of compensating for his passive feminine role in the sexual act. He said he was particularly ashamed of having a man penetrate him with an artificial phallus or by inserting a fist into his rectum, despite the intense pleasure he derived from it, because it emphasized his femininity. His sexual partners invariably resented the demands he made on them, and after a while left him, while he in turn accused them of ingratitude. In fact the immediate cause of the depression which brought him back into treatment was the desertion by a lover whom he had befriended when he was in trouble with the law. A contributing factor, however, was that the lover was a replacement for his father, who had recently died. He reacted to the lover's desertion as to another bereavement and his turning to me was no doubt, in part, a search for another father substitute. Indeed his depression cleared up shortly after he started therapy.

    The patient wondered if I could make anything of the dream. I asked him what came to his mind in connection with the vacuum cleaner. He said that it was something that sucked in matter. This immediately made him think of fellatio, which was a receptive action like a woman being penetrated or taking the penis in her mouth. The "Jewish people who own the motel" must refer to me, but he did not recall having had sexual fantasies about me. I remarked that by selling me a vacuum cleaner it now belonged to me, as if I was like a receptive woman. In other words, he made me into a woman by emasculating me. He said he did not understand what that could refer to. I pointed out that in the dream he sold the vacuum cleaner in an "underhanded" way. Could this refer to his attempt to have me falsify the insurance form? If I had done so it would have put me in a vulnerable position vis-à-vis him. He would then have succeeded in compromising my authority, so that I would no longer be in a position to pass judgment on him. In other words, it would be like stripping me of my power or castrating me. In this way he might be trying to control me, just as he tried to control all men to whom he submitted. He recognized the parallel. At the end he had failed because I refused to sign the form, as in the dream he was not paid. Could the wish in the dream be to fail, that is, to be punished for his intent to injure me? He was thoughtful but said nothing.

It will be noted the interpretation dealt with what the patient was already aware of, but along with that it attempted to give his actions a broader meaning, by tying them up with his general tendency to put others under his control.

Case 2P: The patient was a man in his fifties who suffered from hypertension and who had been complaining for about a week of intractable headaches. He was worried about the possibility of having a stroke, because of a family history of hypertension and cerebral vascular disease (See Case 4, Ch. 5)

> *Dream:* I am driving a car in the wrong direction. The road is winding and curvy and I am going fast. There is danger of hitting a car coming in the opposite direction, especially on the curves. As I come to an intersection at the end of the road I am afraid I will be caught by a traffic cop, and although I am not caught, I wake up feeling worried and upset.

Day Residue: The patient had a minor car accident on the previous day and was overly concerned about it. He felt the accident must have been his fault, a result of some negligence, although there was no evidence of it. He was worried and dejected before going to sleep.

Background: The patient had an obsessional character problem. It was essential to his peace of mind to be in everyone's good graces. He was constantly on edge lest his business associates find fault with him. As a result he maintained a low profile, avoided the limelight, and meticulously withdrew from doing anything that could be considered hostile or self-serving. On the surface he gave the impression of being diffident and self-effacing. It seemed though as if he had adopted a passive attitude toward life in order to counteract his underlying hostility and aggressive competitiveness. People came to regard him as a competent but rather shy person who ostensibly never sought praise.

Associations: The road on which he was traveling was the scene of a recent accident in which a friend of his had been killed. The latter had been having an affair with a married woman. The curviness of the road reminded him of a woman's curves. It was on the curves that he was afraid an accident would occur. Actually he himself was in the midst of an extramarital affair, that is, he was doing something forbidden, like driving his car in the wrong direction. The car coming the opposite way might refer to the husband of his paramour. Although he felt fairly safe in his relationship with the woman, there was always an outside chance that the affair would be discovered, in which case there would be a confrontation with her husband—a collision. He felt he was treading on thin ice and was in constant fear that people suspected him of doing something wrong.

The patient regarded the affect in the dream as a copy of the guilt he had felt the previous day when thinking about the car accident. In the dream he was expecting something to happen and the fear woke him up. Although the car accident was a minor one, he took it as a warning that something more serious might be lying in wait for him, namely, that he might have a stroke. By awaking it was as if he did not want to face the danger of being discovered with the goods, as it were, by the traffic cop. By going in the wrong direction he was rebelling against authority (father) figures. If the external authority didn't catch up with him, he said, his conscience would. There were worse things that could happen to one than being arrested. The pricks of one's conscience could cause him to be plagued by superstitious forebodings or even lead to physical illness.

The patient actually did have a mild stroke several days later. When he returned for treatment, a philosophic calm had come over him. It was as if, having paid for his sins by the illness, he was now forgiven and had nothing further to fear. Felix Deutsch (1939) and Fenichel (1945) also speak of the resolution of conflicts by the onset of somatic disorders.

The interpretation of punishment dreams is as a rule readily accepted by the dreamer, since it satisfies his need for confession and atonement. The problem is to determine whether the dream wish is one of punishment. The frequent occurrence of such dreams in an individual points to the masochistic aspects of his character. If the masochism becomes sexualized, however, the patient may get enough satisfaction from his dreams, so that their repetition comes to serve as a resistance.

Case 3C: The following dream was reported in Chapter 5 (Case 8):

A woman dreamt that she was in her apartment with her paramour. In the bed there were two men covered with a brown shiny plastic material, as though they had been dipped in it. They were in agony. One could hear them screaming as they tried to free themselves. She was horrified and ran out of the room.

On an initial survey of the dream one is immediately struck by a discrepancy: the patient is horrified by the sight of the tortured men, but instead of trying to help them she runs out of the room. It recalls the story of the beggar who comes to the wealthy man seeking charity and relates a heartrending tale. When he is finished, the wealthy man rings for his butler and says, "Throw this man out, he's breaking my heart." This was my fantasy and indicates the way I understood the dreamer's reaction, or to put it in other terms, how my unconscious understood hers. One may understand a dream pretty much as he understands a joke, that is, by putting himself in the other person's place and recognizing that, under similar circumstances, he might have behaved the same way. The faculty by which one mind comprehends another, throwing itself into the feelings of the other, is what is meant by empathy. The situation in the dream also reminds one of those who try to avoid the scenes of accidents because they cannot stand the sight of blood. We are accustomed to understand this as a reaction to their own sadism. In other words, by running away from the situation the dreamer may be attempting to deny her guilt and fear of retaliation, as indicated by the horror that awakens her.

Observations such as these can often be made by a third person as the material is being presented, particularly if he has the knack of seeing resemblances quickly. In addition, being relatively detached from the immediate situation he can be more objective. During the analytic session one works with one's intuitive and empathic understanding as one listens to the patient's associations. After making such observations he then subjects them to an objective and rational evaluation.

Background: The patient had been in analysis for about two years, having come originally because of dissatisfaction with her interpersonal relationships. These were characterized by intense emotional involvements with sadomasochistic overtones. She was overly possessive of the men to whom she was attached and became abusive if they showed an interest in other women. This often led to quarrels and an exchange of physical blows. At the time of the dream she was living with an artist, but was beginning to find the sexual relationship to be bland and unexciting and was entertaining the idea of having affairs with other men. She had two men in mind, one of whom was experiencing a failure in his marriage, while the other was in the process of getting a divorce. She felt that they were both vulnerable and her involvement with them would further complicate their lives, since she was only interested in flirting with them.

Day Residue: The patient had recently thought of inviting one of the men to her apartment at a time when her paramour was at work, but then thought that if the latter lost his job, he might return home and find her with the man. The day before the dream she was trying to decide how to arrange a meeting with the latter.

Associations: The patient gave few associations. Her first thought upon awaking was that her paramour was responsible for what happened to the two men in the dream. This was obviously a projection of her guilt, since her next thought was that if he learned of her flirtations he would blame her if things went wrong.

I said that if the patient's intentions toward the two men were good, she would not feel guilty. We therefore had to assume that her guilt was the result of unconscious hostility. In escaping from the room she revealed her conflict. It was noteworthy that she was planning to get involved with men who were already attached to other women. The presenter added that her paramour was also living with another woman when she first met him.

[This would suggest that the patient's problem was an oedipal one. What could be her unconscious reason for wanting to hurt the men, though? Could it be related to her need to deny her affection for her father, in the way an adolescent boy might torment his mother as a means of fending off his affectionate feelings for her? One could ask the patient why she ran out of the room instead of trying to help the men.]

The presenter offered additional data about the patient. [In the absence of the patient's associations it is frequently necessary to fall back on what is known about her.] Despite her physical attractiveness and her mental superiority, the patient held herself in low esteem. If a man showed an interest in her, she assumed that it was for purely sexual reasons. She was also competitive with men; for instance, she believed she ought to know as much as her instructors at school. [This suggests that her desire to hurt men might be motivated by her envy of them. She could also have felt inferior in comparing herself to her mother, as children often do, and concluded that her father preferred her mother because of her greater attractiveness.]

In keeping with the rule of analyzing defense before content, I suggested that attention be directed first to the horror which the patient experienced in the dream. One could say to her that it was understandable for a person to want to shrink from the sight of someone being tortured. Had she ever undergone a similar experience? Later one could ask whether the two men in the dream could refer to the two men with whom she was thinking of having affairs, since she was also afraid that they would be hurt if she got involved with them.

The patient was clearly hesitant about doing anything that might further upset the men, and by calling attention to her fear rather than to her wish we would be both reassuring her and lending support to her ego in the conflict. Her abhorrence in the dream indicated that she did not approve of what was happening to the two men, and therefore could not really be held responsible for it. The dream, however, seemed to reflect her conflict about getting involved with the men. If such a conflict existed it meant that part of her wanted to inflict some injury on them, but if so, it must be unconscious, since mature people do not, as a rule, entertain such thoughts consciously. One could also add that children often think of inflicting physical injury on others, so that the horror she felt in the dream could be a mature reaction to a more primitive tendency, which dated back to childhood. Did she recall having ever entertained such thoughts as a child? This type of approach could help to enlist the patient's cooperation in working on the problem.

Comment: The dream has further implications which could come up for later consideration. The brown plastic covering suggests anality and could refer to the anal nature of the patient's sadism. This adds another dimension to our understanding. The horror she experienced in the dream could express a fear of retaliation. Again we learn how important it is to deal discreetly with a dream that is so frank.

Case 4C: The following dream has to do with an inappropriate reaction to the death of the patient's father. It was reported in part in Chapter 5, Case 5.

> *Dream:* I walked into a bedroom. My father is lying on the bed covered by a sheet. He is dead. I begin to have difficulty in breathing and go into the bathroom where my mother is. I open the window and start to breathe much better. My mother can always help me. I think what a wonderful wife I have.

> *Background:* The patient was a phobic individual whose occupation required him occasionally to work at night. At such times he had to assume full responsibility for the work and he was afraid of being criticized by his chief. Strange to say, however, when

his co-workers were present to share the responsibility, his anxiety was not alleviated but on the contrary became more intense. It could be relieved only if his wife accompanied him to work. His phobia was understood to be, in part, the result of a homosexual conflict.

The patient's mother died after a prolonged illness when he was fourteen. He had been quite attached to her and had even had frankly incestuous fantasies about her. After her death he was angry with her for having "abandoned" him. He never got along well with his father, and when he became engaged at the age of twenty, he left home and went to live with his future in-laws. The friction between him and his father was aggravated by this unfriendly act, and when he was married he did not invite his father to the ceremony.

Day Residue: The night before the dream he became anxious while on duty. He felt a sudden loneliness for his wife and had an urgent desire to be with her. He then decided to go home and felt a sense of triumph in having the courage to defy his superior by leaving.

Comment: Beyond relating the events of the previous night the patient gave no associations. We are therefore warranted in looking for other clues that might help us find meaning and purpose in the patient's behavior. One question that arises is why the patient should have felt triumphant, rather than merely being relieved, when he escaped from the anxiety-laden situation at work. Could his anxiety be related to his subordinate position to his chief? If so, why should his wife's presence at work alleviate the anxiety?

There are also certain discrepancies in the dream. For instance, instead of manifesting grief at the sight of his dead father, he exhibits a somatic symptom—difficulty in breathing. Psychosomatic symptoms are frequently taken to be anxiety equivalents (Fenichel, 1945). Is it therefore reasonable to assume that the death of his father is not to be taken literally, and that it means something else? It is of further interest that the patient's respiratory difficulty is suddenly relieved when he opens the window of the bathroom where his mother is present.

In view of the dream stimulus certain inferences may be made. The death of his father could stand for the patient's action in

Dreams with Unpleasurable Affects

"getting rid" of his chief by leaving the job the night before. Death in that case could mean being free of his father's surveillance so that he could be reunited with his mother (returning home to his wife). But then why did he not experience the same feeling of triumph in the dream as he did the previous night, and instead manifested difficulty in breathing? Respiratory difficulties are often associated with sexual excitement, an association which can be readily understood. The feeling of suffocation, for instance, is a prominent symptom of the nightmare where the anxiety has to do with the normal incest wishes of infancy in which there is repression of the feminine, masochistic component of the sexual instinct, and the sexual act is depicted from the woman's point of view, as indicated by pressure on the chest, etc. (Jones, 1931, p. 76). Difficult breathing may also represent the fear of being smothered in a claustrum (Lewin, 1952). If the anxiety in the dream signifies the fear of punishment (castration) for incestuous fantasies, however, why should it be relieved by escaping to mother? Castration frequently stands for separation from mother, so that by running to her, one overcomes the fear of such separation. In the dream the patient was able to breathe much more easily after he opened the window, that is, escaped from the claustrum. Escaping to the mother may also symbolize heterosexuality, which could relieve anxiety brought on by homosexual fantasies. This could account for the patient's freedom from anxiety when his wife accompanied him to work. This idea seems to be confirmed by his thoughts in the dream, "My mother can always help me" and "What a wonderful wife I have" (wife and mother being equated). Having considered all these possibilities we can then be prepared for confirmation or correction by fresh data.

In other words, by understanding the sense of the dream and correlating it logically with what we know about the patient, we can come up with inferences that can cast light upon the meaning of his phobia. If we consider a number of possible explanations we avoid being restricted to narrow interpretations. Freud (1916) suggested that the overt content of the phobia could be interpreted as the psychological equivalent of the manifest dream content. According to Lewin (1952, p. 311), the anxiety of phobias is determined not only by the events of the oedipus complex or the phallic stage, but also by the admixture of pregenital and preoedipal motives, such as the fear of being separated from the mother or of "being eaten."

Our aim is to understand the reasons for the subject's behavior. The validity of our interpretation is determined in part by correlating the logic of our inferences (stemming both from our intuition and empathy) with a knowledge of clinical theory and an understanding of life. We base our conclusions on observational data to which we seek to give a larger, that is, a multidimensional, meaning—one which includes consideration of unconscious and genetic factors. Our hypotheses must be open to new facts and should not be considered final. We need to be sufficiently flexible to modify our deductions in accord with fresh observations, constantly keeping in mind what constitutes adequate evidence or proof.

Several months later, the patient had the following dream:

> I was lying in bed beside my wife who was asleep. I suddenly started to wheeze and had the thought that if a bronchoscope were inserted I would be able to breathe better. I then realized that a bronchoscope wasn't used for this purpose.

Associations: The patient stated that he frequently masturbated with fantasies involving his friends' wives, because he found it difficult to become aroused by his own wife. His wife had recently developed symptoms of peptic ulcer and he thought he was responsible for her illness. At one time he masturbated while reading pornographic magazines which dealt with incestuous relationships. No further associations were elicited.

Comment: The patient's masturbatory fantasies about the wives of his friends could be related to his oedipal problem. His guilt over his wife's illness reflected his unconscious hostility toward her—possibly a wish for her death. Since she was equated in his mind with his mother, intercourse with her brought the question of incest too close to home. This could explain his loss of sexual interest in her.

A bronchoscope represents a phallic symbol. If the bronchoscope is inserted to relieve wheezing, the latter could refer to sexual excitement. To take a phallus into one's mouth (fellatio) means having homosexual relations, perhaps in order to stave off "incestuous" feelings aroused by his wife who was lying next to him. The final observation that a bronchoscope wasn't used for this purpose, that is, to prevent incest, may be intended to reassure himself that he is not a homosexual.

There is no action in the dream; the dream consists entirely of thoughts. Such deliberations are not to be taken at face value, but must be analyzed along with the rest of the dream. "Everything that appears in dream as the ostensible activity of the function of judgment is to be regarded not an intellectual achievement of the dream-work but as belonging to the material of the dream-thoughts and as having been lifted from them into the manifest content of the dream as a ready-made structure" (Freud, 1900, p. 445). It is not an unpleasant dream, so we can assume that the patient's misgivings were for the moment resolved.

The second dream suggests that the anxiety experienced in the first was actuated, at least in part, by a homosexual drive which was ostensibly overcome when the patient escaped to his mother. This seems to validate one of the alternate constructions which were made in considering the meaning of the dream. The fellatio symbolism in the second dream could have been pointed out to the patient, in order to test his response to the subject of homosexuality and the possibility of its being a counterbalance to incestuous fantasies (of which he was already aware).

A follow-up of this case appears in the discussion of Case 3 in chapter 10.

Case 5C: The following is a recurrent embarrassment dream that illustrates the multidetermined nature of its motivation. A thirty-three-year-old housewife had a recurring dream which was characterized by defecating or urinating in the presence of others. She first reported this type of dream in the third hour of treatment.

At that time she dreamt that she had an urge to move her bowels, but the only place she could find was a toilet in public. She nevertheless sat down and defecated, but then became concerned because she couldn't find the stool. Someone pointed it out to her and she awoke feeling very upset and embarrassed. In other dreams she also has either to urinate or defecate, but always finds herself in a public place of some sort, either an auditorium or out in public with people milling all around her. Because of the urgency she loses control and either defecates or urinates where she is.

Background: The patient was pregnant for the second time and expected to give birth within a few weeks, at which time she had decided, for financial reasons, to terminate the analysis. She was an aggressive person who was competitive with men and tended to assume a critical and derisive attitude toward them, particularly when she herself was feeling inadequate. She knew that hers was a supervised analysis, and when she first started treatment she was scornful and patronizing toward the analyst because of his "youth." She also frequently spoke slightingly to her husband about his shortcomings, but then felt guilty. During the period when she was trying to become pregnant she insisted that her husband have intercourse with her every night so as not to miss any opportunity of being impregnated. When, after a time, he became temporarily impotent she reacted angrily, charging him with a lack of manliness and telling him that he needed to be analyzed. She automatically assumed that the unborn child would be a boy (her first child was a girl) and said she would name him after the therapist.

Associations: [The patient reported the dream late in the hour. What the patient says before reporting a dream must be included among the associations.]

On the day before a five-day interruption of the analysis, the patient had discussed her thoughts about termination. Upon her return after the break she reported that she had overslept and was racing around in order to get to the doctor's office on time. While driving to his office she became confused and wondered whether she was correct about the time of the appointment. She thought it would be embarrassing if she were to break in on someone else's hour, but then reflected that when her treatment was terminated her appointment time would then be assigned to someone else. This reminded her that at the age of eight or nine she took art lessons from a commercial artist on Saturday mornings. Each time she came for her appointment she had an uneasy feeling that it might be the wrong day. She did not understand why she should be so fearful. The artist was an attractive man of about the same age as her father and it was rumored that he was a roué. As she continued to think of it at this time she thought her fear might have to do with the possibility of intruding on something private that she should not be seeing. She recalled that as a teenager she once walked into her parents' bedroom just as they were about to have intercourse.

At this point she said, "I have been dreaming like crazy but I don't remember my dreams." She followed it by saying, "I do remember a dream now. I woke up and told my husband about it, because I was afraid I would forget it otherwise."

[The patient had been talking about fantasies of breaking in on the primal scene. We can therefore anticipate that the dream will deal with the same topic. Her temporary amnesia for the dream was the result of repression, which she managed to overcome. In such instances the reasonable aspect of the ego is identified with the therapist and becomes his ally in accomplishing the therapeutic task. This was evidenced by the manner in which the patient's associations led unerringly to the recollection of the dream. Telling the dream to her husband may have been in the nature of a confession, which she rationalized by characterizing it as a mnemonic measure.]

> *Dream:* It was another version of the bathroom dream that I have had from time to time. I dreamt that I was in a public place and had to go to the bathroom. I went into a bathroom which turned out to be a men's room. There were two toilets at right angles to each other and men were sitting down in both

cubicles. The doors were open. I don't know if my daughter was with me. I closed the door and locked it, but there were people standing outside waiting to get in. I had to move my bowels but because people were waiting outside I couldn't do it. I was very uncomfortable. Then I woke up.

Associations (continued): The patient added, "The dream portrays a feeling I often have, namely, that I can't have a bowel movement unless I'm entirely alone. It has always been that way. I must have been very upset by the dream if I told my husband about it. I usually save my dreams for you." She thought that she was showing progress in the dream when she closed the door with people around, something that had never occurred in previous dreams of a similar nature. To her this meant that she did not feel exposed or too helpless to protect herself.

Day Residue: She had been having a lot of discomfort at the end of the day before because she was "carrying low." Perhaps she should talk to her obstetrician about it, but she was reluctant to visit his office because he was likely to do an internal examination. She tied up her fear of vaginal examinations with fantasies of a sexual attack. She knew that the doctor did not do vaginal examinations routinely on all of his patients, but she thought she might have encouraged him to do them on her because she found it pleasurable. This made her feel guilty. [The fact that she could discuss this so openly showed that she felt sure of the therapist's noncritical attitude.] Thinking of the examination made her recall her childhood. The entire family was accustomed to walk around the house in the nude and she thought she might have been very stimulated. When she returned from college for her first Thanksgiving Day vacation, however, she became upset and berated everyone for their immodesty. She added that her father used to discuss general affairs with her and she had the fantasy that he preferred her to her mother because she was more understanding.

Another instigator of the dream was the fact that the patient's daughter, age two and a half, had walked into the bathroom while her father was urinating. The patient was uncomfortable and was in doubt about how to handle the situation. The little girl was constantly preoccupied with the subject of penises and repeatedly asked, "Do I have a penis? Does Daddy have one? Do you have one?" She would also go through a list of all their acquaintances and distinguish those who had penises from those who did not, often at the most inopportune times. On the one hand, the patient wanted to deal with her daughter's questions straightforwardly, but on the other, she had the impulse to tell her to leave the room. She was conflicted about giving her daughter the correct information because she did not want her to feel that she was lacking something.

Associations (continued): As a child the patient herself was constantly curious about what went on in the bathroom, and even now felt uncomfortable in looking at her husband's penis when he urinated.

[The word "uncomfortable" raises a question because it is unexpected. If the patient's curiosity were motivated merely by a desire to discover something or to be aroused, she should have experienced no discomfort with her husband. What could have caused this uneasiness? Did looking at her husband remind her of seeing her father in the nude? From her need to shield her daughter from the knowledge of her anatomical defect, one could also assume that she was distressed by her own lack of a penis. Looking may at times have the sadistic aim of destroying (Fenichel, 1953) or of robbing men of their genitalia (Nunberg, 1952). As we have said, the patient was abrasive in her relationships with men, and it was not inconceivable that she might have wanted figuratively to castrate them. This then could account for her discomfort.

Since the dream was stimulated both by thoughts of visiting her obstetrician and by her daughter's curiosity, it must have represented both the desire to expose herself and to look. Looking was arousing for her and presumably for those to whom she exhibited herself. Another motive for exhibiting oneself is to draw attention to the penis, illusory in this case.

The focus of the little girl's interest in observing her father urinate was his penis. *Defecation* may mean having a baby—the cloacal theory of birth. In the dream the patient enters a man's bathroom, as if she was a man, so that having a bowel movement could also mean having a penis. According to Nunberg (1961, p. 74) infantile sexual curiosity has to do with such questions as where children come from, the difference between a boy and a girl, and what goes on between father and mother. He draws attention to the aggressive component in curiosity—the need to know the relationship between cause and effect being equivalent to mastering reality in an active way (See also Freud, 1905, p. 194). The patient's feeling of being inhibited apparently resulted from her conflict about doing something forbidden, namely, seducing or castrating men, or pretending that she had a penis.]

The patient's associations occupied the entire hour. They appeared to be so appropriate and flowed so easily that the therapist thought it advisable not to interrupt them. He felt, however, that the patient was withholding something. Her feeling of satisfaction upon awaking could mean that she had succeeded in overcoming her infantile wish to expose herself, but could "closing the door" also imply that she was well enough not to need further treatment? He wondered how the dream might have been handled.

In this type of case it is helpful to review the general principles of interpretation. With the wealth of associative material presented by the patient, one must be selective and determine what is currently significant to her. Again, as in all anxiety dreams, the instinctual drives have risen to the surface and can be recognized with little difficulty. We should therefore be doubly on guard against offering premature interpretations. A safe rule to follow in such cases is to ascertain the nature of the patient's defenses in the dream and then make the patient aware of them. Her defenses appear to be her embarrassment and her feeling of inhibition. One could proceed by asking her what she thought the dream was saying, in order to encourage her to take an objective view of the material. Once the type of resistance is known, the analyst interprets it by relating it indirectly to the repressed drives against which it has been set up.

In the present instance one could start with the episode that triggered the dream, namely, the patient's embarrassment when her daughter walked into the bathroom, and her fear that the sight of the father's penis would have a traumatic effect on the child. She might be asked what made her think that the girl would be traumatized. Since there was no evidence that the child was troubled, could she have been projecting her own sensitivity about the lack of a penis onto the child?

The next issue to be taken up could be the exhibitionistic nature of the dream. The motive behind exhibitionistic dreams is to show off something, usually one's genitals. By entering a man's bathroom she behaves as if she were a man, that is, someone who possesses a penis. In the dream she was either defecating or urinating, which means that she was doing both ("either-or" in dreams is to be understood as "both-and"). In urinating, one's genitals are exposed: defecating may also have the same significance. The bowel movement, among other things, may represent a penis, because of its shape. If she were disturbed by the fact that women do not have penises, the dream could be designed to relieve the tensions stirred up by the incident in the bathroom. It would be the fulfillment of a childhood wish and not necessarily one which she was entertaining at the present time, although in the dream she reacts in an embarrassed manner, as if it were taking place now when she was a grown woman.

[Of course, embarrassment associated with exhibitionism has other determinants as described above, but discussion of them could be put off to some future time.] The patient in her associations mentioned the fact that she was "carrying low" and that this was causing her some discomfort. This made her aware of the fact that she would soon be giving birth. Bowel movements are often equated with babies as well as with penises. This explains why many women feel fulfilled and proud when they give birth. In other words, if she has a baby (a symbolic penis) she no longer has to pretend by exhibiting herself; she now possesses the real thing and can afford to shut the door in the dream. Her inability to move her bowels might imply that her conflict was not entirely resolved. In any event, her satisfaction about having made progress may indicate her awareness of being more self-sufficient.

CHAPTER 10

Validation of Interpretation

Waelder (1960) in his chapter on validation, discusses with his customary lucidity, the difference between the physical and behavioral sciences. According to him, the former have achieved a high degree of acceptability because their criteria of validation are measurable and the number of variables in laboratory experimentation can be controlled. In the behavioral sciences, on the other hand, the number of variables is so great and so inconstant as to make it unlikely for them to be amenable to experimental verification, at least for the present. Furthermore, the psychoanalytic tool of investigation is an introspective one, so that the effect of human influence cannot be ruled out, even though provision is made to limit it. We, therefore, cannot expect to have the general acceptance that the physical sciences do, even were we to overlook a major obstacle, namely, that psychoanalysis deals with the unconscious. Waelder concludes that if introspection is combined with restraint of free speculation and validation of hypotheses by the application of strict objectivity and cross-checking, one can arrive at results which are quite convincing and which can be repeated by other well-trained and experienced psychoanalysts. This applies to validation not only of interpretations, but also of analytic concepts and metapsychological theory.

In the present context we are concerned only with the validation of conjectures which we form as we listen to the patient, and the subsequent interpretations which we transmit to him. Since we are dealing with a body of empirical theory which has been derived from clinical findings, our observations must be geared to this theoretical point of reference, if they are to be relevant and comparable to the findings of other qualified workers in the field. Psychoanalysis is a psychology of the unconscious; we must therefore accept the reality of the unconscious, as well as the principle of psychic determinism, namely, that there is a relationship between two psychological events which follow one another in time, and that the association of ideas is governed by an unconscious purpose. We must also accept the fundamental concepts of transference and countertransference, resistance, and intrapsychic conflict.

Without doubt one obtains the greatest conviction of the soundness of dream interpretation from an analysis of one's own dreams, either in one's personal analysis or by subsequent self-analysis. One is reminded of Freud's advice to someone who asked him how one could become an analyst: "By analyzing one's own dreams." By means of one's own associations one is able to recognize the connection between personal experiences and the content of both the manifest and latent dreams. One becomes convinced of the validity of analytic concepts and can better appreciate what his patients are coping with and what is necessary to help them gain insight. Consistent practice in this form of self-training prepares one to comprehend and interpret the dreams of others. One can also appreciate the cogency of Freud's comment that it was only his success in confirming the hypothesis that a neurosis could become intelligible through dream analysis that enabled him to persevere in the face of complete isolation by the Viennese medical fraternity (1914b, p. 20).

Case Illustrating the Mental Processes of the Analyst

In discussing validation it may be useful to inquire how the analyst arrives at his conclusions, in other words, how the mind of the analyst operates. For this purpose I wish to return to a dream which I mentioned in the chapter on "The Manifest Dream." I have

Validation of Interpretation

chosen for discussion a dream which, although not fully analyzed, contained features which enabled me to make certain conjectures which seemed valid, and to indicate the direction in which validation could be sought. It thus seems to be suitable for didactic purposes.

> A man dreamt that his mother asked him to look for something in her handbag. He did not recall what it was, and instead found a box which he opened and saw that it contained a watch. His mother then said, "But don't open the box; don't touch it." He wanted to replace the box without letting her know that he had looked into it. Later his curiosity again got the better of him and he opened various drawers in her room and found a number of watches in them.

After reporting the dream, the patient added that it was typical of his mother to ask him to do something and then blame him for doing it. In his eyes she was a deceptive woman who had repeatedly tricked him. According to the dream, however, he seemed to be going beyond his mother's instructions, and was furthermore defying her by opening the other drawers in her room, which was presumably forbidden. I recognized in his attitude his habitual way of avoiding criticism by attacking his accusers. This was a cognitive response on my part, but it also contained an affective component which was one of disapproval.

Another factor was present, however, which was not discussed when I first reported the dream. On further consideration of the dream, the patient seemed to have some justification for his attitude. When his mother first asks him to look in the handbag she does not mention the box. It is only after he opens the box that she tells him not to do it. She also adds the injunction, "Don't touch it," after she has already cautioned him not to "open" it. The additional prohibition is unnecessary, since in opening the box he would necessarily have had to touch it. We know that dreams do not use superflous words. A discrepancy of this kind immediately attracts our attention. When do mothers tell children not to touch something? When it is something dangerous or forbidden. How could that apply here? In thinking about a handbag and a box, it occurred to me that they both symbolize the female genitalia. I had an instantaneous image of a child lying in bed with his mother and trying to explore her genitals by "touching" them. In my fantasy, the mother then becomes upset and calls him a "naughty boy." I also thought of a woman who once told me that she and her young son used to bathe together and play "games" with each other—the idea of a mother exposing her young son to temptation and thereby arousing his sexual curiosity. These thoughts at once made the situation in the dream clear to me: the mother first permits the child a certain degree of intimacy (by asking him to look for something in her handbag) and when he becomes sexually stimulated to the point of wanting to go further she forbids it ("Don't open the box; don't touch it"). This understanding came to me without any deliberate effort on my part, in the manner of a free association. By placing myself in the role of the passive listener I was enabled to feel an empathic resonance with what the patient was saying. The patient then related the day residue which confirmed my surmise. On the previous day he made a sexual pass at one of his co-workers, a flirtatious girl who was wearing an abbreviated skirt. She became indignant and told him off. He felt guilty and chagrined, but upon further reflection justified himself by thinking that she had invited his overtures by kidding around in a suggestive fashion.

The patient gave no further associations. I then asked myself if this experience could throw any light on the patient's tendency to project his feeling of guilt onto others? If we were to judge from the reaction of his co-worker, it is conceivable that she was dimly aware of her own seductiveness and was trying to deny it by rebuffing him. By analogy I could imagine that the patient's mother may have also tried to deny her complicity by blaming the little boy. In projecting his guilt feelings onto others the patient could therefore have been identifying with her and reacting the way she did.

By the assumption that the patient had experienced a rebuff at the hands of his mother when, as a child, he approached her sexually, I was attempting to reconstruct the situation as it may have happened at that time. Before this reconstruction could be fully accepted, however, it had to be verified. Otherwise it could only remain a hypothesis.

Validation of Interpretation

The patient remembered that he often came to his mother's bed until he was five years old. A that time when his father, in anger, once told him to get out, his mother failed to protect him, an experience he frequently mentioned with great bitterness. Although the dream suggested that his skepticism about the trustworthiness of women began with his mother, it would seem from this that his mother was the permissive one and his father the one who disapproved. There is therefore no evidence that she criticized him for being too forward. Furthermore, it was known that in later life the patient had an unreasonable fear of the fathers of the girls he dated. It is also true, however, that he was always cautious about approaching girls for fear of being turned down. On the one hand, he was unsure of himself in expressing interest in a girl; on the other, he became frightened when the girl was forward. On one occasion when he called on a girl at her home, she met him at the door wearing a very revealing housecoat. He was so unnerved by the confrontation that he left without entering the house. He rationalized his behavior by saying he was afraid of getting involved with her because she was merely leading him on and really did not mean to "come across."

He might then be afraid of both his father and mother. How could these conjectures be confirmed? One could boldly confront him with the direct interpretation that his mother must have rebuked him for showing a sexual interest in her when he lay in bed with her at the age of five. This might have enabled him to recall a confirmatory memory that had been repressed. In that case, the immediacy of his response would indicate that I had succeeded in overcoming his repression. Such direct confrontations do not always work, however, and may even have some unfavorable results. The element of surprise may, for instance, evoke a strong negative reaction in the patient, because he may be totally unprepared for the suddenness of the revelation and its unpleasant connotations. It thus often falls short of its purpose. It also tends to create an unrealistic image of the analyst as a magical figure who is omniscient.

In this case the patient was informed of the reconstruction and then asked if anything of that nature might have occurred. His immediate reply was that he did not recall. That is where the hour ended. felt, however, that if the interpretation had any validity the proof would be forthcoming sooner or later.

To summarize the analyst's activities, he tests his psychological "hunches" by subjecting them to strict logical scrutiny and seeing how they fit in with his previous knowledge of the patient, as well as with his understanding of the current situation. His hunches are best arrived at by withdrawing all critical activities of the mind while he is listening to the patient and gathering data; logical thinking comes later. Hs ability to understand the patient depends upon his intuitive reactions to the patient's productions. He must be able to experience what is going on in the patient by identifying with him—putting himself in his place, in this instance, being the "little boy" who feels he has a justifiable grievance, because he has been misled and confused by the inconsistent behavior of his elders. Such empathic identification with the patient must necessarily be partial and temporary, so that the analyst can be free to detach himself and view the material objectively and logically. He must, as it were, have one foot in the unconscious and the other in consciousness, and be flexible enough to shift from one to the other. There is thus a constant interaction between affective (empathic) and cognitive functions, both being of equal importance. By empathy we come to understand the patient's unconscious; by cognition we correlate our empathic impressions with reality, thereby contributing the objectivity which is essential for validation.

When the analyst comes to his conclusion he regards it as being provisional and subject to change on the basis of additional information. He also realizes that his conclusion is only one of a number of alternative explanations, all of which may be relevant, realizing that there are a number of determinants of human motivation. In other words, he constantly checks his evidence and takes nothing for granted, adhering to his own scrupulous standards by submitting his conjectures to objective proof. He must first be convinced himself before he can hope to convince the patient. When he has completed his work everything should fit in as if to complete a jigsaw puzzle "so that the picture acquires a meaning" (Freud, 1923b, p. 116).

Validation of Interpretation   209

I have drawn an analogy between this procedure and the method of qualitative analysis in chemistry. By means of presumptive tests various chemical groups are successively eliminated until the substance being tested is isolated. The role of the analyst may also be compared with that of a detective who tracks down and examines all available clues, discards those which he considers irrelevant, and finally comes up with the one which meets all the requirements for solving the problem. He must have a sharp eye for discrepancies in the evidence, since these point to the proclivity of individuals to make "accidental" slips. In analysis such discrepancies likewise point to the surfacing of unconscious material and represent a breakthrough of that which is repressed. In considering alternative explanations and subjecting them to successive elimination, we use a form of Socratic reasoning. The realization that one cannot rely completely on first impressions, exercises a sobering influence on the tendency to speculate too freely.

Before leaving this discussion, one more comment must be made. I said that my recognition of the similarity between the patient's criticism of his mother and his customary way of denying responsibility was both an affective and cognitive reaction, the affective response being one of disapproval. This was an expression of my countertransference, an unconscious superego reaction to something that appeared to be improper. Is I had allowed myself to be influenced by the affect alone it would have interfered with my objectivity in pursuing the further implications of the dream. I was able to regain my objectivity and undo the judgmental and emotional response brought about by the countertransference. The possibility of reacting only affectively, without the leaven of impersonal detachment, can thus lead to basic misjudgments and, at times, to alienation of the patient.

Criteria of Validation

Generally speaking the interpretation of a dream, as well as other interpretations offered during the course of an analysis, can be confirmed only by the patient's responses. These are particularly impressive if they include the recall of past memories. Such recall is facilitated if the patient's current resistance is overcome, thereby allowing repressed material to be released and come to the surface.

The removal of a resistance following an interpretation may be indicated by the sudden appearance of a forgotten dream fragment, a free flow of associations, or recollection of childhood experiences. Another type of favorable response is the analysand's instantaneous recognition of the correctness of an interpretation, even in the absence of associations or recall of specific memories. Such immediate perception is often accompanied by a feeling that something has "clicked," or by a comment to the effect that the thought had never occurred to him. This type of reaction often stems from experiences of the preverbal period, at a time when the child was incapable of memory in the usual sense (Waelder, 1937). Fantasies and visual images which occur after an interpretation may also be related to this time of life.

Other significant responses to an interpretation which may provide corroborative testimony are inappropriate outbursts of weeping, anger or other emotions, or a need for comforting; physical manifestations such as blushing, facial grimacing, muscular twitching, or other involuntary bodily movements, sighing, abdominal cramps, borborygmus, etc.; and the appearance of a negative therapeutic reaction with aggravation of symptoms or increased resistance. In one case, reported below, the patient responded to an interpretation with an outburst of laughter. Sudden laughter following an interpretation usually results from a lifting of a repression and represents the release of the tension which was necessary to repress the forbidden thought.

Since dreams furnish us with invaluable keys to the unconscious processes in the individual, the appearance of a corroborative dream, that is, one which confirms the analyst's interpretation of an earlier dream or other material, can be a most valuable form of validation (Freud, 1911). Such dreams often carry the interpretation to greater depth. If they are to be convincing, however, they must be supported by recall of genuine memories from the past. This is clearly demonstrated in some of the dreams reported below.

Validation of Interpretation

Otherwise the possibility exists that the dream's reliability is marred by having been suggested by the analyst, or that the dream is the outcome of the patient's wish to be compliant. These doubts are reinforced if the patient reports corroborative dreams habitually. On the other hand, dreams as well as associations which verify the analyst's working hypotheses before they have been discussed with the patient, are singularly convincing, since it cannot be said that the patient was influenced by the analyst. It is equally impressive when a patient provides evidence which succeeds in completing the picture of his problem with unmistakable clarity.

A patient, for instance, who had been closely attached to her father as a child, suddenly turned against him during her latency period and openly flaunted her preference for an uncle. She was unable to account for the change. This had been discussed many times but no conclusion had been reached. On one occasion I happened to be present at a social affair to which she had been invited. I observed that she danced often and kept looking in my direction. During the following analytic session she ridiculed the women with whom I had been talking and acknowledged that she wanted to arouse my jealousy by dancing with attractive men. She recognized the resemblance between her behavior and her attitude toward her father as a child, and was instinctively able to realize that her hostility toward the latter resulted from her jealousy of his close attachment to her mother.

Symptomatic improvement cannot be regarded as a reliable criterion for an interpretation, since such changes may be brought about in a number of other ways, such as suggestion, positive transference, or a flight into health, and are not necessarily the result of the resolution of conflicts. This is further attested to by the fact that symptoms can be cleared up by forms of psychotherapy other than psychoanalysis.

Confirmation of a memory by a member of the patient's family or other person can be an excellent source of corroboration, but we would hesitate to complicate the analytic situation by making it a routine part of analysis. Validation by direct observation can also be very convincing, but it is possible only in the case of children.

The patient's simple assent to an interpretation, unaccompanied by supportive details, cannot be accepted at face value, without an appraisal of the intent which lies behind his words. Such agreement may be used by the patient as a means of concealing unpleasant thoughts, of currying favor with the analyst, or of denying his ambivalence. It may result from a need to believe or it may represent a purely intellectual acceptance of an interpretation which has no affective significance for him. On the other hand, an outright rejection of an interpretation may similarly not denote an actual negation or a legitimate dissent, but may be an expression of resistance. In either case, acceptance or rejection, one must wait for what follows in order to determine whether new memories emerge which may serve to complete and extend the analyst's interpretation or effectively refute it (Freud, 1937).

Case Reports

Case 1C: The following case is reported in order to demonstrate the confirmation of the analyst's hypothesis by the patient without the assistance of a corroborative dream.

The patient was a young woman.

Dream: A woman who was once your patient walked into the office during my hour. You didn't say much. You were just sort of calm. I turned around and saw her sitting behind your desk. You talked very slowly when you realized that she wasn't going to leave. When she recognized me she said, "I'm sorry," and left very quietly. She was wearing bright red lipstick.

After relating the dream the patient added, "I thought you would lose your cool, get physical, and push her out. I don't know whether I'm afraid you might get mad at me and throw me out or that you might not want to see me again. My problem is sexual. Sometimes I really think that all I would have to do to get cured is to go to bed with Ron, but I'd have to stop my analysis and never see you again. I want to have intercourse with him but I can't allow myself to do it."

[The patient's comments after she related the dream must be considered as part of the latent content of the dream. In the dream the therapist disapproves of the other woman's presence, and she leaves. The patient thinks that he might also get angry with her and make her leave. This suggests that she identifies herself with the other woman. The reversal, among other things, is a defense mechanism designed to conceal the patient's motivation from herself. The patient also implies that the dream is concerned with sex and doing something forbidden for which she will be put out of treatment.]

Association: The bright red lipstick reminded her of a painted woman, a prostitute. The former patient was an attractive woman whom she used to meet in the waiting room. They often conversed in a friendly manner and the patient became fond of her. The woman was beautiful and had an attractive figure. The patient was certain that she lived a full sexual life and was more appealing to the doctor. In the dream the patient was impressed by the fact that the woman was sitting behind the doctor's desk, but when she tried to associate to this detail she became extremely anxious. She said she felt a blockage in her thinking and could not go on any further.

Day Residue: On her previous visit the patient had removed her coat in the inner office instead of in the waiting room as she had always done. In doing so, she stood at an angle which displayed her bustline, made more prominent by the close-fitting sweater which she was wearing. When the patient assumed her position on the couch, the therapist remarked that it was unusual for her to take off her coat in his office and noted that she had exposed the outline of her figure. The patient said she thought she had taken off her coat with her back to him. She later realized that this was not so and said she really wanted him to see her as a woman. She again spoke of her desire to go to bed with Ron, but was afraid of the disapproval of the therapist who, she believed, preferred her to remain virginal.

[Traditionally it is the father who prefers his daughter to remain virginal. Also, in mentioning Ron immediately after saying that she wanted the therapist to find her attractive, suggests that the two were identified in her mind, and that she would really like to go to bed with the therapist.]

Discussion in Seminar: When the dream was thrown open for discussion one student commented that the situation appeared to be oedipal in nature. I said he was no doubt correct, but to give the interpretation to the patient at this point would have no meaning for her, since she was probably not ready to accept it. A more appropriate procedure would be to start with a clarification of the purport of the manifest dream and then apply it to the surface of the patient's problem, that is, to what was currently disturbing her. In the dream the patient expects the therapist to be angry with the intruder and to ask her to leave. One can ask oneself under what circumstances a similar situation might arise. It could occur, for instance, if someone barged into a room where a man and woman were engaged in an intimate relationship. In such case the man could very well get angry and order the intruder out. Experiences like this are likely to come up when a child walks into the parental bedroom. If this had happened in the patient's past we would have to think that an inversion of persons has taken place in the dream: the intruder would then represent the patient who had once incurred her father's anger, while the patient herself would represent her mother lying in bed (the couch). There are other indications which suggest that the patient is identified with the intruder. For instance, immediately after relating the dream, she expressed fear of the therapist's anger and then talked of her guilt about sexual fantasies. Again, in exposing the contour of her body to the therapist on the previous day, she may have been trying to arouse his interest in her, as if she were a "prostitute." We can therefore assume that the patient was preoccupied with sexual fantasies about the therapist and start from this point.

When the associations stopped, one could have asked the patient, for instance, why she should become anxious in the dream if the therapist were to get angry with the other woman. It would make more sense if she were glad to get rid of the intruder. Could her anxiety be understood if she herself were the person being dismissed?

Validation of Interpretation

The therapist at this point stated that the patient's presenting symptom when she started the analysis was that she suffered from severe anxiety whenever she visited her parents' home. While there she frequently woke up during the night in a state of anxiety, wondering where she was, what she was doing there, and what was going on. [As described, it seemed to be a state of derealization. In such states there is a sharp conflict between the ego and superego. The impressions of the ego are totally unacceptable to the superego, and as a result the latter denies them by refusing to give them the sanction of reality (Nunberg, 1937, p. 172)]. Because of these experiences the patient had not visited her home for over a year, although her mother was seriously ill with chronic renal failure and was on dialysis. She felt guilty but nevertheless could not get herself to go home.

The patient's anxiety about going home could be related to a fear (wish) that her mother would die. She might be afraid that her mere presence could in some way bring about her mother's death. Since dismissal of a person, getting rid of her, can be equated in the unconscious with the death of that person, the intruder in the dream could also be a substitute for the patient's mother. This could have been an additional reason for the patient's anxiety in the dream. It is also possible that the patient may have had a latent homosexual attachment to her mother and might have been wary of displaying too much tenderness toward her as she lay ill in bed. In this connection, Freud (1900, p. 327) states that reversal in dreams frequently arises from repressed homosexual impulses. This would fit in with the fact that the patient became fond of her rival, the therapist's former patient. These considerations, however, are not of immediate concern in discussing the dream and can be put aside for the present. It is rather of interest that the therapist responded to my conjectures about the dream by recalling certain pertinent facts of the patient's history, just as frequently occurs with patients in the course of analysis.]

A member of the seminar asked how one was to understand the patient's remark that having intercourse with Ron would spell the end of the analysis for her. According to the therapist the patient realized that her statement was "silly" because, as she well knew, she could then analyze her behavior. Nevertheless, she could not get over her feeling that the therapist would be angry. I asked the student how he understood it. He replied that it could have meaning if in talking about Ron she was unconsciously referring to the therapist. Intercourse with him would definitely spell the end of the analysis. If it were to happen she would be unable to face her guilt and in addition she would probably be punished by being put out of treatment.

Another student suggested that, on the basis of her attempt to arouse the therapist the day before, one could assume that as a sexy little girl she may have tried to seduce her father. In time she might be able to recall memories of breaking in on the primal scene. Someone else said that in the dream the patient could be both the mother (on the couch) whom the father prefers, and also the provocative seductress.

All of these comments were appropriate, but it was necessary to distinguish the conjectures "from above," that is, those which were near consciousness, from those "from below." We are concerned with how to proceed pragmatically. We could return to the inquiries that were suggested above, or start in another way by dealing with the day residue. The patient could be asked, for instance, if she recognized any connection between the dream and the last session. Her attention could be directed to the fact that she had tried to arouse the therapist's interest in her as a woman by displaying her figure. Furthermore she expressed a desire to go to bed with Ron. Could she be the woman with the painted lips, the prostitute, in the dream? Since both incidents were part of her conscious awareness, the reference could not be considered too remote. If the patient accepted this interpretation she might be able to give further associations, or one could ask her how it could be understood in the context of the dream. Had she ever regarded herself as an intruder, for instance? This could open the path to a discussion of her fantasies about the therapist and explain her anxiety in the dream. If the patient failed to bring up similar incidents from the past the therapist could inquire about them. Such questions do not have to come up all at one time; the process can be spread over an indefinite period, since the road is bound to be strewn with obstacles (resistances), each of which must be overcome in turn.

[It should be noted that in all of this discussion with the patient an attempt is made to include her as an active partner. If she were inclined to be afraid of the therapist's reaction to her flirtatiousness, she could be reassured by his objective but friendly attitude. Such considerations are intended to support the patient's ego and persuade her to become less defensive.]

I added that it might suffice for the time being if the patient were to accept her identification with the prostitute-intruder. The therapist then recalled that the patient's father often accused her mother of "running around." When she went to Monday night novenas, for instance, he would say, "The only reason you are going is to see the priest."

[This may have accounted for the patient's fear of her father's disapproval of her sexual fantasies. This was repeated in her fear of the therapist. Although she behaved as if she were not sure of the latter's attitude, the fact that she could discuss her fantasies openly suggests that she was encouraged by his nonjudgmental attitude, and took it for granted that he was allied with her ego against the recriminations of her superego.]

Follow-up: Several weeks later the therapist gave a further report of developments in the patient's analysis, which he believed confirmed a number of the conjectures made during the presentation. It is entirely possible that he passed on to the patient some of the inferences that had been made at the seminar, although he cited no specific instances. In any event, the patient's reactions and recollection of data from the past could not have been foreseen.

Shortly after the above session in which her case was discussed, the patient fantasied that the therapist would look "cute" in a turtleneck sweater. She did not report her fantasy, however, until a week later when he actually wore one. At the time she became extremely anxious because she felt that he had read her mind and wanted her to find him attractive. [The patient's anxiety seemed to be a reaction to her intuitive belief in the compelling power of her fantasy. There are also elements of surprise and uncanniness when something in one's unconscious finds confirmation in reality.] At the end of the hour she became confused about the change of time of her next appointment that had been agreed upon previously, thinking it was for 11 o'clock instead of 10. She expressed fear that if she arrived at 10 she would be breaking in on another patient's hour. This reminded her of the dream. [She thus confirmed the surmise that she was the intruder.]

During the next session she became progressively more anxious as she spoke of her attraction to married men. She said she could not figure it out. On the following day she expressed her annoyance with the therapist because he would not change her 7 A.M. appointment to a later hour. When she came in at 7 she felt she was barging in on him. It recalled the time when she was taking lessons from a tutor and was concerned that when she arrived at 8 or 9 A.M., people in the house would not be up and she would be intruding. [Her repeated protestations against invading other people's privacy suggests an attempt to deny her underlying tendency to pry.]

Subsequently she expressed her fear that the therapist would become impatient with her. She thought of the impatience of men who were waiting for sex and was afraid he might say that he couldn't waste any more time on her. [She may have meant by this that the therapist was losing patience with her for not talking more freely about her sexual fantasies concerning him.] At this point she became aware of a distressing sensation of shaking in her legs, although there was no outward sign of it. She said she had the same sensation after she had gone to bed the night before; just before then she had entertained the idea of going down the hall to Ron's room. (The patient was a college student and lived in a mixed dormitory.) She then recalled that she often had the same symptom at home and had to be helped to bed. This was one of her reasons for being afraid of going home. As if apropos of nothing, she added that it made her feel good to be more assertive and less fearful of the therapist's reaction.

[The episode of the shaking sensation, coming immediately after she spoke of men waiting for sex, was apparently related to sexual excitement and implied that she had erotic feelings for the therapist. It now becomes clear why she felt that having intercourse with Ron would mean the end of the analysis; Ron was merely a substitute sex

Validation of Interpretation 219

object for the therapist. In other words, she could not continue the analysis if she were to have intimate relations with the therapist. The fact that she experienced the same sensations in her parents' home points to the oedipal nature of her fantasies. Her remark about being more assertive could have been intended to assure the therapist that she was making progress, in view of her fear that he was becoming impatient with her.]

One evening she went down the hall and actually entered Ron's room, half expecting to find another woman there. [Again, the fantasy of being an intruder!] Two days later she had intercourse with him for the first time. As she was relating this she had a severe episode of the shaking sensation in her legs. She was afraid the therapist would strongly disapprove of her for having had intercourse, just as she was afraid of her father's attitude toward sex. She then added that as a child she was afraid while lying in bed lest she hear her father coughing in the next room. She often heard sounds in her parents' bedroom and worried that her father might die. To reassure herself she got up frequently and, pretending that she had to go to the bathroom, would stop at the door of their room and call to her father to see if he was well. Sometimes in doing so she became so frightened that her legs shook.

[We may infer from the shaking of her legs that stopping at her parents' room had a sexual implication. A child's awareness of sounds coming from the parents' bedroom at night is typical of its curiosity about what they are doing in bed. Under the guise of being worried about her father's health she was able both to satisfy her curiosity and to interrupt anything that might be going on.]

Comment: The patient by her subsequent productions thus confirmed our inference that she was a voyeur and an intruder who was curious about her parents' sexual relations. She was also sexually interested in married men, and specifically in the therapist. The patient's evident attachment to the therapist and her trust in his benevolent neutrality allowed her to discuss her innermost thoughts freely. She was even emboldened to believe that he was susceptible to erotic feelings, despite her fear of his disapproval of her sexual behavior. In announcing her intention to have intercourse with her friend, she was apparently testing the therapist's reaction. There was obviously a change in the balance of inner forces through modification of the severity of her superego which permitted her actually to engage in intercourse. The most convincing corroboration consisted of the patient's recollection of what had been forgotten, particularly when the memories helped to complete the picture which we had constructed.

Case 2P: This is a follow-up of the previously reported dream (Case 1, Ch. 9) of the homosexual patient in which he experienced fear of being overwhelmed by a large wave when he was stranded on a sandbar with his mother and aunt. In the interpretation given at that time the wave was regarded as an elemental force representing sex which threatened to engulf all three persons. The following dream occurred several weeks later.

> The dream took place in my bedroom. The room looked even prettier than it really is with vivid, radiant hues of bronze paint on the walls, crisp, clear chintz print draperies, and lighted by a sparkling chandelier. I was proud that it was my creation.
> I was lying on my back and was aware of a very pleasant, warm, moist sensual feeling in my penis. I was also observing myself from a vantage point in the ceiling, looking down to see what was causing the good feeling. I saw my dead grandmother materializing into life, like a cloud solidifying, and descending from midair to sit on my penis. The sight was startling and rather unreal. The "observing me" immediately remembered that Dr. Sloane had spoken of my sexual attachment to my mother and aunt and I thought this must be it, returning to my conscious mind. The "me" to whom all this was happening was a little horrified and wanted to stop the activity despite the fact that my grandmother's vagina felt tight, like a toothless mouth sucking on my penis and I was enjoying it. After the "observer-me" reassured me not to be frightened, the other "me" worked my penis about to even more erotic feelings. There was no orgasm.

Validation of Interpretation 221

The "observer-me" then indicated that the other "me" seemed to tolerate this fantasy well, and told me to stop thrashing in and out of my grandmother. He then caused my grandmother to rise up off my penis into the air and to disappear through a closed window.

The "observer-me" then wondered who exactly was the object of my interest—grandmother, aunt, or Mom. All three were of great importance during my early formative years. With the idea of testing me with each of these women, in an attempt to discover which was the object of my fantasy, the "observer-me" called Aunt May into the room through the window, and she in turn descended on my penis. This also gave rise to good feelings, although not as wonderful as those felt with my grandmother. I tolerated the experiment well and was deriving much pleasure. The "observer" then dismissed my aunt as he had my grandmother.

Lastly, Mom entered the room in the same manner as the others and sat on me. My sexual exultation was complete, just as I had always sought, even sublime with a tighter vagina, more moist than the others, and sending powerful electrical impulses through my entire body. This was the most sexually stimulating of all. It was obvious to both the "observer" and "me" that she was the real object of my fantasy. Each of us, however, reacted in a different manner. I became frightened and ashamed and felt apologetic toward Mom. I do not recall what happened to her; she may have remained in the room, disapproving of all that had just happened. The "observer," on the other hand, tried to reason that this was only a dream, a testing dream, and reiterated that attention should be paid to it for it revealed something important that I could learn.

After minor struggles between the two "me's," one reasoning and the other recriminating, the dream came to an end. Once awake, I reflected with serious concern as to what all of this could mean. I had no feeling of guilt, only one of perplexity.

Comment: On the face of it, it is an unusual dream. The dreamer is split into two figures, the observer and the one who acts out, while each figure, in turn, is subdivided. The observer seems to represent both the patient's ego and superego. On the one hand, he is a grandiose magical figure, a deus ex machina who manipulates people—causing them to appear and disappear and to go through sexual maneuvers. He also behaves like a director who conducts experiments, shows scientific curiosity, and is interested in validating my interpretations. On the other hand, he appears to be an authority figure who passes judgment, grants permission, and is generally tolerant. The "me" who acts out represents other aspects of the ego. He thus gratifies the instinctual drives emerging from the id, but also judges his behavior on the basis of the reality principle, not allowing himself to be taken in either by his self-indulgence or by the rationalizations of the other aspect of his ego. In other words, one part of the ego is influenced by the id, another by the superego, while the other (the integrating ego) tries to effect a reconciliation between the conflicting aims of the two. The dreamer is apparently unable to resolve the differences and wakes up in a state of perplexity, although in the meantime he has gratified his desires. The perplexity at the end of the dream may be the ego's attempt to blunt the satisfaction it has enjoyed, in order to avoid the condemnation of the superego. We would thus have to say that the dream discloses the fulfillment of the patient's infantile wish to possess his mother—infantile, because it is unacceptable to the adult part of the patient. This is evidenced by the reactions of the acting self: he is horrified by his behavior and wants to put a stop to it; he attests his innocence by remaining passive and permitting things to happen to him (the women descend on his penis); he appears frightened, ashamed, and apologetic toward his mother; he attempts to clear himself of responsibility by displacing it onto the "observer" and the analyst as scapegoats, as if to say, "I do it only because I am being persuaded to take part in an experiment. I'm not entirely to blame." He also reassures himself that "this is only a dream, a testing dream," as if to diminish the horror of the situation.

The patient reported the dream enthusiastically as if it constituted a breakthrough in the treatment. However, he gave no associations. In his eagerness to understand the nature of his problem he seemed

Validation of Interpretation

to be ready to accept anything I said without any sign of resistance. His positive reaction may also have been a continuation of his need to deny responsibility for the instinctual gratification depicted in the dream. Since it was also likely that the dreamer was trying to appear agreeable and cooperative, one was naturally cautious in interpreting the dream.

Despite the above reservations, the thing that comes through in the dream, is the fact that the patient actually has incestuous relations with his mother and enjoys it. From this point of view the dream can be regarded as a corroboration of the sexual significance of the previous dream. In this connection, it will be recalled that for several months after his father died he avoided contact with his mother. When I expressed surprise at his attitude toward her, he apparently accepted my comment as permission and proceeded to shower her with attention. He began to see her regularly several times a week, escorting her to dinner, dances, and other social events. Although he said that he felt an aversion to being close to her, he now seemed to enjoy socializing with her. In relating this to me he protested that he had to do it because she refused to seek companionship among people of her own age. I got the impression, however, that he was happy to find a reason for annulling his self-imposed isolation from her. It therefore appeared likely that he took my interpretation of his sexual interest in his mother and aunt as permission to experiment with his fantasies, as if he were pleasing me by carrying out my suggestions. I was thereby also identified with the "observer."

The splitting of the patient's ego into participating and judging parts resembles the tendency of some children to create an imaginary companion as a means of overcoming the frustrations and restrictions of everyday life. We regard this device as a temporary scaffolding which enables the child to get over some of the rough spots of life without developing a neurosis. Although the phenomenon usually occurs between the ages of two and a half and ten, it has been described in adults in whom, according to Nagera (1969), it is an expression of underlying conflict. In younger children it serves as a forerunner of the superego and contributes to the building up of the superego structure. In older children it acts as a prop to assist an already established superego. From this aspect the patient's dream utilizes a regressed form of fantasy in order to gratify a forbidden impulse.

Another aspect of the dream to be noted is the resemblance made between intercourse and fellatio, that is—in this case—between heterosexuality and homosexuality ("my grandmother's vagina felt tight like a toothless mouth sucking on my penis.") This suggests that the patient's homosexual partners might have been surrogates for the incestuous object, thus forming a bridge between the latter and the patient. In this oblique fashion, the patient manages to gain access to the oedipal object.

Several months later I had occasion to refer back to the dream. When the patient realized that his mother's dependency on him was increasing and that she sought no other companionship, he began to withdraw from her, although he continued to have dinner with her several evenings a week. This did not satisfy her and she accused him of being ungrateful in view of the fact she had given him a considerable sum of money for his business. The patient, becoming indignant, thought that her demands were excessive and that she was seeking to have an "impossible" relationship with him. His attitude appeared reasonable until it turned out that he had recently asked her again to lend him a large sum of money, knowing from his previous experience that she would probably refuse to accept repayment and would insist that he accept the money as a gift. In that case, he said, he naturally would keep the money, since one could always use capital in his business. I remarked that if he were in earnest about making a break from her he would want to avoid putting himself further in her debt and thus give her more ground for complaining of his ingratitude. Despite his protest about the unfairness of his mother's demands he seemed to be playing into her hands and keeping up the game. I reminded him that on several occasions he had attached himself to wealthy elderly widows and had even considered marrying them in order to inherit their wealth. The situation with his mother recalled to my mind the situation in the dream where, despite his inner protests, he was enjoying the sexual gratification.

I asked him what he would have done if the "observer" in the dream had asked him to rob a bank which might involve the shooting of a security guard. He immediately replied that he would not have gone along with it. He added that if the suggestion were made that it would advance the treatment, he would have considered it immoral and would have sought another therapist. It was therefore clear that the "observer's" suggestion in the dream was in accord with the patient's own wishes. When I pointed this out to him he agreed and added, "I could have gone through with the sexual act, but I didn't have to enjoy it!"

It occurred to me that the "observer" might also refer to his mother, or more accurately to the mother-representation in his superego, the permissive aspect. In his childhood she was the head of the family, and his father was completely dominated by her—a not uncommon family constellation in the background of male subject homosexuals (Sperling, 1954). A motherly superego formation may be anteceded by a female ego-ideal formation, which is then used as a defense. To a large extent the mother's omnipotence is sufficient to overcome the prohibitions of the father (Nunberg, 1932, p. 124). In confirmation of this his mother was a kleptomaniac, and during his entire adolescence made him her accomplice by having him conceal the stolen articles on his person. She thus relieved him of responsibility for his behavior.

The obvious motive of the dream was the wish fulfillment of the oedipal fantasy by overriding the reality principle. Since there was no impairment of reality testing we must assume that the fantasy existed at a time when structuralization of the superego had already occurred. This was manifested in the dream by the patient's realization that he was doing something wrong. The superego, however, was permissive and, although it recognized reality, minimized it. It was thus at the service of the impulses from the id. According to the principle of multiple function (Waelder, 1930) the gratification of the instinctual impulse thus satisfied the id, the ego, the superego, and the compulsion to repeat the infantile fantasy, although the patient made some obeisance to the reality principle by appearing to be "perplexed." In this instance, the "observer," like the imaginary companion of older children, served as a prop for the superego, as an externalization of unacceptable impulses, and as a scapegoat. In real life this took the form of aim-inhibited incestuous fantasies (close tie to the mother and the idea of marrying a wealthy widow) which were partially disguised as anal drives (receiving gifts of money or inheriting the widow's wealth).

On the other hand, he was also on guard against his mother, since by insisting that he remain closely attached to her she threatened his freedom and independence. This in effect both appealed to his regressive tendencies (desire for infantile, preoedipal dependency on older women) and restricted his masculinity (castration threat). Up to the time of his father's death the patient made no effort to liberate himself from his mother. He continued to live a leisurely, hedonistic existence. However, following his initial period of treatment with me after his father's death, he began to apply himself to work. Since he had definite aptitude for the work, he became quite successful and gained many personal compensatory rewards. In this instance I seemed to become a protection against his "terrifying and engulfing mother," and probably also a sublimated homosexual object as an escape from her dangerous seductiveness (Bibring, 1953, pp. 282–283).

The question arises how the dream could be interpreted meaningfully to the patient. It was clear that the thought of actual incest was abhorrent to him and the only way it could be accepted was to present it in terms of an infantile fantasy, or at least as part of his past experience. When I suggested this to him, he recalled that until he was thirteen he and his mother regularly undressed themselves in each other's presence. At that age, however, she once joked about the beginning appearance of his pubic hair and in his embarrassment he withdrew from her completely. He frequently slept in the same room with his grandmother and until his mid-twenties often stayed over in his Aunt May's home and slept in the same bed with her, despite her husband's protests. These recollections confirmed the fact that the women in his life were permissive and had overruled the prohibitions set up by the men. This would explain the relative ego-syntonicity of the incestuous fantasies in the dream, as well as his intimacy with his various mother figures.

Case 3C: Dream 4 of Chapter 9 concerned a patient who experienced sudden difficulty in breathing when he saw his dead father lying in bed, and who obtained relief when he escaped to his mother's presence in the bathroom. It was assumed that the respiratory difficulty was an anxiety equivalent related to the patient's homosexual attachment to his father and was relieved by the patient's escape to heterosexuality.

> In a later dream the patient reported that he started to wheeze as he was lying in bed beside his wife. He thought that the insertion of a bronchoscope would relieve the wheezing, but then realized that a bronchoscope wasn't used for this purpose.

When I discussed the dream with the supervisee it was assumed that the patient's wife represented an incestuous object and that resort to homosexuality (insertion of a phallic object in the form of a bronchoscope) could counteract the forbidden incestuous impulses. In both dreams the respiratory difficulty was taken to represent anxiety associated with sexual excitement.

Neither dream was interpreted to the patient. Several months later, the patient later recalled in another connection that as a child of five or six he had observed his father taking a shower and at the time was impressed by the great size of his father's penis, which he described as being "vicious-looking." He also had a fantasy of his father forcing his penis into the patient's mouth. He connected these fantasies with the fact that at about the same time he began to suffer periodic asthmatic attacks; these continued to occur until he reached puberty. He also recalled becoming angry with his mother at the age of thirteen, when she reprimanded him for masturbating and soiling the bedsheets. It would therefore appear that the patient's asthma was related to fellatio fantasies and that it cleared up when he began to masturbate with heterosexual fantasies.

These associations confirmed our suppositions that the patient's respiratory difficulty was related to sexuality, particularly to homosexuality. Since no interpretations were given to the patient it cannot be said that he was influenced by our inferences. This form of validation is particularly impressive. It again emphasized the cogency of empathic understanding of the patient, as well as the importance of determining the sense of the manifest dream and of applying it in a logical manner to our knowledge of the patient.

Corroborative Dreams and Validation

Case 4P: I was showing someone girlie magazines in my file drawer. They were in a small stack. I showed him two at the top—one was *Playboy*—but after that I became very reluctant to show him the remainder of the magazines and felt very embarrassed.

Day Residue: The day before the dream we had discussed the patient's naiveté and inhibition in his sexual relations with his wife. He could not allow himself to look at her in the nude. On the wedding night his wife had vaginismus, but he felt that if he had been more aggressive and forceful he could have entered her. Since he understood the nature of vaginismus, I remarked that he could not possibly believe that. The patient took offense at my remark and said he resented being spoken to as if he were "stupid." He said he would ultimately have arrived at the same conclusion if I had left him to his own devices and not intervened.

Associations: "Showing someone": Yesterday, he said, he was telling me about the nature of his sexual relations with his wife.

Playboy at that time was an "innocuous" magazine that just showed girls with breasts exposed, but did not display the genitalia. In the bottom drawer of his locked desk where he kept the girlie magazines was an advertisement for pornographic books showing women's vaginas.

Validation of Interpretation

"Two on the top" referred to women's breasts. He was ready to admit his interest in breasts but not his interest in the vagina. (I showed him two at the top... but... became reluctant to show him the remainder.)

I remarked that he showed me the "innocuous" part of his mind, namely, that which contained thoughts about breasts, but that he concealed his real interest, which was female genitalia. I went on to say that the locked desk was like his mind where he kept his real secrets locked up. He smiled and said he had had intercourse with his wife the previous night and was more aggressive than he had ever been. For the first time he spread her legs apart and exposed her vagina. She liked it. He also had an unusually strong erection, but he was embarrassed to tell me about it (in the dream he was embarrassed to show... the remainder of the magazines).

[The patient had apparently been stung by what he considered to be my taunt about his "stupidity" and as a result became aggressive with his wife. He had not completely overcome his guilt, however. He had been touched on a sensitive spot and his response was quite specifically in line with the directness of my comment. Thus far he had satisfactorily explained the current situation. But dreams deal with more than what the patient consciously knows and in offering interpretations we attempt to do likewise. What was the dream trying to say? Why all the curiosity about female genitalia? Could it be referring to something in the past that was being repressed?]

I asked the patient why he felt free to look at breasts or to talk freely about them. He was unable to say. I continued that breasts usually symbolize the mother, in that she breast-feeds her offspring. Could they refer to his mother? He then recalled having seen his mother's breasts as a boy. Had he ever seen her genitalia? He replied it had happened once, but he was too ashamed to discuss it. I said that he was reacting to his wife as he did to his mother; he could not look at his wife's genitalia, at least until the previous night, just as he could not look at his mother's. He agreed.

This brought the discussion to a close. It seemed the patient had inadvertently revealed a character trait when he complained of my comment about him. It was frequently observed during the course of the analysis that for an intelligent person the patient often behaved in an obtuse, guileless manner, as if he did not know what the score was. This tendency was most likely to appear whenever he wanted to conceal his knowledge of sex. I reminded him that during his adolescence his mother frequently drew attention to his ineptness, as if he were "stupid." At this point he laughed aloud, a frequent sign that a repressed truth has been brought to consciousness. He said he would rather be known as stupid and inept than as one who was knowledgeable about sex. As a matter of fact, his mother often wondered whether he would ever get married or know what to do with a woman if he did marry. His roommates at college likewise regarded him as a person with little knowledge of women and never included him in their bull sessions or escapades.

[In laughing after I recalled his mother's comments about him, the patient not only experienced the release of tension which always accompanies the undoing of a repression, but seemed to have overcome his resentment at my reference to his "stupidity." He apparently realized that I was interested in helping him and not in judging him. Finding protection in the analyst undoubtedly played a big part in the patient's ability to abandon his resistances. His response to my interpretation provided assurance that we were on the right track.]

A few days later the patient reported the next dream:

> I was looking very hard for something. I walked all around the back of the house and looked in the grass to see if it had been dropped.

Day Residue: During the previous session I had contrasted the ease with which he discussed masturbation earlier in the analysis with his reluctance to discuss it at the present time. He replied that formerly he had isolated the guilt associated with it so that he could talk about it more easily. Now he could do so no longer. In addition, the urge to masturbate was not as strong as it used to be. These answers, however, did not satisfy him and he kept searching for another explanation.

Associations: I drew an analogy between his use of the word *searching* and the idea of looking for something in the dream.

"Grass": The patient recalled an earlier dream in which grass was associated with pubic hair. He once dropped a screwdriver in the grass.

The "back of the house" reminded him of the anogenital area, the perineum. When he discussed masturbation in the past he mentioned a fear that it might lead to impairment of potency. For several days after masturbating, for instance, he would find himself unable to maintain an erection during intercourse. This difficulty had been overcome, however, and he no longer felt that masturbation caused impairment of function.

The previous day he had spoken of the fact that his father did not trust him to go to school alone. He took this to mean that his father suspected him of masturbating. He identified himself with Justice Fortas who at the time had been compelled to resign from the Supreme Court; in his opinion, no one should have held anything against Fortas as long as he was a good judge. Likewise as long as the patient was a good student his father should not have objected to his interest in sex. As an adolescent his curiosity took the form of paying attention to girls' legs and wanting to lift their skirts.

The patient's masturbatory fantasies included looking at girls in the nude. During intercourse the previous night his wife had asked him why he kept a small light on in the next room. He told her he was more stimulated if he could see her in the nude.

I remarked that "looking," like searching, was a form of curiosity. [My purpose was to draw attention to the fact that he might be looking for something specific in his curiosity about nude women.] He said he knew what his wife looked like in the nude, but he seemed to be searching for something more. When he masturbated he would look at pictures of nude women in magazines. After a while, the pictures failed to arouse him and he would get new ones. It turned out, however, that the new pictures satisfied him no better. It was the same old thing! I asked him what he expected to find. He said he was fascinated by the pubic hair. He was at a loss to know what he was seeking—perhaps a penis—but he was not aware of any such thought at the time of looking.

I said, "Perhaps you are looking for something that is *lost* in the pubic hair." He thought of the dream, in which *something was lost in the grass*. The pubic hair concealed the clitoris but he was not aware of wanting to look at the clitoris. He then corrected himself by saying that formerly he did want to look at the clitoris but he was inhibited by his wife's embarrassment. I suggested he might still want to look at it if he were not afraid of offending her. He agreed, saying he knew he could become more aroused if he saw her clitoris. Indeed this was the content of his fantasy when he first masturbated at the age of twelve; at that time he only wanted to see what a girl's bottom looked like. All he could picture was pubic hair.

I commented that "looking very hard" could be related to his earlier compulsion to masturbate. He replied that when he saw girls in miniskirts he had a compulsion to look which was beyond that of the average man's curiosity. I repeated the thought in the dream of something having been lost or dropped. He replied it could refer only to a penis. He recalled wondering, between the ages of seven and nine, whether or not his mother had a penis with which she urinated. He could never be certain about it.

[According to Freud (1908, 1910) children believe that everyone, including girls, is born with a penis. In girls, however, the penis has been lost or mutilated, or it is very small and will grow later. The patient's acceptance of my interpretation would not in itself have constituted sufficient confirmation. Being in a cooperative mood, he might have wanted to believe I was correct. The recapture of a confirmatory memory from childhood, however, was most convincing, even though it may be said that I was leading him on to a preconceived goal. On the other hand, as already mentioned, in interpreting dreams one tries to tell the patient something more than he already knows. The intention is not to take giant steps but to point out something that seems to be just beyond the patient's grasp and has thus far eluded him. I was also careful to use his own words in drawing parallels to his associations.]

At this point, I reminded him that he once found a screwdriver in the grass, that is, something to "screw" with. He laughed aloud and said, "Yes, a screwdriver is a long rod that you screw with." I then

Validation of Interpretation 233

offered the following reconstruction: just as he was once afraid that masturbation caused a loss of potency, he may also have thought at one time that girls were punished for masturbating by losing their penises. If so, it was also possible for him to lose his penis.

There was no response to this interpretation. I therefore reworded it: if girls could lose their penises it was also possible for him to lose his, as if to say, the penis was not a permanent fixture. In his urge to look at the pubic hair of girls which might conceal a penis, was he really seeking reassurance that he had nothing to fear? He immediately recalled his fear of dogs, specifically, that they might bite off his penis. As he said this he became anxious and wondered how men could submit to a transexual operation.

[The first interpretation was intellectual and too remote from the patient at the time. The second interpretation mentioned his fear of castration directly; its effectiveness was indicated by the recollection of repressed but unmistakable memories from early childhood. It is questionable whether this material could have been learned without the dream, or at least as quickly and as relevantly.]

On the succeeding night the patient had the following dream:

I bought something and received some change. In it I found a 1963 silver quarter. There were also two or three other quarters that seemed interesting.

Associations: The analysis began in 1963. A silver quarter dated 1963 was considered valuable among coin collectors. The patient added the dream must refer to the analysis. He said that following the previous hour he developed a dull headache and sharp precordial pains which he thought might be coronary in origin. (His father had died from a coronary infarct.) He also had a sensation of epigastric bloating and he felt like belching. After the last session he said he felt "anxious as hell" and was afraid something would happen to his penis. He had once heard of an exhibitionist who said he could solve his problem by cutting off his penis so that he would have nothing to exhibit. The patient was horrified at the idea. Yesterday he felt he was making progress in the analysis and that the analysis was helping him. This, he said, could fit in with his association that 1963 silver quarters were considered valuable. I asked him in what way he thought he was making progress. He replied he thought he could stop masturbating if he was able to master his fear of injuring his penis. He could then finish his analysis.

He recalled that as a small boy, sometime between the ages of four and ten, he looked at his mother's genitals and, not seeing her penis, wondered where it had disappeared. As he was saying this he developed a splitting headache.

[The previous day's discussion apparently helped to lift further repressions and the patient was able to recall specific childhood memories and fantasies. Along with this he began to show somatic symptoms, namely, precordial pains, gastric distress, and headache. The memory recalled was even more explicit than the one of the day before. (It is characteristic of infants in the preverbal period to express emotions by means of somatic symptoms.) The pairing of the patient's headache with thoughts of castration suggest that the two were equated in his mind. Henceforth we could assume that at least one of the determinants of his headaches, which he complained of for years, was castration fear as a punishment for masturbation—pain in the head being equated with pain in the genitals.]

To further extend the significance of the headache, I suggested that there might be a connection between the headache and the precordial pains of the previous day. Had he ever associated his fear of getting a coronary attack with my recent illness? [My intent was to establish a possible connection between his precordial pain and his identification with me, as well as with his father who had died from coronary disease.] The patient hesitated at first and then replied it was his impression that I did not look well when I returned from my summer vacation. He was embarrassed to mention it but he thought my face looked brownish and washed out, as if I were suffering from a liver or blood disease. As a matter of fact, I was suntanned and others had remarked that I looked very well. I suggested that in having a thought which he felt might upset me, he might be revealing his ambivalence. He said he was not aware of harboring any hostile thoughts toward me. On the contrary, he was grateful because I had been very helpful the day before. He remarked, however, that when he read about the exhibitionist suggesting the idea of having his penis cut off, he thought the man might as well be dead. According to him, his anxiety about losing his penis, having a coronary attack and also a stroke (pounding headache) all had the same significance. [This must refer to punishment for death wishes against his father and me.]

I recalled that his father had died from coronary disease and suggested that, in his mind, he had to suffer the same way his father did, as if he were responsible for his father's death. To this he said it must refer to a wish he might have had. He remembered wishing to be free of his father's authority and surveillance. He also recalled having been curious and anxious when he saw his father's penis, so much larger than his own. He felt he shouldn't be looking at his father's penis because he might have a hostile thought just as he did when he observed that I was not looking well. [In other words, to look was tantamount to killing or castrating—the destructive aspect of curiosity and scopophilia.]

Comment: What was the dream wish? The dream is a pleasant one. Essentially it said that he had obtained a valuable coin and several others that were interesting. According to him, this referred to what he was currently experiencing in his analysis. He had expected me to be angry when he reported his thought that I might be very sick. If I died he would not have to return and remain under my surveillance. But instead he found I was actually friendly. He was furthermore being more cooperative in the analysis by giving good associations. That would make me feel more kindly toward him. I would forgive him and help him get well. He did not have to be afraid that I would castrate him. On the contrary, he found a silver quarter, that is, his penis. Following the previous hour he felt he could finish his analysis. This would relieve him of his castration fear.

This might have been an appropriate place to show him that since his current fears in the transference were unrealistic, they could really apply to his childhood fear of his father. Such an interpretation, however, should not be expected to produce an effective result at once. A good deal of working though would still have to take place. For instance, the patient's father died just before the patient's Bar Mitzvah and he anticipated that he, too, would die before his son's Bar Mitzvah. This fear was reactivated after I became ill, and continued without modification even after his son's Bar Mitzvah had taken place. His guilt had to do with wanting to get rid of me so that he could continue to masturbate, which he had not done for many months. He now realized that I did not forbid masturbation as his father did. The dream demonstrates how dependent we are on the patient's associations, despite all we know about him. It was thus the patient's associations to the 1963 quarter which gave us the clue that the dream referred to the analysis. Such an association also carries the ultimate conviction for the patient.

The correctness of the previous day's interpretations was evidenced by the further dispelling of amnesias and elaboration of the same subject. The first dream pointed to the patient's progress in that he could admit that he was interested in looking at women's genitalia. In other words, his superego had become less severe as a result of the previous discussion, thus permitting some lifting of the repression. In the dream that followed, it became evident that the patient's scopophilia was motivated by his desire to assure himself that the penis was still there, that nothing could really happen to the penis, and that his penis would remain intact after he confessed his hostile thoughts and was forgiven for them. In the immediate situation this referred to completing his analysis successfully; in the past, to the fact that his father really loved him and would reward him by allowing him to become a man. In other words, each dream appeared to be part of a series which expressed the fulfillment of an infantile wish to retain the penis.

CHAPTER 11

Terminal Dreams

The terminal phase of analysis represents for the patient the end of a close relationship with a person who has come to mean something beyond his actual self. In the course of the analyis the analyst has served as a replacement for the most important people in the analysand's life. It is therefore only to be expected that the breakup of the relationship will affect the analysand keenly. The nature of his reaction is determined largely by his early life experiences.

When the analyst suggests that the analysis may soon come to an end, it can be considered a favorable response if the patient is encouraged, that is, takes it as an indication that the analyst has confidence in his capacity to become self-sufficient and shift for himself. Being assured of the approval of the analyst may induce the patient to identify even more closely with him, so that he strives to achieve as much as possible in the time remaining. An increased flow of previously repressed material usually ensues, which extends to the deeper reaches of the unconscious. The prospect of having to be on his own induces him to make a determined effort to restrain his instinctual drives, evaluate his potentials realistically, direct his energies toward realizable goals, and begin to deal with his emotional problems on a more mature level. Such reactions are evidence of greater ego strength, possibly supported by a modification of the severity of the superego, which has hitherto not permitted him to succeed or to assume the mantle of complete adulthood.

On the other hand, the patient may regard the approaching end of the analysis as a separation from the analyst, in which case he goes through a period of mourning or weaning. If he feels he is being abandoned, he may become angry or depressed. His ambivalence shows through, both in his clinging to the analyst, on the one hand, and his hardly concealed death wishes, on the other. He may depict the analyst in derogatory terms. One patient for instance felt betrayed; he said he could no longer trust people who left him; it reminded him of his childhood when his mother always seemed to be running off and leaving him—as if he were being thrown to the wolves. As a result he was in a constant rage and by alienating people attempted to deny his need for them and to protect himself against the possibility of being deserted. Such reactions are not uncommon and may be difficult to overcome, particularly in instances where a previous analyst has died during the course of therapy. Where termination is looked upon as a weaning process, the patient may regress to a state of complete dependency, with the reappearance of the symptoms of the transference neurosis. Resistances which have been dormant may flair up anew along with the reactivation of symptoms. This usually expresses an unconscious desire to cling to the analyst by appearing still to need his help.

In favorable cases, repressions are finally overcome with recall of memories which permit the childhood history to be reconstructed. The number of alternative explanations of the patient's symptoms are narrowed down until we come upon the nuclear core of the infantile neurosis. In those patients who have experienced severe psychic traumata during the developmental period, particularly at the preverbal level, however, we find varying degrees of alterations of the ego which affect object relationships and cause difficulty in giving up infantile gratifications. These individuals utilize the analytic situation to satisfy their infantile and narcissistic needs, and show little concern about establishing their individual separateness and autonomy. They have serious problems in detaching themselves from the analyst, often becoming panicky. In their reproaches for his leaving them, all of their suppressed resentment against him comes into the open. Such patients need much support and should be offered the opportunity to talk to the analyst after the formal sessions are over. In such cases one must be content with limited results.

In the terminal phase, the patient's dreams follow the trend of his waking thoughts and frequently anticipate them. In view of the separation aspects of termination, it is not surprising that transference elements are particularly prominent in dreams. Dreams of the analyst's death, usually much distorted, indicate preparation for the actual separation, hostility, or impatience to gain independence and be free of surveillance. Dreams may also consist of fantasies of rebirth and reveal anxieties about growing up. As the patient's resistances disappear with the progressive interpretation of his dreams, the manifest dreams tend to become clearer and less distorted, while the patient's associations reveal that he has gained access to a wider range of his unconscious. Infantile memories, especially screen memories related to the primal scene, are often recalled, with evidences of their traumatic effect on later development. The depth of memory recall, as well as the reduction in the number of recurrent dreams, indicate that termination may be approaching. There is also evidence in the manifest dreams of increased ego strength, along with modification of severity of the superego and a tendency to restrain instinctual gratification.

The transference regression in the dreams recapitulates the patient's relationship with his parents in the earliest stages of infancy, and provides us with data that cannot be recovered in any other way. From such information we are in a position to determine the patient's ability to establish mature and adequate object relationships and to tolerate further analysis (Glover, 1955).

Case Report (P)

The patient was a young, unusually intelligent woman who had originally come for analysis because of marital discord, which was caused by her unreasonable dissatisfaction with her husband. Although the latter was a dependable and tolerant individual who seemed in the main to be quite capable, she repeatedly provoked him by drawing attention to his flaws. The merest sign of inadequacy on his part, such as a trivial show of absentmindedness, was sufficient to lead to an outburst of immoderate anger. She said that it was essential that her husband be "perfect" so that she would not be embarrassed in the eyes of others. The unreasonable nature of her faultfinding became evident when she attacked him even after he had clearly demonstrated his superior competence in other areas. She found it difficult to express tenderness for him, except during periods when she was being unfaithful to him. On the other hand, after having provoked him to the point of violent anger, she could submit to him sexually with heightened pleasure.

The patient was the older of two children, having been three when her brother was born. Her attitude toward the latter all through her childhood was one of competitiveness and resentment. She strove to impress her father by her intelligence, and also tried to outdo her brother in physical sports until he was old enough to surpass her. Although she mothered him in a protective way when he was young, she had repressed this memory until the latter part of the analysis. She recalled only that her hostility toward him never quite disappeared. Even when he developed a serious physical illness in later years she was unsympathetic and resented her father's concern for him, while deriving secret satisfaction from her father's distress over his "favorite" child. During her latency years she remained detached from her father and openly displayed her preference for a maternal uncle. At college she considered herself to be a "towny," that is, a girl from town who was taken out by fellows when they could get no dates with college girls. She was attracted to her husband because he appeared to be strong and reliable. Her mother disapproved of him, but her father, who had always allowed his wife to dominate him, came through at this juncture and supported his daughter. Her disparaging attitude toward her husband first appeared soon after the marriage, when she thought that he fell short of her mother's expectations. When she became pregnant shortly afterward she insisted on having an abortion because she feared her mother's censure; later, in a perverse mood, she criticized her husband for permitting her to go through with the abortion.

Terminal Dreams

At the beginning of the analysis the patient appeared to be a sedate, socially proper person. Her attitude toward men was competitive; she enjoyed matching wits with them and coming out ahead. An abrupt change, however, occurred soon after her father's death. At the time she experienced no grief, but instead expressed concern that her mother might become too dependent on her. Shortly thereafter she began a liaison with a socially prominent man and revealed a recklessness that was quite unexpected in her, exposing herself to public gossip by meeting her lover openly. When I cautioned her against jeopardizing her marriage and home life, she became defiant and willful. She said she would sooner stop the analysis than give up the relationship. She hoped to marry the man and was offended when I said her expectations might be unreasonable, as if I were downgrading her. The affair continued for several years, though more circumspectly, until, in response to her direct inquiry, the man told her that he could never marry her. She thereupon became depressed and broke off with him.

A short time later she became involved with another equally prominent man. She realized that the analysis was not making any progress, but said she would not give up the relationship and withdrew from the analysis. The interruption continued for several years while the affair was going on. It was finally terminated by the man, when he felt that his own marriage was becoming shaky. She again thought of herself as the "towny," a plaything for men who had to take a back seat for the women of their real choice.

After the affair was broken off the patient came to see me several times for individual sessions because of persisting resentment against her lover and because of her wish for reprisal, even though she realized this was unreasonable. When she found that she could not get over her longing for him, she finally returned for therapy on a more regular basis. She was still having the same problem with her husband for which she had come originally, namely, her ambivalence and inability to feel tenderness for him. This period of analysis continued for six months, during which time the patient sat up, as she had done on her occasional visits.

The following dreams were reported during this time, and

occurred seriatim over a period of a single month. Their significance lies in the fact that they seemed to follow one another logically with the elaboration of one central theme, and ended with the termination of the analysis:

Dream 1: I'm on the fourth floor of a hotel with Jim but we are in different rooms. He has one bed in his room and is planning to bring in a woman with him but the hotel can't get him another bed. He comes into my room and asks me to give up my bed. I get angry. Not only does he spurn me by taking in another woman, but he wants to take my bed so that I will have nothing to sleep on. I tell him I would not have asked him for such a favor. In the end I don't know whether or not I give him my bed.

Associations: Jim was the second lover. When he had broken off the relationship in order to return to his wife, the patient felt spurned and angry. On the day of the dream she had met him casually, but nothing of significance had passed between them.

When she was five or six her family lived in a *fourth floor* apartment. When climbing the stairs she was often afraid of being attacked by a man, and would run up as fast as she could. She recalled that she once walked into her parents' bedroom and observed her father embracing her mother. Although the parents were not having intercourse, her father withdrew his arm guiltily, and the patient felt both embarrassed and angry.

Her next association had to do with the previous session. I had anticipated this, since I was silently trying to figure out whether something similar to the situation in the dream had arisen in the analytic situation. I had been seeing the patient in the study of my home, but in the preceding hour, for some reason, I had to see her in the living room. The patient said nothing about it at the time and appeared to be taking it in her stride. In associating to the dream, however, she remarked that she felt uncomfortable sitting in my living room because she could hear my wife walking upstairs. She said, "I realize that you didn't intend to embarrass me. You must have had good reasons for not seeing me in your study." I asked her whether, despite her reasonable attitude, she might not have been angry with me. She thought a moment and said she was not aware of any anger. She then added that after the previous hour she had remarked to her husband, "I wonder if I'm not finished with Dr. Sloane." She went on to say that when she heard my wife moving around she felt like a stranger and an intruder, and became angry with me for having exposed her to such a situation. If I really cared for her, she said, I would have seen her in the other room. It indicated that my wife meant more to me than she did.

The patient's thought of terminating the analysis impressed me because it showed the strong effect the situation had had on her. It seemed to be an exaggerated overreaction and one that had to be understood and analyzed if the analysis were not to go on the rocks at this late date. I felt her reaction should be met head-on. I said that she must have felt she had been left out by me and had taken it as a personal offense. I added, to judge from the dream, her response to this experience was similar to the one she had had when Jim left her for his wife. She agreed. I went on to say that she had felt such rejections several times before in her life. Her father, for instance, had always made a fuss over her as a child because she was a bright little girl, but she felt he had turned away from her when he began to pay attention to her brother, and also when she saw him embracing her mother. She had reacted to these situations by withdrawing from him and turning to her uncle. I also reminded her that at the time of her first extramarital experience, when I told her that her continued acting-out was interfering with the analysis, she became resentful and said I had no right to meddle, since I myself had not responded to her affection for me. Her first lover also turned her down when he said he could never marry her. Both paramours had thus passed her over for their wives, just as I had presumably shown preference for my wife. The episodes with her two lovers and with me, I said, were repetitions of the trauma she had experienced at the hands of her father as a little girl. She accepted the interpretation without a demurral.

The dream, however, seemed to have further implications. Since, in the dream, the man passed her over for the other woman, we must assume that this is the dream wish. This could be understood as a masochistic punishment for the patient's oedipal guilt. But the dream also stated that she did not know whether or not she gave up her bed. In other words, it was as if she had not made up her mind what to do. This indicated her ambivalence about complying with Jim's request and showed that she was still angry with him. It could also explain her anger toward me following the previous hour and her indecision about leaving treatment. In endeavoring to seek clarification, I returned to a question the patient had raised in the previous hour, namely, why she could not have tender feelings for her husband or tell him that she loved him. I reminded her in this connection that she was unable for a long time to express positive feelings for me. It was only in the last few months that she could allow herself to say that she did not know what she would do if she ever lost contact with me. She then recalled how upset she had been when she heard I was ill a short time previously. Incidentally, since the more formal aspects of the analytic situation (such as the use of the couch) had been dispensed with and there seemed to be a good therapeutic alliance, I had allowed myself to be a little more free with her, and on one occasion had loaned her a magazine article which I thought might interest her. Although she seemed to accept the gesture in the spirit in which it was made, it turned out to have a greater significance for her than had appeared on the surface. She had referred to it several times and it seemed to have stimulated her fantasies about me. I, therefore, assumed that she might be feeling threatened by her positive feelings for me, and was looking for a reason to become angry with me, in order to keep me at arm's length and not allow the relationship to become too intimate. In other words, her fondness for me threatened to become eroticized. After having made these silent conjectures, I pointed out to her that the adding of insult to injury by Jim in the dream not only served her masochism, of which there had been previous evidences, but by providing her with a reason for getting angry, protected her against her positive feelings for him. Her overreaction to my changing of the room might have had the same motive. To express love or tenderness was equivalent to making a commitment to me, thus placing herself in my power and exposing herself to the possibility of being rejected. (In order to avoid complicating the interpretation, I purposely said nothing about her possible erotic feelings.) She offered no objection to this interpretation.

I went on to say that she had reacted in the same way to her father. Despite her statements that he was never close to her, it could be clearly deduced, from other remarks she had made, that he was quite devoted to her. She, however, had kept him at arm's length and tried in many ways to make him jealous. This had continued throughout adolescence. In that sense *she* had rejected *him*. She might be following the same pattern with her husband, in which case he would represent an incest object. In looking for reasons to criticize him, she could be seeking protection against feelings of tenderness. (This, of course, could have been only one of several motivations.)

The dream was a transference dream, stimulated by the events of the previous hour. By inference it depicted her husband, Jim, and myself as incest objects and cast light on her pattern of acting out. It also brought to the surface many details of the transference neurosis that had been obscure, particularly her hostility toward me which seemed to be a protection against sexual feelings. It also helped to explain her ambivalent attitude toward her husband in a way that was meaningful to her.

The second dream occurred a week later. The patient supplied few associations to this dream and most of my interventions were based on my own understanding of what was going on.

Dream 2: I'm coming into your office. My friend N. is also there, as if she were visiting. As I'm coming in the door, you are going out through the same door and we try to avoid bumping into each other. But as often happens, we manage to get into each other's way. We move together in the same direction until we finally manage it correctly and each goes his way.

Associations: When she came in that morning, I remarked that she was not wearing stockings, despite the fact that it was a cold day. She was also wearing a miniskirt that exposed her thighs in a suggestive way. This was unusual for her. By mentioning her appearance I hoped to bring her seductiveness to her attention. She did not take the hint, however. Instead she said, "We seem to be going over the same ground repeatedly. I know I am reacting to you the way I reacted to my father and to all the men in my life. It's a repetition of what you call the infantile trauma. I recognize it and yet I can't get over feeling the way I do. Intellectually I can see that the pattern has been repeated over and over again with various men, with my father, with Bob and Jim and now with you. I seem to pick out men who I should know are going to reject me, but even so, when the situation actually arises, I think it's real. I can't believe it's all fantasy. When you had me sitting in your living room, I really believed you were doing it deliberately in order to show me my place, even though my better sense told me otherwise."

In other words, she was saying that despite the reasonable part of herself, something was preventing her from distinguishing fantasy from reality. She was thus expressing what to her was a real problem.

In associating to the dream she characterized her friend *N.* as being a girl who was rigid, proper, and reserved. *N.* thus represented one part of herself. She gave no further associations.

The detail of the dream that impressed me was her statement that, as we were trying to avoid each other, we managed to get in each other's way by *moving together in the same direction.* I intuitively took this to mean that she thought I was having the same fantasies about her that she was having about me; in other words, I was going along with her, which was a manifestation of countertransference. I therefore ventured to ask: "Is it possible that you feel I am encouraging your fantasies in some way?" She then recalled that on one occasion I had asked her to come in a few minutes later for her session, but instead she had come in early. When she entered my home, I instinctively took her by the arm and led her into another room. She later realized that I was attempting to keep her from encountering the previous patient, which might have been embarrassing to both of them. She said: "That was the first time you ever touched me and I felt it was a very intimate thing, that there was something, a secret, between us." She also referred to the magazine article that I had loaned her. She felt uneasy about accepting it and thought it, too, was a gesture of intimacy. She stated that she also felt uncomfortable when I addressed her as if she were an adult.

It occurred to me that she might have reacted similarly to my comment about her appearance that morning, namely, that I was responding to her seductiveness. I asked her if she was surprised by my remark about her bare legs. She replied: "No, I expected it, because you always make some comment if I dress differently." (This was not altogether true.) I then asked: "Did you give it any thought this morning while you were dressing?" She replied: "Yes, I thought it was somewhat immodest but I thought 'Who cares?'" I said: "So you may have had a seductive motive in mind, hoping to get a response from me. You even anticipated that I would react to it. In other words, you seemed to take it for granted that I would respond to you." She agreed with me at once.

I then added: "You seem to be out to seduce me. I remember you once said that you never gave up. If you are out for a man, you feel that you must gain your end." I reminded her that she had done the same thing with her father when she was sixteen. At that time she had teased him by playing coy, and when he tried to put his arm around her with what she considered an improper gesture, she drew away in a shocked manner, even though she knew that she had invited his action.

Since we know that the dream is an attempt to resolve a current problem as well as one from the distant past, I asked myself what could be preoccupying the patient at this time. She had started the hour by saying, in effect, that recognizing her repetitive pattern of acting out did not make it disappear. It then occurred to me that one of the reasons for the failure to resolve the problem might be her fantasy that I was responding to her. She might then be persisting in the hope that she could win me over as she had won over other men, including her father. This, of course, could be helping to keep the fantasy alive and making it appear part of reality. I said to her: "You are apparently not ready to give up the hope that something can actually happen here." She agreed with me. I then made a connection with what she had said at the beginning of the hour to the effect that when certain situations arise she thinks they are real and not fantasies, despite her better judgment. I wondered whether her feeling that I was encouraging her responses could be instrumental in keeping her fantasies alive and making them appear real. She had nothing to say to this.

If my interpretation of the dream was correct, the dream was revealing something about the nature of the transference and countertransference that was being overlooked. It could also have accounted for the failure of the analysis to come to a satisfactory conclusion. At the end of the hour, I offered her an extra hour the next day, saying that it would be important at this time to continue the discussion because significant material was coming up. She accepted my suggestion and came in with the following dream:

Dream 3: I had promised to buy my son a pair of shoes but then found that I was physically unable to drive him to the store. He became angry and said, "You shouldn't promise anything if you can't deliver it." There was a second part to the dream which was long. I recalled that in it I was a little girl and was talking with Jim. He wanted to cure me by bleeding my foot. I refused because I wanted the relationship to continue and he got annoyed with me.

Associations: She had the impulse to call Jim yesterday but realized that it would have been acting out and she restrained herself.

Being a little girl referred to her childhood.

She was reading in a book on medieval France about the general practice of *bleeding* people in order to relieve congestion. Very often people died from the bleeding. Marie Antoinette was bled from the legs when she fainted after childbirth.

During the last hour I had remarked that her face was flushed; flushing of the face, she said, could result from either embarrassment or sexual excitement.

She said that since Jim was "treating" her, he must refer to me. She felt the dream might have to do with the last hour, but she could not recall what we had discussed. She did remember, however, that she had expressed dissatisfaction with the repetitious nature of our discussions which led nowhere.

When I reminded her of the last dream, she expressed surprise that she had not remembered it. I suggested that she might not have wanted to remember it. I reminded her of the details of the dream and repeated the interpretation, saying that it was as if I were responding to her fantasy and that this could be the reason for the persistence of her neurosis, namely, that she felt I was accessible and there was still a chance that her fantasy might come true. I wondered whether my objective discussion of the subject might not have taken some of the romance from it. She had some difficulty in seeing this. I asked her how she reacted to my comment about her bare legs and miniskirt. She said she did not like it because she felt foolish and embarrassed. Her response after leaving the hour was, "Screw him! Next time I'll be bundled up." I said, "In other words, I was attempting to cure you by *decongesting* your passion. You may have regarded this as a destructive thing since the idea of living without having fantasies would make life very dreary and you might as well be dead." I suggested that today's dream in which she refused to be bled because she wanted the relationship to continue could refer to the fact that she did not want to give up her fantasies, and in that sense did not want to be cured. She wondered what that could mean. I pointed out that in her associations Marie Antoinette was bled after she gave birth to a child. In the dream she promised to buy her son a pair of shoes. (Previously she had identified her son with me.) Might she have hoped to become pregnant by me? I recalled that she once had a fantasy of getting a child from Bob and that she had recently wanted to give me a gift of a plant. She said it would be foolish for her to think of having my baby because, first of all, she was *physically unable to* have another child. I suggested that the fantasy had nothing to do with reality and that it could be a childish wish to bear her father's child. (In the dream she was a child.)

She then recalled that her mother did not want her to have children. When she became pregnant shortly after the marriage, she was afraid of her mother's disapproval and insisted on having an abortion. She also recalled for the first time that until the age of ten she took care of her brother as if he were her own child. I said this could confirm my surmise that she wanted to have a child by her father. I pointed out that in the dream she was physically unable to drive her son to the store. She was also physically unable to give me a baby. (In the dream, her son says, "You shouldn't promise anything if you can't deliver (sic) it.")

Dream 4: I was trying to replace a round bowl on a shelf, but it wouldn't go in easily. I then realized that there was a lot of dust and debris behind the bowl which had to be removed first.

Associations: She had noticed a lot of *dust* on her piano yesterday and realized that she had neglected her dusting and cleaning. Dusting and cleaning reminded her of *D & C*, which means cleaning out of the uterus. She understood that this was how abortions were performed.

Replacing something on a shelf usually refers to a book. Sometimes if there is something behind a book, the book cannot be replaced. That reminded her that she had "stolen" a book from her mother, in fact the very one that dealt with medieval France and which spoke of the use of drastic bleeding by physicians for therapeutic reasons.

The bowl: Her father-in-law had given her some valuable china. Her husband piles up his old junk in a drawer and then forgets that it is there. He raises objections whenever she wants to clean it up.

She stated that during the past week she had shown some regression in that she had gone back to the practice of eating while reading in bed. We had previously understood this to represent a fantasy of returning to the warmth of her mother and suckling at her breast. The book she was reading in bed was the one she had "stolen" from her mother. She decided that she would have to stop the regression and "put the book back on the shelf."

She then said that she had felt let down after the last hour, because the momentum had died down. She was also angry with me because it had been a fruitless hour.

I reminded her of what she had said about taking care of her brother as if he were her own child—again something she had stolen from her mother. I had interpreted this as a wish to have a child by her father. This was like the gift of china from her father-in-law (father). Instead of having been a fruitless hour, I continued, it seemed to have been a productive one.

I proceeded to say that her recent regression might be compared to the "regression" of the fantasy of having my child, which she had recognized as being entirely irrational. Although she had said she wanted a sexual response from me and had reacted to my "rejection" of her as if it were real, she could not possibly conceive of wanting a baby from me. I said she realized this to be pure fantasy without any reality to it, and she had to overcome it ("replace the bowl"). This was like putting back the book on the shelf, that is, giving it (the baby) back to her mother. But something was obstructing the correction of the fantasy. In the dream the "dust and debris behind the bowl" first had to be removed. I asked her what the debris could refer to. She gave the association of broken fragments of old relics. That could refer to the junk in her husband's drawer that he did not want her to throw out or disturb. The debris could also refer to the detritus that is removed during a D & C, or perhaps to a fetus.

I then said it was as if she could not get rid of the regressed fantasy of wanting my child until she got rid of the "relic" of the past, namely, the infantile wish for a child by her father. In the dream, she only realizes that she must get rid of the debris, but she does not actually do anything about it, as if she is not quite ready to give up her infantile wish.

I then returned to the reason for her dissatisfaction at the end of the previous hour. I recalled that I had offered her that hour as an extra session because we were in the midst of analyzing the infantile neurosis, and I did not want to lose the momentum of the material. I asked how she felt after I had offered her the hour. She replied that she thought I did it because I liked her and considered her someone special. As she drove away from my office that day she felt sexually aroused, although she was not aware that her sexual feelings were directed toward me. When she returned the following day, however, she felt I was cold, detached, and analytical, as if I were dashing cold water on her hopes. In comparison to the disappointment of her expectations, the new findings that were elicited during the hour were of secondary interest to her. Rather than being encouraged by them, she became angry with me.

The next session took place several days later. At that time I was surprised to find that a striking change had taken place in the patient. She reported no dream, but in her attitude toward me she appeared to be less self-conscious and in discussing her problems she was more realistic and self-confident. She said she felt no more interest in Jim and was more concerned about her husband's business problems. She expressed much feeling for him. She had also begun to feel differently about her father. She had many mementos of his funeral which she had never wanted to look at, but she now felt a nostalgia for them and wanted to take them out. She thought a good deal about her past feelings for her father and decided to visit his grave, which she had not done in the many years since his death. She also realized that the response she sought from him as a child was entirely unrealistic, and she felt she could begin to see things in their proper perspective.

I asked her how she accounted for the change in herself. She said she was certain that it must have had to do with her recent dreams. It would have been easy for her to say that she wanted to have her father's baby, but it would have been all intellectual and would really have meant nothing to her. When it appeared in the form of the dream, however, she realized that the wish was real and vital enough to have a great deal of meaning.

I confirmed what she said and added that she could probably feel the reality of her infantile wish for a baby from her father only because she had experienced it in all its vividness as a wish to have my baby. Only then could it begin to have meaning for her. The original conflict with recall of the content and appropriate affect, and its reexperience in relation to the analyst, was now confronted by her more mature ego. he patient could deal with it more effectively because she realized that it was not so "bad," that is, frightening, disgusting, or immoral. She said she had always been irritated with me when I asked her about her feelings for me, but she now realized how meaningful it was for her to face her transference feelings.

She thought she could stop treatment now. I agreed with her and added that if any further problems came up, she was not to be discouraged, but to feel free to come back and discuss them. She wondered why her treatment had taken such a long time. I suggested that to some extent it might have had to do with her continued acting out with Bob and Jim, as well as her interactions with me. She said she was grateful that I had continued to treat her despite her acting out. If I had stopped treatment, she would never have come to this point. As she was leaving, she expressed criticism of the artificial plant in my office and said she was going to bring me a "living" one, which she did shortly thereafter!

Summary of the Dreams: The first dream dramatized my rejection of her in the current situation, from which I drew a parallel with her previous rejections by her father and her two lovers. It also brought up the possibility that these situations were unconsciously contrived by the patient as a means of seeking masochistic punishment for her incestuous wishes, and of protecting herself against these wishes by finding a reason for becoming angry with the man. The dream also explained why she could show no tenderness toward her husband.

The second dream seemed partially to account for the fact that she had not profited from our previous discussions of her oedipal attachment. It opened up the possibility that she continued to maintain her fantasy because she felt I was responding to her seductiveness. Although she had often spoken about her reactions to the interest I was showing in her, the real depth of its meaning emerged only after the discussion of the dream. Her reaction to this disclosure was one of disappointment and anger, because it apparently meant she could no longer hold on to her fantasies.

The third dream brought out her fantasy of wanting to give me a child, which was readily understood as a repetition of her infantile wish to bear her father's child. The patient acted out this fantasy in childhood by taking care of her brother as if he were her own child.

In the last dream she wrestled with the idea of giving up her fantasy of having the oedipal child. Following the interpretation of this dream, there was a return of strong positive feelings for her husband, a loss of interest in her lover, and increased tenderness in thinking of her father. She regarded me in a friendly and more realistic manner, from which unreasonable expectations seem to have been removed.

Discussion: It may be of interest to review the dreams from the point of view of the resolution of the patient's underlying conflicts.

In the first dream the transference neurosis was dramatized in the incident of the patient's lover asking her to give up her bed for another woman. This referred to an occurrence in the preceding session when I changed rooms "in order" to let her know that there was another woman in my life. It was as if I regarded her as an intruder and was asking her to give up her position on the couch (bed) for my wife. My interpretation that the intensity of her reaction during the previous hour might have been a reflection of the way she felt when she found her parents fondly embracing each other in bed (on the fourth floor)—probably a screen-memory of the primal scene—apparently had a strong effect on her. This was reinforced when I pointed out that she was repeating with me a pattern that she had followed with her two lovers, when they left her for their wives. Her ability to accept the interpretation with little or no difficulty indicated, among other things, that there had been a lifting of repression. The fact that in the dream she did not know whether or not she gave up her bed, suggested that she was undecided whether to retire in favor of my wife, that is, leave the treatment. She was apparently not the type of person who readily takes no for an answer.

Terminal Dreams

The second dream disclosed the patient's recognition of her positive feelings for me, and also conveyed a hint that I was responding in like manner to her. In that respect, she was not entirely at fault. I was just as responsible if she fell in love with me. A disengagement followed in which we each went our separate ways. This was probably a response to my interpretation of the previous day, which she tried to disparage by referring to it as hackneyed and without any real meaning for her. It may also have had reference to her recent encounter with her lover in which nothing significant had occurred. Was it perhaps an indication that she had been placated by my frank discussion of her fear that I had an ulterior motive in making her aware of my wife's presence, and was adopting a more realistic view of the transference relationship, anticipating the need to give up her fantasies? If so, it was apparently not yet fully crystallized in her mind, since she still tried to be seductive by coming to the session wearing a revealing miniskirt. When I drew attention to it, she felt let down and angry, as if I were disowning my own emotional involvement with her and dashing cold water on her hopes, causing the "momentum" to "die down."

The third dream brought out the patient's reluctance to give up her fantasies (*bleeding* to relieve congestion was like "decongesting" her romantic feelings). If she were to accept my interpretation that her attachment to me was an aspect of her neurosis, it would mean that she had to give up her fantasies and accept reality, that is, get well and discontinue treatment. She was not ready to do this, however (she wanted the relationship with Jim—who was treating her—to continue). The thought of terminating, however, was in the wind. In the dream she revealed for the first time that her fantasy also included a desire to give me a baby (she had promised to "deliver" something to her son; in addition, Marie Antoinette was "bled" after childbirth).

The fourth dream revealed the patient's progress toward termination, in that she was prepared to give up the fantasy of having an oedipal child (she realized the need to do her dusting and cleaning, that is, to have a "D & C").

The series of dreams thus reflected the patient's attempts to cling to her transference expectations, and followed closely, even anticipated, the fluctuating reactions of her waking state. She wanted to continue to act out her fantasies, as she had been doing for years. The successive dreams, however, led to an uncovering of deeper memories and ultimately disclosed the hidden content of her fantasies, the desire to have a baby by her father—the basic oedipal wish. When she finally realized how unrealistic the fantasy was, she was able to give it up.

The question naturally arises to what extent her readiness to stop acting out and to analyze her fantasies was the result of her frustration in real life, namely, the fact that her lover was no longer an available object. We know that analysis is possible only in a state of abstinence and cannot compete with the enticements of real life, any more than a doctor can hope to cure a diabetic who works in a pastry shop and is constantly exposed to temptation.

As the primal scene memories with the evidence of their traumatic effect were recovered, and the patient relived these experiences in the transference neurosis, she was less able to obtain gratification of her unconscious incestuous wishes through fantasy. From a theoretical point of view, her capacity to comprehend the deep interpretations that were given was the result of the reciprocal weakening of her primitive instinctual drives and the strengthening of her ego, so that the latter became dominant. Her acceptance of a solution that was in accord with reality indicated that a corresponding change had taken place in the functioning of her superego; in other words, in identifying with the therapist in the therapeutic process she had adopted his superego. The reinforcement of the ego and the widening of its field of perception helped to fill in the blank spots caused by the infantile amnesia, and thus to reconstruct the history of her childhood. The number of possible causes of her basic neurosis was finally boiled down to the oedipal problem. These are the results we hope to attain through analysis: "Where id was, there ego shall be" (Freud, 1933, p. 80).

Although the depth of memory recall heralded the patient's decision to terminate, there was also a change in her attitude which indicated that the time had finally come. In the last hour she was speaking more objectively and realistically. She announced her greater interest in her husband's business affairs, said that she felt no more interest in her lover, and, for the first time, began to have nostalgic feelings for her father. She also expressed her gratitude to me, and, more realistically, brought me a symbolic baby—a plant. Some time after the analysis was over she visited me in order to discuss some practical problems that had arisen. She reported that she was showing a spontaneous increase in her working capacity. She had become involved in a project that afforded her much personal satisfaction and a sense of fulfillment.

Should we be content with the outcome in this case? If we are to be reasonable in our expectations, we can say that although not all of the patient's conflicts had been resolved, her outstanding problems had been sufficiently studied and understood dynamically, structurally, and genetically. The patient showed better ego control, a fuller and more satisfying emotional life (i.e. one with less conflict), and greater productivity. In addition we hope that the patient has been protected against a return of her maladjustment, although, in this respect, we are at the mercy of the vicissitudes of life. Freud has said: "As regards their causation, instances of neurotic illness fall into a series within which the two factors—sexual constitution and experience, or, if you prefer it, fixation of the libido and frustration—are represented in such a manner that if there is more of the one there is less of the other.... [In certain patients] their sexual constitution would not have led them into a neurosis if they had not had these [detrimental] experiences...." (1916-17, p. 347).

When the patient began treatment she wrote a fantasy which she showed me. In it she was setting out on a boat ride with a pilot, a sinister figure whom she did not trust. The boat went through dark tunnels and the atmosphere was gloomy and ominous. Her fearfulness and distrust continued throughout the entire trip, but she managed to come through unscathed. Analysis is often depicted as setting out on a journey, while water symbolizes both the womb and birth. In the fantasy the boat went through dark tunnels (that is, the birth canal). The patient was obviously fearful of the analysis and often expressed doubts about my integrity. At the conclusion of the analysis, the uneasiness that she felt at the beginning was no longer visible. The patient had come to the point where she regarded herself as a self-sufficient woman, and the analyst as a well-intentioned and helpful person who had guided the boat to a safe shore. A comparison of her two states of mind shows the distance that she had traveled in the analysis and the level of maturity she had attained.

Many of the points made about the physician's role in the analysis of dreams are abundantly illustrated in the case material. These include the affective interchanges that take place between the analyst and the patient; the oscillation of the analyst's mind between imagination and intellect, fantasy and logical thinking—in short, between the conscious and the unconscious—in the process of formulating conjectures; consideration of the content and form of the manifest dream in determining the meaning of the latent dream, both as a defense and a wish; the continuous amending of conjectures by matching them up with the manifest dream content, one's knowledge of the patient and the patient's associations; the reconstruction of the past; the overcoming of resistances and the use of fluctuations in the patient's transference reactions to further the analysis; the use of present-day or surface material to render interpretations meaningful; and the constructive use of counter-transference. As the analysis approaches its end, it is observed that the analyst can feel more confident about his comprehension of the case material and of the patient's reactions. This is reflected in the assurance with which he makes interpretations.

BIBLIOGRAPHY

Abraham, K. (1913). Should patients write down their dreams? In *Clinical Papers and Essays on Psycho-Analysis,* pp. 33–35. London: Hogarth Press, 1955.

Adler, A. (1911). Beitrag zur Lehre vom Widerstand. *Zbl. Psychoanal.* 1:214. (Quoted by Freud, 1900, 579n.)

Alexander, F. (1925). Dreams in pairs and series. *International Journal of Psycho-Analysis* 6:446–452.

Altman, L. L. (1969). *The Dream in Psychoanalysis.* New York: International Universities Press.

Arlow, J. A. (1969). Unconscious fantasy and disturbances of conscious experience. *Psychoanalytic Quarterly* 38:1–51.

Beres, D. and Arlow, J.A. (1974). Fantasy and identification in empathy. *Psychoanalytic Quarterly* 43:26–50.

Bergler, E. (1943). A third function of the "day residue" in dreams. *Psychoanalytic Quarterly* 12:353–370.

Bibring, G. (1953). 'On the passing of the Oedipus complex' in a matriarchal family setting. In *Drives, Affects and Behavior,* vol. 1, ed. R. M. Loewenstein, pp. 278–284. New York: International Universities Press.

Blitzsten, N. L., Eissler, R. S., and Eissler, K. (1950). Emergence of hidden ego tendencies during dream analysis. *International Journal of Psycho-Analysis* 31:12–17.

Bornstein, B. (1949). The analysis of a phobic child. *Psychoanalytic Study of the Child* 3/4:181–226.

Dement, W. C. and Fisher, C. (1960). The effect of dream deprivation and excess: an experimental demonstration of the necessity for dreaming (abstract). *Psychoanalytic Quarterly* 29:607.

Deutsch, F. (1939). The choice of organ in organ neuroses. *International Journal of Psycho-Analysis* 20:252–262.

Deutsch, H. (1926). Occult processes occurring during psychoanalysis. In *Psychoanalysis and the Occult*, ed. G. Devereux (1953), pp. 133–146. New York: International University Press.

——— (1965). *Neuroses and Character Types*. New York: International University Press.

Eissler, K.R. (1953). The effect of the structure of the ego on psychoanalytic technique. *Journal of the American Psychoanalytic Association* 1:104–141.

Erikson, E. H. (1934). The dream specimen of psychoanalysis. *Journal of the American Psychoanalytic Association* 2:5–56.

Fenichel, O. (1945a). Nature and classification of so-called psychosomatic phenomena. *Psychoanalytic Quarterly* 14:287–312.

——— (1945b). *The Psychoanalytic Theory of Neurosis*. New York: W. W. Norton.

——— (1946). On acting. *Psychoanalytic Quarterly* 15:144–160.

——— (1953). The scoptophilic instinct and identification. In *Collected Papers of Otto Fenichel: First Series*, pp. 373–397. New York: W.W. Norton.

Ferenczi, S. (1912). To whom does one relate one's dreams? In *Further Contributions to the Theory and Technique of Psychoanalysis,* p. 349. New York: Boni and Liveright, 1927.

——— (1923). Stage fright and narcissistic self-observation. *Ibid.,* pp. 421–422.

——— (1926). The problem of acceptance of unpleasant ideas—advances in knowledge of the sense of reality. *Ibid.,* pp. 366–379.

——— (1927). The problem of the termination of the analysis. In *The Selected Papers of Sandor Ferenczi: Problems and Methods of Psychoanalysis,* pp. 77–86. New York: Basic Books, 1955.

——— (1928). The elasticity of psycho-analytic technique. *Ibid.*, pp. 87–101.
Fisher, C. (1965). Psychoanalytic implications of recent research on sleep and dreaming. *Journal of the American Psychoanalytic Association* 13:197–303.
——— (1974). Total and prolonged suppression of REM sleep: is dreaming necessary? In Panel on dreams and dreaming. R. M. Whitman, Reporter. *Journal of the American Psychoanalytic Association* 22:643–650.
Fliess, R. (1942). The metapsychology of the analyst. *Psychoanalytic Quarterly* 11:211–227.
——— (1953). *The Revival of Interest in the Dream.* New York: International Universities Press.
Frank, J. (1955). Indications and contraindications regarding the application of the "standard technique": Dynamic, economic and structural considerations. An attempt at corroboration by clinical examples (Abstract). *Psychoanalytic Quarterly* 24:166–167.
French, T. M. (1958). The art and science of psychoanalysis. *Journal of the American Psychoanalytic Association* 6:197–214.
French, T. M., and Fromm, E. (1964). *Dream Interpretation—A New Approach.* New York: Basic Books.
Freud, A. (1937). *The Ego and the Mechanisms of Defense.* London: Hogarth Press.
——— (1968). Acting out. *International Journal of Psycho-Analysis* 49:165–170.
——— (1974). A psychoanalytic view of developmental psychopathology. *Journal of the Philadelphia Association for Psychoanalysis* 1:7–17.
Freud, S. (1900). The interpretation of dreams. *Standard Edition* 4:1–338 and 5:339–627.
——— (1901). On dreams. *Standard Edition* 5:629–686.
——— (1905a). Three essays on sexuality. *Standard Edition* 7:135–243.
——— (1905b). Jokes and their relation to the unconscious. *Standard Edition* 8:9–258.

―――― (1908). Creative writers and day-dreaming. *Standard Edition* 9:141–153.
―――― (1911). The handling of dream-interpretation in psycho-analysis. *Standard Edition* 12:89–96.
―――― (1912a). The dynamics of transference. *Standard Edition* 12:97–108.
―――― (1912b). Recommendations to physicians practising psycho-analysis. *Standard Edition* 12:109–120.
―――― (1913a). On the beginning of treatment. *Standard Edition* 12:121–144.
―――― (1913b). The claims of psycho-analysis to scientific interest. *Standard Edition* 13:163–190.
―――― (1913c). An evidential dream. *Standard Edition* 12:269–277.
―――― (1914a). Remembering, repeating and working through. *Standard Edition* 12:145–156.
―――― (1914b). On the history of the psycho-analytic movement. *Standard Edition* 14:1–66.
―――― (1914c). Observations on transference love. *Standard Edition* 12:157–173.
―――― (1916-17 [1915-17]). Introductory lectures on psycho-analysis. *Standard Edition* 15:1–239 and 16:240–496.
―――― (1917 [1915]). A metapsychological supplement to the theory of dreams. *Standard Edition* 14:217–222.
―――― (1918). From the history of an infantile neurosis. *Standard Edition* 17:3–122.
―――― (1920). Beyond the pleasure principle. *Standard Edition* 18:1–64.
―――― (1923a [1922]). Two encyclopedia articles. *Standard Edition* 18:233–259.
―――― (1923b [1922]). Remarks on the theory and practice of dream interpretation. *Standard Edition* 19:109–121.
―――― (1923c). The ego and the id. *Standard Edition* 19:1–66.
―――― (1925). Some additional notes on dream-interpretation as a whole. *Standard Edition* 19:127–138.
―――― (1926). Inhibitions, symptoms and anxiety. *Standard Edition* 20:77–175.

―――― (1933 [1932]). New introductory lectures on psycho-analysis. *Standard Edition* 22:3–182.
―――― (1937). Constructions in psycho-analysis. *Standard Edition* 23:255–269.
―――― (1940 [1938]). An outline of psycho-analysis. *Standard Edition*. 23:141–207.
Glover, E. (1955). *The Technique of Psycho-Analysis.* New York: International Universities Press.
Greenacre, P. (1968). The psychoanalytic process, transference and acting out. *International Journal of Psycho-Analysis* 49:211–218.
Greenson, R. R. (1967). *The Technique and Practice of Psychoanalysis,* vol. 1. New York: International Universities Press.
―――― (1970). The exceptional position of the dream in clinical psychoanalytic practice. *Psychoanalytic Quarterly* 39:519–549.
Guttman, S. A. (1965). Some aspects of scientific theory construction and psycho-analysis. *International Journal of Psycho-Analysis* 46:129–136.
Hartmann, E. L. (1973). *The Functions of Sleep.* New Haven: Yale University Press.
Hendrick, I. (1958). Dream resistance and schizophrenia. *Journal of the American Psychoanalytic Association* 6:672–690.
Isakower, D. (1938). A contribution to the psychopathology of phenomena associated with falling asleep. *International Journal of Psycho-Analysis* 19:331–345.
―――― (1957, 1963). Minutes of faculty meeting, New York Psychoanalytic Institute. Quoted by Lillian Malcove. "The analytic situation: Toward a view of the supervisory experience." *Journal of the Philadelphia Association of Psychoanalysis* 2:1–14.
Jacobson, E. (1971). *Depression: Comparative Studies of Normal, Neurotic, and Psychotic Conditions.* New York: International Universities Press.
James, William (1890). *The Principles of Psychology,* vol. 1. New York: Dover, 1950.
Jones, E. (1931). *On the Nightmare.* London: Hogarth Press.

Jones, R. M. (1965). Dream interpretation and the psychology of dreaming. *Journal of the American Psychoanalytic Association* 13:304–319.
Kanzer, M. (1954). A field theory perspective of psychoanalysis. *Journal of the American Psychoanalytic Association* 2:526–534.
Kanzer, M. and Blum, H. (1967). Classical psychoanalysis since 1939. In *Psychoanalytic Techniques,* ed. B. Wolman, pp. 93–144. New York: Basic Books.
Kernberg, O.F. (1975). *Borderline Conditions and Pathological Narcissism.* New York: Jason Aronson, Inc.
Kubie, L. S. (1952). Problems and techniques of psychoanalytic validation and progress. In *Psychoanalysis as Science,* ed. E. Pumpian-Mindlin, pp. 46–124. Palo Alto: Stanford University Press.
Langs, R. J. (1971). Day residues, recall residues, and dreams: Reality and psyche. *Journal of the American Psychoanalytic Association* 19:499–523.
Lewin, B. D. (1948). Inferences from the dream screen. *International Journal of Psycho-Analysis* 29:224–231.
––––– (1952). Phobic symptoms and dream interpretation. *Psychoanalytic Quarterly* 21:295–322.
––––– (1954). Sleep, narcissistic neurosis and the analytic situation. *Psychoanalytic Quarterly* 23:487–510.
––––– (1955). Dream psychology and the analytic situation. *Psychoanalytic Quarterly* 24:169–199.
Lipton, S. (1967). Later developments in Freud's technique. In *Psychoanalytic Techniques,* ed. B. Wolman, pp. 51–92. New York: Basic Books.
Loewenstein, R. M. (1951). The problem of interpretation. *Psychoanalytic Quarterly* 20:1–14.
––––– (1954). Some remarks on defences, autonomous ego and psycho-analytic technique. *International Journal of Psycho-Analysis* 35:188–193.
Lorand, S. (1948). Comments on the correlation of theory and technique. *Psychoanalytic Quarterly* 17:32–50.

Maeder, A. (1912). Uber die Funktion des Traumes. *Jb. Psychoanal. Psychopath. Forschung* 4:692 (quoted by S. Freud, 1900, p. 579n).
Mahler, M.S., Pine, F., and Bergman, A. (1975). *The Psychoanalytical Birth of the Human Infant. Symbiosis and Individuation.* New York: Basic Books.
Marmor, J. (1955). Validation of psychoanalytic technique: Report of panel. *Journal of the American Psychoanalytic Association* 3:496–505.
Nagera, H. (1969). The imaginary companion, its significance for ego development and conflict solution. *Psychoanalytic Study of the Child* 24:165–196.
Nunberg, H. (1931). The synthetic function of the ego. *International Journal of Psycho-Analysis* 12:123–140. Also in *Practice and Theory of Psychoanalysis.* New York: Nervous and Mental Diseases Monographs, 1948, pp. 120–136. Also in *Practice and Theory of Psychoanalysis*, vol. 1, chap. 8. New York: International Universities Press, 1965.
——— (1932). *Principles of Psychoanalysis.* New York: International Universities Press.
——— (1937 [1936]). Theory of the therapeutic results of psychoanalysis. *International Journal of Psycho-Analysis* 18:161–169.
——— (1954). Evaluation of the results of psychoanalytic treatment. *International Journal of Psycho-Analysis* 35:2–7. Also in *Practice and Theory of Psycho-analysis,* vol. 2, pp. 140–151. New York: International Universities Press, 1965.
——— (1961). *Curiosity.* New York: International Universities Press. Also in *Practice and Theory of Psychoanalysis,* vol. 2, pp. 168–206. New York: International Universities Press, 1965.
Pederson-Kreg, G. (1956). The use of metaphor in analytic thinking. *The Annual Survey of Psychoanalysis* 7:82–83.
Ramzy, I. (1974). How the mind of the psychoanalyst works: An essay on psychoanalytic inference. *International Journal of Psycho-Analysis* 55:543–550.
Reik, T. (1949). *Listening with the Third Ear.* New York: Farrar, Strauss.

Schur, M. (1966). Some additional "day residues" of the "specimen dream" of psychoanalysis. In *Psychoanalysis—a General Psychology,* ed. R. M. Loewenstein, L. Newman, M. Schur, and A. Solnit, pp. 45–85. New York: International Universities Press.

Sharpe, E. F. (1949). *Dream Analysis.* London: Hogarth press.

Spanjaard, J. (1969). The manifest dream content and its significance for the interpretation of dreams. *International Journal of Psycho-Analysis* 50:221–235.

Sperling, O. E. (1954). An imaginary companion, representing a prestage of the superego. *Psychoanalytic Study of the Child* 9:252–258.

Spitz, R. A. (1965). *The First Year of Life: A Psychoanalytic Study of Normal and Deviant Development of Object Relations.* New York: International Universities Press.

Sterba, R. F. (1934). The fate of the ego in analytic therapy. *International Journal of Psycho-Analysis* 15:17–126.

Stone, L. (1954). The widening scope of indications for psychoanalysis. *Journal of the American Psychoanalytic Association* 2:567–594.

Tartakoff, H. (1974). Discussion in panel on advances in psychoanalytic technique. Abraham Freedman, Reporter. *Journal of the Philadelphia Association for Psychoanalysis* 1:45–46.

Tausk, V. (1924). Compensation as a means of discounting the motive of repression. *International Journal of Psycho-Analysis* 5:130–140.

Waelder, R. (1930). The principle of multiple function. *Psychoanalytic Quarterly* 5:45–62. Also in *Psychoanalysis: Observation, Theory and Application* (Selected Papers of Robert Waelder, ed. S. A. Guttman, pp. 68–83. New York: International Universities Press, 1976.

—— (1937). The problem of the genesis of psychical conflicts in earliest infancy. *International Journal of Psycho-Analysis* 18:406–473.

—— (1960). *Basic Theory of Psychoanalysis.* New York: International Universities Press.

——— (1962). Psychoanalysis, scientific method and philosophy. *Journal of the American Psychoanalytic Association* 10:617–637.

Waldhorn, H. F. (1967). Reporter: *Indications for Psychoanalysis: The Place of the Dream in Clinical Psychoanalysis.* (Monograph II of the Kris Study Group of the New York Psychoanalytic Institute), ed. Edward D. Joseph. New York: International Universities Press.

INDEX

Abraham, K., 150
Adler, A., 74
affects
 in manifest dream, 43–44
 unpleasurable, 173–99
Alexander, F., 165
Altman, L.L., 13
analyst, role of, 18–21
Aristotle, 21
Arlow, J.A., 88
associations, 23–25, 48–49, 57–58, 156–57, 166–68, 213, 228–35
 to dreams with unpleasurable affects, 179–89, 192, 194–98
 to early dreams, 95–97
 to terminal dreams, 244–47, 250–55
 to transference dreams, 120–21, 124–29, 131–34, 137–38
attention, evenly suspended, 18–21

Bergman, A., 30
Bibring, G., 226
Blum, H., 16
Bornstein, B., 31, 92, 164

compulsion to repeat, 70
condensation, 35
corroborative dreams, 228–36

day residue, 22–23, 28–29, 37, 47–48, 56–57, 161–64, 213–14, 228, 230
 of dreams with unpleasurable affects, 179, 182, 184, 187, 190, 196
 of early dreams, 95–96, 99–100, 103–6
 of transference dreams, 119, 131, 137
Dement, W.C., 71
Deutsch, F., 185
Deutsch, H., 6–7, 176
displacement, 35
"dream screen," 36

dream wish, 35, 62, 67–83
  case reports on, 75–83

early dreams, premature interpretations and, 87–106
ego psychology, 16
Eissler, K.R., 158
Eliot, T.S., 43
empathy, intuitive, 7
evenly suspended attention, 18–21
externalized superego, 30

Fenichel, O., 104, 185, 190, 197
Ferenczi, S., 104–5, 109, 110
Fisher, C., 71
Fliess, R., 6, 13
Frank, J., 159
free association, 15–18
  regression and, 16–17
French, T.M., 26, 37, 74, 83
Freud, A., 30, 148, 157
Freud, S., 13–15, 18–19, 21, 26–28, 30, 31, 35, 37–40, 42, 57, 67–75, 87, 91, 97, 110, 124, 129, 148, 150, 165, 174–76, 191, 193, 198, 204, 208, 210, 212, 215, 232, 258–59
Fromm, E., 26, 37, 74

Glover, E., 241
Goethe, J.W. von, 68
Greenacre, P., 8
Greenson, R.R., 13, 94
Guttman, S.A., 9

Hartmann, E.L., 70–71
Hendrick, I., 165

interpretation
  in depth, 59–61
  premature, 87–106
  preparation for, 21–23
  technique of, 26–32
  on superficial level, 58–59
  use of manifest dream content in, 38–39
  validation of, 203–36
intuitive empathy, 7
Irma's injection, dream of (Freud), 26–27, 40, 68, 71–73
Isakower, D., 20, 36
"Isakower phenomenon," 36

Jacobson, E., 155
James, W., 21
Jones, E., 191
Jones, R.M., 68

Kanzer, M., 16
Kernberg, O.F., 6, 159
Kubie, L.S., 19

latent dream content, manifest dream content and, 26–29, 35–38
Lewin, B.D., 36, 89, 149, 191, 192
Lipton, S., 16
Loewenstein, R.M., 31, 91, 97, 164
Lorand, S., 30

Index

Maeder, A., 74
Mahler, M., 30
Malcove, L., 20
manifest dream, 35-52
    affects of, 43-44
    demonstration of use of, 47-52
    dream specimens illustrating sense of, 43-47
    latent dream content and, 26-29, 35, 38
    sense of, 39-42
    use of, in interpretation, 38-39

Nagera, H., 223
Nunberg, H., 42, 174, 197, 198, 215, 225

"objective correlative," 43

Pederson-Krag, G., 8
Pine, F., 30
premature interpretations, early dreams and, 87-106
psychic reality, 87

"reconstruction upwards," 31
regression, free association and, 16-17
Reik, T., 19, 74
REM sleep, 71
repetition compulsion, 70
repressed unconscious, 14-15
resistance
    dreams and, 147-70
    transference and, 111-12

secondary revision, 35
Sharpe, E.F., 113
Spanjaard, J., 26
Sperling, O.E., 225
Spitz, R., 30
Stone, L., 158
supervisory session, demonstration of, 55-63
symbols, 25-26

Tartakoff, H., 15
Tausk, V., 110
technique of interpretation, 26-32
terminal dreams, 89, 239-60
transference, resistance and, 111-12
transference dreams, 109-43
    case reports of, 113-43
trial identification, 6

unconscious, repressed, 14-15
unpleasurable affects, dreams with, 173-99

validation of interpretation, 203-36
    case reports of, 212-28
    criteria of, 209-12
    corroborative dreams and, 228-36

Waelder, R., 8, 203, 210, 225
Waldhorn, H.F., 13
wish fulfillment, 35, 62, 67-83
Wolf Man case (Freud), 68, 89